A CASE TO
ANSWER

David Bevan is a journalist who followed
the prosecution of Australia's first
European war crimes defendant from
its first day to its last. He now reports
politics for ABC radio news.

A CASE TO
ANSWER

The story of Australia's first
European war crimes prosecution

by DAVID BEVAN

Wakefield
Press

Wakefield Press
Box 2266
Kent Town
South Australia 5071

First published 1994

Designed by design BITE, Melbourne
Typeset by Clinton Ellicott, Adelaide
Printed and bound by Hyde Park Press, Adelaide

Cataloguing-in-publication data
Bevan, David, 1964–
A case to answer: the story of Australia's first
European war crimes prosecution

ISBN 1 86254 323 2

1. Polyukhovich, Ivan. 2. War crime trials – Australia.
3. War crimes. 4. World War, 1939–1945 – Atrocities.
I. Title.

345.940238

Publication of this title was assisted by the
Commonwealth Government through the
Australia Council, its arts funding and
advisory body.

Promotion of this title has been assisted by the South Australian Government
through the Department for the Arts and Cultural Development.

*We are not placing people on trial as a symbolic
gesture or to serve some larger purpose of conscience.
We are putting them on trial because they broke
the law. That is the only reason people should
be put on trial.*
Allan Ryan Jnr
United States war crimes prosecutor

*I cannot say to my children, when asked about
my attitude to such loathsome crimes,
'I just forgot about it.'*
Australian Democrat senator
Michael Macklin

*It's been a tragedy to watch. As his neighbours said a
long time ago, 'He is a lovely man whatever he may
or may not have done fifty years ago.' They said,
'He's a lovely old bloke and he's suffered.'*
Ivan Polyukhovich's lawyer
David Stokes

CONTENTS

Author's note

This book would not have been written without the faithful support of my wife, Janette. I am deeply grateful to her and my son, Joshua, for their patience, love and support.

Those people who helped in my research know who they are and, I hope, know how grateful I am. I'm also grateful to publishers Michael Bollen and Stephanie Johnston for taking on an untried author and a difficult subject. Thanks also to my parents, John and Marlene Bevan.

Preface

A Case to Answer tells the story of Australia's first European war crimes prosecution. I have tried to keep myself out of the narrative as far as possible, preferring to let the characters, circumstances and events speak for themselves as they did at the time.

There has been much debate about war crimes prosecutions, and I hope my book will throw new light on the issues by giving an insight into the actions, throughts and feelings of those who were caught up in this remarkable case. Whatever the political motives behind the legislation, the prosecution was born of real suffering, and it was played out in court at great cost to the witnesses, the investigators, the defendant and his family.

A Case to Answer is not offered as a *de facto* retrial: Ivan Polyukhovich has had his day in court.

———

The book is based on a variety of sources. For three years I followed the Polyukhovich case as a court reporter for the Adelaide *Advertiser*. Just before the trial was due to begin I returned to work for my former employer, the Australian Broadcasting Corporation, and I'm grateful the ABC gave me time to observe the final stages of the case. So I was an eyewitness throughout the prosecution. The court transcripts were invaluable. Wherever the reader comes across direct speech in the courtroom, this has been taken from the court record. I have also used statements made by various witnesses, including a record of the interview between the SIU and Polyukhovich on the day he was arrested. That record allowed me to give Polyukhovich a voice of his own, even if only for a few pages. The first portion of the book is a recreation of events in the Serniki area during the war. It is based on largely uncontested evidence given during the committal hearing. The section dealing with the war crimes debate was drawn from the *Hansard* record and media articles published at the time.

Part way through the committal hearing I began a series of off-the-record interviews with some of the key players. The aim of the interviews was to preserve memories during an important moment in Australian legal history. It soon became apparent that there was enough material to begin work on a book. Many of the people involved in the case were not able to speak to me while it was still before the courts, but eventually most agreed to be interviewed.

———

The central character, Ivan Polyukhovich remains virtually silent throughout *A Case to Answer*, just as he did during the proceedings which stretched over more than three years. On several occasions I asked Polyukhovich's solicitor, Craig Caldicott, for an opportunity to speak with his client but the offer was declined by Polyukhovich and his family. I respect their position.

Because of his age, education and poor health it seems unlikely that Ivan Polyukhovich actually understood much of what went on around him during his prosecution. His days in court were spent sitting silently, sometimes leaning on his walking stick, occasionally sharing a word with his translator. At times, it was easy to believe he had, in a way, become superfluous to the proceedings and theatre into which he had been thrust.

David Bevan, May 1994

Chronology

---

23 Aug 1939 . . . Germany and the Soviet Union conclude a non-aggression pact and sign a secret protocol dividing eastern Europe.

1 Sep 1939 . . . The second world war begins with Germany's invasion of Poland.

22 Jun 1941 . . . Germany attacks the Soviet Union.

Jul–Aug 1941 . . . About 100 Jewish men executed by Germans in the Ukrainian village of Serniki.

Aug–Sep 1942 . . . About 850 people from the Jewish ghetto in Serniki executed not far from the village.

9 May 1945 . . . The war in Europe ends.

28 Dec 1949 . . . Ivan Polyukhovich, his wife Maria, and two step-daughters arrive in Melbourne on board the Castel Bianco.

26 Dec 1986 . . . The Adelaide *Advertiser* receives a telex from Soviet Ukraine outlining war crimes allegations against Polyukhovich.

29 Dec 1986 . . . Polyukhovich denies the crimes outlined in the telex.

20 Dec 1988 . . . Australia's federal parliament passes the War Crimes Amendment Bill which allows prosecutions against suspected European war criminals in ordinary Australian civilian courts.

25 Jan 1990 . . . Polyukhovich is arrested. He appears in the Adelaide Magistrates Court the next morning charged with having murdered twenty-four people and with taking part in the murder of 850 people.

13 Jun 1990 . . . An Australian–Soviet team begins exhuming the mass grave outside Serniki. They stay at the site until July 13.

27 Jun 1990 . . . Polyukhovich withdraws his permission for overseas, on-commission hearings. All witnesses will now have to be brought to Adelaide.

29 Jul 1990 . . . Polyukhovich shot in Adelaide's western suburb of West Lakes. His committal hearing had been set to begin the next morning.

3 Sep 1990 . . . The High Court begins hearing a challenge to the Constitutional validity of the war crimes legislation.

14 Aug 1991 . . . The war crimes legislation is endorsed by the High Court.

5 Sept 1991 . . . Mikolay Berezowsky and Heinrich Wagner appear in the Adelaide Magistrates Court charged with war crimes.

28 Oct 1991 . . . The prosecution opens its case against Polyukhovich in the Adelaide Magistrates Court. The committal resumes again for two weeks in November.

8 Mar 1992 . . . Polyukhovich's committal resumes with the first overseas witnesses.

5 Jun 1992 . . . Magistrate Kelvyn Prescott commits Polyukhovich for trial on just six murders. The rest of the charges are dismissed. The director of public prosecutions decides to re-lay the charge alleging Polyukhovich's involvement in the mass execution and two more murders.

29 Jul 1992 . . . Magistrate David Gurry finds there is insufficient evidence to place Berezowsky on trial.

22 Dec 1992 . . . Justice Cox rules on the Polyukhovich abuse-of-process application. The pit-killing and six murders can be tried but before two juries.

1 Mar 1993 . . . Pre-trial argument begins in the Polyukhovich case.

18 Mar 1993 . . . Polyukhovich's trial before a Supreme Court jury begins.

18 May 1993 . . . Polyukhovich is acquitted of all charges.

10 Dec 1993 . . . The Director of Public Prosecutions decides to drop the case against Heinrich Wagner on the grounds of the defendant's poor health.

Serniki

Serniki

The strangers looked frightened and exhausted. They said they'd travelled far but couldn't stay long. It wasn't safe. They'd seen Germans gather a group of Jews, herd them into a Polish synagogue and set it alight. Everyone inside – men, women and children – had been burned alive.

The small crowd who'd gathered listened quietly and offered hospitality, but the strangers insisted they must move on. The Jews in Poland were being slaughtered and Serniki was too close to the border for safety. They would continue heading east.

After the strangers left, a few of the men looked up at their own synagogue, then noticed some of the local children looking at them. They too had heard the strangers' story. The men told the children not to worry. Serniki was a small village, a long way from the trouble. The children should go and play.

———

About five thousand people lived in Serniki before the war started. It was one of many small villages found in the Polesie, an expanse filled with forest and marshes that stretched from Byelorussia to northern Volhynia.

The area was very poor, inhabited mostly by Ukrainian farming families. Large Polish and Jewish communities lived mainly in the towns. Jews had lived here for about eight hundred years. For twenty years after the end of the first world war the region had been controlled by Poland.

In September 1939, however, it had fallen under Soviet control when Adolf Hitler and Joseph Stalin divided Poland and the rest of eastern Europe between them. In German-occupied Poland hundreds of thousands of Jews had become refugees, their businesses confiscated or plundered. Massive populations were forced into ghettos, and Jewish men were sent to labour camps. Killings had become commonplace. But only the occasional rumour from the German side of Poland filtered through to Serniki.

On 22 June 1941, the Nazi policy of annihilating the Jews spread across the border as Hitler turned against the Soviet Union. His armies advanced quickly and Serniki was behind German lines within three weeks. As they retreated, the Soviets passed through Serniki and offered to take with them anyone who wanted to leave. Very few locals took up the offer. They felt no more loyalty to communist Russia than they did to fascist Germany. Instead they waited, only to find the Germans considered Serniki a place with no strategic value. It could be ignored, at least for a while. Bands of Ukrainian men, often very young men touting guns, set themselves up as the local 'police'. In fact, they were thugs who terrorised the Jewish population, breaking into their homes at night, stealing from them, beating the men and boys, raping the women and girls. These men would later be recruited by the Germans to form the basis of the official local police force.

———

When the Germans finally did arrive in Serniki, Jack Kriniuk recognised them immediately. The thirteen-year-old had never seen German soldiers, but there was no mistaking them. They were on horseback and wore uniforms. He saw other soldiers walking from door to door through the Jewish section of Serniki shouting orders and taking men – only the men – from their homes at gun point.

Jack's father, Moyshe Kriniuk, was a shrewd but generous man who ran a wholesale grocery store from the front of a large home on the outskirts of Serniki. Moyshe had a reputation for giving credit which often wasn't repaid, and was respected by both Jews and Gentiles throughout the region. His popularity had allowed him to survive the Soviet assault on capitalism. When nearly all the small businesses in the area had been confiscated by the state, Moyshe's workers had voted for him to remain in control of his business. His family had suffered at the hands of the Ukrainian gangs but now, as the soldiers made their way through Serniki, Moyshe saw that German rule was not about to restore law and order – not for Jewish citizens anyway.

Moyshe knew that he and Jack had to escape. He grabbed his brother, a neighbour and Jack, and headed for the forest a few kilometres away. He knew the woods. They'd have a better chance there.

They had been in the forest a few days when the Ukrainian police caught up with them. Jack was holding his uncle's arm when he heard a shot. His uncle fell to the ground dead. Another shot was fired and the neighbour was dead as well.

––––

Moyshe and Jack were arrested, beaten and ordered to begin walking in the direction of a town Jack had never visited. The officers had ordered Jack to wear his father's boots and now, forty kilometres later, the boy's feet were raw as he walked up the steps into the police office.

The exhausted father and son stood silently as the chief of police walked over. He seemed to recognise them. 'Moyshe. You know me?' he said.

'No,' Moyshe answered.

'I know you,' the commander said. 'I'll see you later.'

Moyshe and Jack were led away to a cell.

The boy wasn't sure how much time had passed when his father woke him. 'I've had a dream,' Moyshe said. 'A rabbi came to me and said, "As soon as you get up someone will come and take you away. Go with them." '

Serniki

A few hours later the cell door opened. The chief of police walked in, looking decisive. He turned to Moyshe and spoke quickly. 'I remember one day before Easter I came to you, and I said, "I have no money and I want you to give me credit for food for my family." You gave it to me. I never paid it back. Now, come and see what I can do.'

It was night. The chief took them outside to a horse and wagon. They climbed on and the chief began driving. He stopped at the edge of the town, turned to them and said, 'Run.'

Run where? Moyshe decided to return to Serniki where the rest of his family remained.

When they reached the village, Moyshe and Jack learned that all the Jewish men who'd been rounded up by the Germans had been taken to the cemetery and shot.

———

After four or five months, notices written in German began to appear around Serniki. They were put there by the Ukrainian police, now officially established in the village. Although German wasn't his first language, Jack found that, if he read slowly, he could understand most of the decrees. All Jewish people living in the surrounding areas were to be brought to Serniki and housed in the predominantly Jewish part of town. This section was to become a ghetto. Jews found outside the ghetto would be shot. All Jews had to wear a yellow star on their clothing and be inside their homes by 5 PM. They had to walk in the middle of the road; the sidewalks were forbidden to them. Any Gentiles living within the ghetto were not required to shift, but Jews were not allowed to go to Gentile homes.

Jack had seen only a few Germans in the town. The Nazi chiefs had decided that a permanent German garrison was not necessary, and that enforcing the ghetto's boundaries would be left to the local police force.

Among those forced back to Serniki was the Kaz family. Tsalykha Kaz was a widow. Her husband had died several years ago and left her with a family of four children. Her eldest, Luba, was now a widow and mother of a baby girl. Luba's husband and brother had been killed when the local gangs had been in control. Tsalykha's next eldest was Pepe, a single woman of twenty-five who was shy of authority, but learning to control her fear. Tsalykha's other daughter was Sonja. The Kaz family had fled Serniki several months before and lived with a friendly Gentile family a few kilometres away on a farm near Alexandrovo.

Some time after the ghetto was formed orders were circulated that all Jews fit for the journey were to travel to the town of Vysotsk, about thirty kilometres away, for 'registration'. Only the elderly and infants were exempt. Luba was allowed to stay at home to look after her baby and, somehow, Tsalykha was allowed to stay and look after Luba. These days Tsalykha was rarely far away from Luba and the baby. Pepe, however, had to make the journey along with several hundred others. Somewhere in the moribund line stretching out of Serniki was Jack Kriniuk.

No one knew what was meant by 'registration' and, as they walked, some speculated they would be killed on reaching their destination. Others thought they might be put on trains and taken out of the region.

When they arrived they were taken to a building with German soldiers standing outside. The line led through the soldiers up to the building. They discovered more soldiers inside. One was sitting at a desk. Pepe noticed his blond hair as he asked her name, age, occupation and address. Then she followed the other villagers through another door, and someone said they were free to go home.

Jack Kriniuk was in the office. Then he was outside. The questions were the same for everyone. No explanation was asked for and none was offered.

They began the long journey home not knowing for what they had been 'registered'.

———

Months passed. It was late August 1942 and only a few days before Rosh Hashona, the Jewish New Year. Jack's eldest sister was doing the accounts when some Ukrainians who had worked for the Kriniuks came into the store, saying that fresh graves had been dug outside the village. The Germans, they said, intended to kill every Jew. All Jews must escape now. The Kriniuks found this suggestion fantastic, in spite of all they'd endured. They didn't believe it could happen. So they stayed.

———

At midnight Pepe Kaz sat at the window staring out into the darkness. The rest of the household was asleep, but she was restless. When she had been walking with her mother near the post office two days ago, they'd been approached by a Ukrainian man, a former neighbour. He had stopped for a moment and told Tsalykha that a large grave had been dug outside the village.

'Tsalykha, take the girls and run,' he'd said. 'Leave. Ditches have been dug and today or tomorrow the Germans will liquidate the ghetto.'

'How can I?' Tsalykha had replied. 'We have a small baby, my eldest daughter's baby.'

'Take the baby with you and leave her with somebody on the farms,' the man had said.

It had been arranged the next day that Pepe and Sonja would escape. Tsalykha, Luba and the baby would take their chances in Serniki, or perhaps find their own way out.

Pepe forced herself not to look back as she left. She and Sonja had intended to make for the woods, where they knew other Jewish families were hiding, but had gone only a few kilometres along the road to Alexandrovo when they heard someone calling, 'Halt, *Stoi*, Halt'. Two policemen on horseback rode up to them from behind. One was scarred by chicken pox. The women recognised him immediately as Kutcher from Serniki. Kutcher told them that they wouldn't be killed, but must be escorted back to the village. At Serniki, Moyshe Kriniuk appeared and, somehow, the shopkeeper persuaded the two policemen not to take the women to the police station. They were left in Moyshe's custody instead.

After dark Moyshe took his and Pepe's families across to an abandoned house and told them to spend the night. They found another family already there, the Silbermans. Everyone settled down, but Pepe couldn't sleep and that was how she came to be staring out at the darkness through the window, thinking about their futile escape and rumours of a grave dug on the outskirts of town.

She could make out the road to Alexandrovo, stretching into the distance. Her eyes picked out pairs of lights: faint lights coming towards her, growing stronger.

The Germans were on their way.

Pepe rushed into the room where the families lay sleeping, shouting at them to get up. Amid the panic, Pepe took control. 'We're not going to wait for them to put us on the trucks,' she said, thinking as she spoke. 'Get out the back door. Run for it. If you hear shots, lay down in the brush. If you don't, run.'

Then Pepe's command faltered and gave way to Moyshe's experience. She had no idea of how to get to the woods in the dark.

———

They were running through the darkness. Moyshe Kriniuk was leading the way, looking for landmarks, listening for pursuers, and helping his wife, who was struggling to keep up. All the time, he was trying to keep the large group together. Moyshe's three daughters and Jack followed, then Pepe, who was clutching a bag containing a loaf of bread and her family photographs. With her other hand she gripped her sister Sonja's. Behind her ran the Silberman family and, finally, Luba and Tsalykha Kaz, who was carrying the baby.

Luba and Tsalykha were falling further and further behind. Finally Pepe realised that her mother and sister had stopped. She tracked back and found them exhausted, Tsalykha still cradling her grand-daughter. They looked at each other and knew it was time to part. Pepe's and Sonja's only chance was to stay with the Kriniuks until they reached the forest.

Half a century later, Pepe could still remember the sound of the baby crying as she turned and left, a whimpering that became fainter and fainter.

Moyshe was also eventually forced to stop; his wife was sick with exhaustion. As the group waited for her to catch her breath, Pepe looked back into the darkness hoping her mother and sister would appear. They didn't.

———

Pepe dropped her bag as the group walked into the night. Moyshe made them walk back until they found it. They had food again and incidentally had preserved Pepe's family photographs. They came to the edge of the forest at dawn. Not far in they found other Jewish families. Pepe took out some of the bread and gave a piece to some children. Then they continued deeper into the forest. Early in the morning it rained.

———

Eleven-year-old Vera Grigoryevna Polyukhovich walked in the autumn sun beside the heaps of orange sand, keeping a close eye on her sheep. She often brought her animals here, within sight of her home. A few days before, she had seen men digging what seemed to be a gigantic rectangle in the ground. She'd played among the piles of sand while her sheep grazed.

Vera didn't see her younger sister, Anna, standing barefoot in their front yard watching a crowd of people pass by. There were old men and women and tiny children, younger than Anna, walking down the road weeping and yelling. Anna began to cry, then felt someone grab her hand. It was her father. In his fear he hit his small daughter, who was standing so foolishly close to the road, and rushed her away.

Vera heard the sounds of yelling and looked up. She saw the column of people walking past her home. A small, dark car was in front of the people, who were coming toward her. Some were crying, some yelling out; others tore at their clothes. She chased her sheep away from the pit and down the road.

————

That night Moyshe said that they needed to go deeper into the forest – they had heard shots coming from the direction of Serniki most of the day.

Three nights later Moyshe announced that it was time to find out what had happened. He said that he would go to the farmers and ask, and that either Pepe or Sonja should come with him. A mother with four children who had joined them should make the journey as well. She might be able to find some food for her children.

It was very late when the group returned. At first Pepe and the others were happy to see Moyshe and his group alive, but then they saw their faces. Moyshe, standing there in the darkened woods in his dirty clothes, told them slowly that only those who had escaped had survived. The ghetto had been liquidated. Men, women and children had been gunned down into a gigantic grave just outside the village.

————

They were moving again, but now as if in a dream. Moyshe said they couldn't stay in the woods and so they walked.

After a time Moyshe stopped and told them they would have to split up. The group was simply too big. Moyshe had many friends among the Polish farmers; perhaps they would help rescue his family. Pepe and the others understood and moved off in another direction.

————

Pepe was walking back towards Serniki for the first time since the escape. It was still 1942, about November. The ground hadn't frozen yet. Pepe was with a group of Jewish men, one of whom, Motl Bobrov, would later become her husband. The group had to watch out constantly for the local police, who were roaming the countryside looking for Jewish escapees. During the previous four months more than a dozen Jewish ghettos had been liquidated within seventy-five kilometres of Serniki. Only a few days before nearly twenty thousand people had been exterminated in the city of Pinsk.

Several trees had been cut down around Serniki. The group walked past them and a burnt house. As they crossed the boundary of the village, they saw it for the wasteland it was. The ghetto had been destroyed. Only a few Gentile houses remained standing.

Pepe followed the street, rebuilding the village in her mind from the charred sticks. At one shell of a house, she recognised a lilac bush growing near a window. This had been her home.

———

Pepe and the others left the rubble of Serniki behind them. They came across a large area where nothing was growing. They walked through the brush to the perimeter of four hundred square metres of sandy grey and brown dirt. The lumpy surface showed that the ground had been dug over sometime before. Their eyes picked out cracks and fissures where the soil had dried out and split apart.

At first Pepe couldn't work out what this place was, but it dawned on her slowly that this was the grave, the site of the mass execution.

'Let's get out of here,' she said, starting to shake.

The men agreed.

———

Pepe knew that her mother, sister Luba, and the baby were dead. She had been trying to find them since their separation in the forest weeks earlier, but now she'd learned they had been killed. A girl from a friendly Gentile family had offered to take her to where the three were buried. Walking from the direction of Alexandrovo, Pepe and the girl crossed farmland and came to the spot not far from the Serniki–Alexandrovo road. The girl told Pepe that a local Ukrainian employed by the police had shot them not long after the ghetto was liquidated and not far from Serniki.

Reporters, politicians
and investigators

Reporters, politicians and investigators

Decorations hung on the walls surrounding the large editorial floor of the Adelaide *Advertiser*. It was the day after Christmas, 1986, the middle of the silly season, and staff at the newspaper were relaxed. Business and the government were on holidays, and only the most enthusiastic back-bencher would send a press release today.

Sometime during the afternoon the telex machine on the far side of the room chugged into life. Peter Hackett, one of the newspaper's senior reporters, picked up the document and read:

Polyukhovich, 70, resident of Seaton, a township in the country's south, was forest warden before the second world war. Serving in the Gebietspolizei under Nazi occupation. He killed several dozen civilians, mostly Jews, in 1942 and 1943, and took part in the shooting of 725 civilians in Serniki village. The many eyewitnesses who now testify to the Nazi collaborator's crimes, refer to him by the diminutive 'Ivanechko', as he was known in Alexandrovo and Serniki villages.

The telex claimed to be from a community in Ukraine. It appeared that a meeting had been held in a town called Zarechnye, where several hundred people had called for this Ivanechko's extradition from Australia back to his homeland, so he could face war crimes charges. One of the citizens quoted in the telex described Ivanechko as 'inhuman . . . a beast'. Another said, 'The wolf in sheep's clothing lives a quiet life in Australia and his neighbours think him a respectable man.' A clergyman was quoted as saying, 'The Nazi criminal must fall into the hands of the law in the country where he committed his crimes.'

The telex had appeared on the machine from nowhere and Hackett had doubts about its *bona fides*. He feared that it was a hoax perpetrated by an extremist group. Why would such a message be sent to Adelaide's morning newspaper?

War criminals living in Australia were news. Only a few weeks before, a commonwealth report on the issue had been tabled in federal parliament. The report had found that serious war criminals probably had entered Australia after the second world war. Seventy suspects had been identified to the government as warranting further examination. The report recommended that the government take action to bring any war criminals living in Australia to justice. There was talk that a special unit would be set up to conduct further investigations.

Hackett's telex carried the name 'Andrei Bezruchenko'. He was able to confirm its Ukrainian origins through Telecom, but not its exact source. He sent his own telex to the source number shown on the print-out. When he hadn't received a reply by that evening, the paper decided to err on the side of caution. An article would appear on page three the next day outlining the contents of the telex, but without the name 'Polyukhovich'. Perhaps a story would flush out more information.

———

On 29 December 1986 an *Advertiser* reporter and photographer found Ivan Polyukhovich in the house he had built in the western suburb of Seaton.

More than forty years earlier Polyukhovich had left the Ukrainian city of Pinsk on a goods train filled with hungry people moving west to war-time Germany. With him had been Maria Polyukhovich and her two young daughters, Anna and Luba. In Germany, Polyukhovich worked on a farm near Hamburg and after the war the family spent four years in displaced persons' camps. They had been among a million Ukrainian refugees scattered throughout western Europe. The Polyukhovichs had initially considered moving to Brazil, but then were accepted by Australia. On 28 December 1949 they'd arrived in Melbourne, along with nine hundred other displaced persons, on the Italian ship *Castel Bianco*. For two years Polyukhovich had served out an immigration contract picking grapes in South Australia's Riverland, then he'd been employed as a carpenter with the Department of Marine and Harbours at Port Adelaide. During the 1950s huge ships carrying passengers and cargo filled the port, giving Polyukhovich and hundreds of others steady work. The Polyukhovichs found a house in nearby Wingfield, and settled into a new life. On 28 May 1958 Polyukhovich became an Australian citizen.

Very few people lived in Wingfield during the fifties. Of those who did, many had migrated from Eastern Europe soon after the war. The land was cheap and harsh. There was no shade. The salty dirt had little nourishment to support trees. Only saltbush was hardy enough to weather the hot dry winds which blew in each summer, hitting Wingfield before any of the comfortable suburbs to the south. A boiling-down works dominated the area. Hundreds of animal carcasses were processed there each week for their fat and tallow. Skinning and tanning sheds dotted the flat landscape. The smell was overwhelming. On local government papers Wingfield was designated as a noxious trade area. Its most famous feature was the Wingfield tip, where Adelaide dumped its garbage.

The Polyukhovichs lived at Wingfield for nearly twenty years before moving to the more comfortable suburb of Seaton in the early 1970s. Their house was near a golf course, but Polyukhovich didn't play. Probably few of his neighbours knew where the family hailed from. Ivan lived a quiet life. People in the street only knew him to say hello.

Polyukhovich retired after twenty-nine years with Marine and Harbours and settled into tending his garden and keeping bees.

The reporter and photographer from the *Advertiser* found Polyukhovich had trouble speaking English; he was helped by his wife, Maria, one of his step-daughters and his son-in-law.

The next day an article appeared on the front page of the paper. The headline read, 'I'm that man, but I'm no war criminal, says pensioner.' The article said that Polyukhovich was confused by the allegations and frightened the police were about to knock on his door and have him extradited to Europe. It claimed that he admitted he was the man referred to in the telex as 'Ivanechko', admitted he'd been a forest warden in the Rovno region of Ukraine for about a year during the Nazi occupation, but denied that anything else in the telex was true. He and his family were 'shocked and numbed' about the allegations. According to the article, Polyukhovich said that he'd lived in a village called Alexandrovo at the start of 1942 but had been sent later that year to another village sixty kilometres away. He'd said that he hadn't been based in Serniki when the villagers were massacred; in about February 1943 he'd been relocated to a German labour farm by the occupying German forces.

Maria was quoted as saying, 'The Germans killed a lot of people and at the time you never knew exactly where or when it was happening. Whenever it did, rumours would fly and the finger would be pointed everywhere at people scared of each other.' The article claimed that Maria had said her husband had been singled out unfairly because 'he'd carried a gun' and held an unpopular position as one of those policing his own people during the occupation.

Polyukhovich had told the reporter that he and his family had been writing to relatives in Ukraine for forty years and that the allegations in the telex stemmed from rumours and grudges. The article said Polyukhovich suspected that his first wife might have spread rumours. She had left him in 1940 and was not liked by the locals in Ukraine.

Polyukhovich was quoted as saying, 'So many terrible things happened during the war. There were Russian, German and Jewish partisans all killing people, confusion, accusations and hatred . . . I'm totally shocked.

I never killed anyone. I wasn't even in the regions that they are talking
about and I don't know why this has all surfaced after forty years ...
If I am so well-known as a monster in this region why hasn't anything
been said for so long? Why does it take forty years for something like this
to come out?'

———

Jeremy Jones, an officer with the Executive Council of Australian Jewry,
read the *Advertiser* articles into the telephone. On the other side of the
world Australian broadcaster Mark Aarons listened carefully and took
notes. Aarons had been investigating claims of war criminals living in
Australia for years and was now in Yugoslavia preparing a book on the
subject. He was negotiating a visit to the Soviet Union.

By the end of January 1987 Aarons, Andrei Bezruchenko – the Soviet
reporter named in the telex sent to Adelaide – and Australian Broadcasting Corporation correspondent Pierre Vicary were in Zarechnye, not
far from Serniki. One of the local Soviet officials introduced Aarons to
more than twenty villagers. Aarons insisted that the procurator not be
present during the interviews. He feared the witnesses might be intimi-
dated if an official was present. During the interviews Aarons produced
Bezruchenko's black-and-white photograph of Ivan Polyukhovich. This
was shown to the villagers. Aarons went with two of the local men to a
field. There he showed each of them the photograph while within earshot
of each other. The photograph had apparently been published in Soviet
newspaper articles throughout the region.

———

Aarons's work was part of a world-wide 'rediscovery' of the Holocaust.
The United States had carried out a handful of investigations into war
crimes suspects during the 1950s and 1960s, but they had been hap-
hazard and reluctant affairs. In the 1970s the US government had made
greater effort, but the cases remained badly prepared and tended to drag

on embarrassingly through the courts. After years of pressure from a few individuals, and on a wave of renewed public interest, the United States government in 1979 set up an Office of Special Investigations dedicated to investigating war crime suspects with a view to deporting them.

A series of cases attracted international attention. The most famous was that of John Demjanjuk, an automobile worker from Cleveland, Ohio, who was accused of being 'Ivan the Terrible', the guard who had operated Treblinka's gas chambers.

The United States had been only one destination in the massive post-war migration out of Europe, so it was inevitable that the same issue would arise in other countries. In February 1985 the Canadian government appointed an enquiry that eventually recommended about two hundred people be investigated for war crimes. Two years later Canada's parliament passed war crimes legislation and the first charges were soon laid.

Australia had received about two hundred thousand 'displaced persons'. Allegations that some of them had been Nazis had been made since soon after the war but it was Aarons's work that forced the government to act. He began investigating suspected war criminals in the late 1970s, travelling the world conducting interviews and searching archives. In 1986 he'd produced a series of radio programs for the Australian Broadcasting Corporation. This was followed by a feature on ABC television's 'Four Corners'.

The federal government responded to Aarons's work and lobbying by members of the Jewish community by appointing Andrew Menzies, who had been a senior official with the Attorney General's department, to conduct an official enquiry.

In late 1986, after five months' work, Menzies produced a report confirming that war criminals had almost certainly entered Australia. His findings, however, only served to create more problems than they solved. What was Australia to do with these suspects? Ignore them? Deport them, as the United States had done? Prosecute them in Australia? Menzies suggested the government confine its interest to the most serious allegations.

It was too late, he believed, to take action against mere collaborators or minor offenders. But the passage of time had never been sufficient reason not to prosecute murderers, and Menzies urged the government to take action to bring serious war criminals to justice.

The problem was that most of the suspects had migrated from what were now Eastern bloc countries. Both major political parties – Liberal and Labor – agreed it was unthinkable that old men who had become Australian citizens should be sent back to communist states for trial. At best the Soviet justice system was different; at worst these men would be given show trials. The Liberal opposition spokesman on legal affairs Peter Reith summed this up when he told parliament that those who disagreed with trials being held in Australia had to explain which alternative they preferred, 'turning a blind eye or extradition to Russia'.

Australia already had a war crimes act dating back to the end of the second world war, but it had only allowed for the creation of military tribunals to try Japanese defendants accused of crimes against Australian personnel. The act would need to be completely overhauled before it could be used against suspected Nazis. The Hawke Labor government spent several months drafting legislation to deal with war criminals in Australian courts; at the same time it continued investigations into the suspects.

In February 1987, queen's counsel Bob Greenwood was given the job of setting up a Special Investigations Unit. Greenwood had been a former member of the government's National Crime Authority, recently set up to fight organised crime. He'd also been a deputy director of public prosecutions. His small war crimes unit faced a daunting task. It wasn't long before several hundred cases had been lodged with the SIU and the volume of material made it difficult to know where to begin. Most of these cases would eventually be put aside as investigators discovered that suspects had died, never been in Australia or left the country. Some allegations were clearly unsubstantiated. By late 1988 the field had been narrowed to about two dozen very active files.

The government's bill was passed fairly swiftly by the House of Representatives. Although the Liberal opposition had expressed some reservations, both sides had agreed that war criminals could not be ignored, that there was no statute of limitations on murder and that any trials would have to be conducted by ordinary Australian courts. One minister had gone so far as to claim that the bill was 'one of the three greatest things that the Hawke government has done'.

By the time it reached the Senate in early 1988, however, opposition to the bill had grown. Now several senators described it as the 'most abhorrent bill' and the 'most dangerously and badly drafted bill ever seen'. One detested the legislation; another described it as 'un-Australian'. Each senator who damned the bill was quick to acknowledge that the Holocaust had occurred but what, they asked, would be gained by prosecuting its perpetrators so late in the day? West Australian Liberal senator John Panizza said, 'It may be wiser to let them be judged by their Maker . . . Who are we punishing by hauling these geriatrics before the court? We are punishing their children, their grandchildren and their great-grandchildren . . . who never saw these countries and never had anything to do with Nazi Germany'. Some senators said that Prime Minister Bob Hawke was repaying favours with the legislation. Others said that the government wanted to compensate the Jewish lobby for the recent policy shift towards recognising the Palestinian Liberation Organisation. National Party senator John Stone said that the bill was simply an attempt by the government to woo the 'Jewish vote'. Stone said that the ensuing trials would tear Australia's judicial system apart and bitterly divide the community. They would be show trials sustained by evidence from the Soviet Union, whose aim was to divide Australia's ethnic communities. National Party senator David Brownhill said the legislation had 'the potential to destroy the social fabric of Australian society'.

These dreadful warnings were mirrored by the media. In November

1988 a full-page feature in the *Australian Financial Review* began with the statement: 'Australia is now preparing to be torn apart by some of the most sensational trials the country has ever seen.' The article quoted an unnamed government source as saying, 'The nice seventy-five-year-old German man who has lived next door for forty years could suddenly turn into a dreaded Nazi accused of committing unthinkable atrocities on Jews during the war and of crimes against humanity. And I'm personally not convinced Australia will be able to cope.' A government adviser was quoted as saying that both sides of politics would be quietly happy if the issue disappeared for another five years. By then, most of the suspects and witnesses would have died, taking with them the hard decisions. A poll published in the Melbourne *Age* on 8 December 1988 declared that the majority of Australians didn't want war crimes trials. One thousand people had taken part in the survey. Only thirty-nine per cent wanted war crimes suspects prosecuted. Fifty-four per cent had opposed prosecution.

Many community leaders also opposed the bill. Archbishop of Melbourne David Penman urged Australian Democrat senators to vote against it. 'Will we become a nation who can exercise forgiveness and mercy or will we become a people committed to vengeance?' he asked. Retired South Australian judge Frank Moran QC predicted that the bill would become a 'blot on Australia's criminal jurisprudence which will never be erased'. The chairman of the Human Rights and Equal Opportunity Commission, Justice Marcus Einfeld, was repeatedly quoted as warning that justice would not flow from the bill. The national president of the Returned Services League, Brigadier Alf Garland, was quoted in the *Financial Review* as saying, 'You can't try people for 1940s' crimes with a 1980s' morality. We are now making people guilty of crimes that at the time they did not know were crimes.'

At this level of the debate those in favour of the bill were very effective. Although the bill was technically retrospective, they were able to argue that the mass killing of men, women and children was at all times a crime against humanity. The bill, supporters argued, was not about attacking ethnic communities; it was about holding individuals to account for their actions.

The bill was also attacked because it was restricted to Europe during the second world war. What of the millions of other innocents who had been slaughtered in other wars? What of Pol Pot's victims, Idi Amin's, or Stalin's? The government answered this in two ways. At a practical level the legislation was aimed at answering specific allegations that European war criminals had entered Australia. There was no evidence of any other type of war criminal living in the country. If such evidence arose the act could always be amended again. Philosophically, it argued that the Nazis were unique. They had set themselves apart with a policy of wiping out whole races and sections of communities – not just Jews but gypsies, homosexuals, and the intellectually disabled – on the basis that they were sub-human.

The debate in parliament was frequently passionate, particularly when the horrors of the Holocaust were recounted in detail. At times it was also astute. Independent senator Irina Dunn pointed out that the arguments against the trials were largely practical, legal and social whereas the arguments for the trials were ethical and emotional. Most of the time the antagonists were talking to each other from different levels. There was very little overlap.

Some members of the opposition feared that the legislation had greater potential to create injustice than justice. It was a complicated piece of legislation which, in a tortured fashion, made people who were now Australian citizens liable for prosecution for crimes committed in another country nearly fifty years before against victims who were not Australians. The government might claim that the atrocities described by the bill had always been crimes against humanity, but Australians had never seen anything like this. Wasn't there a danger that, once forced to do the impossible, the legal system would never quite be the same again?

The Liberal leader in the Senate, Robert Hill, feared that the 'easiest' cases would be prosecuted rather than the most serious ones. After a few high-profile trials the government would close down the investigations, claiming that it had done what it could. That, said Hill, was not justice. But while Hill believed that the government should 'go down the whole path' once it had started, the opposition had in fact pushed for the Special Investigations Unit to have a limited life – probably two years. It did not want the unit 'meandering around the world into the foreseeable future'.

In the end the opposition said it could not support the bill – although it still agreed that war criminals should be prosecuted – because it did not exempt former Australian service personnel. The opposition claimed that if any Australian servicemen and women were ever accused of war crimes they could be handled by military tribunals. There was no need for them to be included in the proposed act. The prospect of Australian personnel being charged had been raised throughout the debate. Airmen who had taken part in the bombing of Dresden in Germany were regularly cited as being at risk. The government had said there was no reason to believe any Australian personnel would be charged. ALP senator Chris Schacht went further and said it was an insult to suggest the actions of any Australians during the war could be equated with the Nazi atrocities. On principle, however, the government couldn't specifically exclude Australian personnel from the bill. To do so would be discriminatory. The government was prepared only to limit the bill to Europe, since this was where the war crimes covered by Menzies's report had occurred. This offered a measure of protection, because most Australians had served in the Pacific or Africa.

A year before the bill had reached the Senate and opposition to it had reached a crescendo, Attorney General Lionel Bowen had acknowledged all the problems it would create. Even so, he'd been philosophical. 'If we have even a handful of trials our courts will be overworked,' Bowen had said. 'Public opinion will be divided on the issue; juries will have the horrendous task of assessing problems that they do not really want to face up to themselves. If that is the way it has to be, that will have to be done, because Australia will not be put in the position of people here being allowed to escape the penalty of justice.'

The distinguishing feature of the Australian legislation, compared to the American approach, was that Australia's own judges and juries would decide the cases. That was also the government's standard answer to accusations that the trials would be unjust. The problems that evidence might be affected by time, language and Soviet interference could be happily left in the hands of the courts. The legislation fulfilled a moral obligation. If unfair trials followed it was the fault of the legal system, not the parliament. The Senate debate closed with the minister for justice, Michael Tate, saying that the matter would now be handed to the independent federal Director of Public Prosecutions. 'We are confident,' he said, 'that those protections and safeguardings of our judicial system will ensure that there will be no show trials with predetermined outcomes and that those persons who find themselves accused of these crimes will find in our courts the justice which they are entitled to find and which was so denied when the rule of law collapsed under the Nazi regime, unleashing war and destruction on Europe.' The War Crimes Amendment Bill was passed thirty-eight votes to thirty-three on the evening of 20 December 1988.

The Special Investigations Unit now had a law under which charges could be laid.

———

Outside it was ten degrees below zero, but the central heating in the Rovno procurator's office was stifling. The Australian investigators had walked through the snow wearing woollen underwear and thick coats. Inside the three-storey building, they stripped off their coats and the men worked in their shirt sleeves. The only woman among the investigators, Anne Dowd, opened a window to allow icy air into the room, despite protests from the senior official from Moscow, Mrs Koleznekova, that they would all die of pneumonia.

Mrs Koleznekova was a very thin woman who seemed to live on her nerves, always needing to be the centre of attention. In Rovno, she was a powerful person, but she didn't look at all well. She didn't look comfortable in her high-heeled shoes and Muscovite clothes.

The Special Investigations Unit had been trying to get into the Soviet Union throughout 1989. The Soviet government had sent permission to enter late in the year. Almost all the unit had then gathered in Moscow, before splitting up to investigate their respective cases. Some had gone to Latvia, others to Lithuania. Bob Reid, Graham Blewitt, Bruce Huggett and Anne Dowd had gone south to Ukraine.

The Rovno office had been used by the Gestapo as a regional headquarters during the war, but the SIU group were in the 'new' section that had been built during the past thirty years. It was used for meetings and addresses. Pictures of past local officials hung down one wall; at one end were a podium, the hammer and sickle and a bust of Lenin. The trappings of communism still adorned Ukrainian buildings in 1989.

Mrs Koleznekova, still concerned about the dangerously open windows, asked how the Australians wanted the room set up. Their response was to remove most of the chairs and arrange the remaining furniture so that they would be seated on one side of a long table with the windows behind them. This would allow their video equipment to take advantage of any natural light, which would shine on the faces of the witnesses about to enter.

It was ten in the morning. The room was ready for the old men and women waiting outside. Dozens of them would file through the office during the next three weeks. The majority of witnesses were from villages in the Rovno district, but others were from Kiev in the east and Kirovograd in the south. Some had been bussed in from Serniki and Zarechnye three hours to the north. The men wore worn-out suits over their flannel shirts, and caps on their grey heads. The women wore dresses with thick shawls. They took off their coats and gloves before entering the interview room.

Bob Reid had joined the Special Investigations Unit in July 1987. Like many of its investigators, he had been recruited from the National Crime Authority. Before that, he'd been a New South Wales homicide detective. He was a keen sportsman, hated flying, laughed a lot and smoked too much. He always gave the impression that he liked people. Until May 1989, when he'd been appointed to the investigation into Ivan Polyukhovich, he'd been investigating a number of German suspects. At the time very little work had been done on the Polyukhovich case, but over the last few months it had emerged as one of the most promising investigations. Polyukhovich had not been among the initial seventy suspects identified by Menzies. Rather, the case had originated from a meeting held in Ukraine in 1986 to mark the fortieth anniversary of the Nuremberg trials. The first the Australian government had heard of it had been the telex to the Adelaide *Advertiser* three years ago.

The original brief had consisted of the Soviet telex, the Australian newspaper articles, a petition from a group of Ukrainian villagers, and tape recordings Mark Aarons had made with alleged witnesses in early 1987. Reid's first move had been to visit Israel, where he'd asked the SIU's consultant there, Miri Drucker, to contact any survivors from the Zarechnye region who might have made their way to Israel after the war. Reid had also visited Yad Vashdm, the huge Holocaust museum in Jerusalem, where thousands of testimonies of second world war survivors were kept. Two names had emerged from there of people who might have been able to throw some light on the Zarechnye claims – Isaar Glazer, who had lived in Haifa, and David Zaltzmann. It turned out that Zaltzmann had died some time before, but his widow had suggested that Miri Drucker should contact a man named Zelig Keufmann. Keufmann was the secretary of a group called the Serniki Survivors' Organisation. Members of this group met each year in Israel to commemorate atrocities not unlike those marked by the remembrance day ceremony at Zarechnye in late 1986.

The SIU's consultant in the United States made similar enquiries and a list was compiled of survivors from the Zarechnye region, who were now scattered across the western world. Reid spent September interviewing these witnesses in Israel, the United States and Canada. On his return to Australia on 3 October 1989 he'd been presented with a pile of statements from the Soviet Union. These had been apparently made by witnesses from the Zarechnye region between May and August 1987. The statements lasted from two to five pages and in some cases they appeared to come in pairs. One statement outlined the evidence of a witness, while another consisted of a re-enactment of what the witness described.

Reid, Blewitt and Huggett had met quickly with senior members from the Office of the Director of Public Prosecutions. On paper, at least, there appeared to be a case against Ivan Polyukhovich. The Ukrainian villagers and the Jewish survivors in the west appeared to remember similar events, and these two groups had not been in contact for more than forty years. The Ukrainian witnesses, however, would need to be interviewed by Australian personnel. Apart from one Jewish witness in Israel, a very old man by the name of Ze'ev Erdmann, none of those interviewed in the west had been able to give eyewitness evidence linking Polyukhovich to any crimes. The Ukrainian statements, by contrast, appeared to name a number of eyewitnesses to nearly thirty separate allegations. Any prosecution would end up relying on the Ukrainian witnesses. But the Special Investigations Unit and the Director of Public Prosecutions were wary of information coming from the Soviet Union. No matter how strong the case appeared, the Ukrainian witnesses would have to be approached as if their evidence was the product of a Soviet plot.

———

When Graham Blewitt had joined the Special Investigations Unit in September 1988, he'd doubted whether they would ever be able to gather sufficient evidence to mount a murder trial. But investigating war crimes suspects had got into his blood. He'd been caught up in the enthusiasm shown by his boss, Bob Greenwood, who had declared that prosecuting war criminals was a great 'civilising' activity.

Blewitt had worked as a prosecutor and solicitor for the New South Wales crown nearly all his life. He'd joined the Office of the Director of Public Prosecutions straight from school in 1965, and had worked there as a clerk while studying law at night. He'd been promoted gradually, until he was working on the most senior cases. In the mid-1980s, Blewitt had been asked to join the National Crime Authority, where he'd met Greenwood. They had worked together closely on the extradition of one of Australia's most notorious criminals, Bruce 'Snapper' Cornwall. Blewitt had developed loyalty and respect for Greenwood, who believed in everything he did and whose beliefs were infectious. Blewitt was confident that, if there was evidence against any suspect, Greenwood would find it. He was a very good lawyer, quick to perceive a fool or a villain. Greenwood had wanted his friend to join the SIU for a long time and eventually Blewitt agreed. He became Greenwood's second in command.

Blewitt's greatest concern had always been the issue of identification. He failed to see how, after nearly half a century, any witnesses would be able to identify a person now in his seventies or eighties. But he had learned very early in the Special Investigation Unit's life that International Refugee Organisation documents had been discovered in the official Australian archives. These documents had been used during the selection of migrants wanting to enter Australia from Europe after the war. They contained photographs of immigrants that would have been taken at the same time as, or shortly after, any of these people had committed offences during the war

——

Senior assistant procurator Vasily Dmitrie Melnishan was a highly disorganised person. Investigator Bob Reid fell into the habit of calling him

'Mel'. Each morning, on the way to the procurator's office, he would ask, 'How many witnesses we got today, Mel?'

'Two,' Mel might reply.

Good, the Australians would think, easy day today, only to find the interviews were still going a dozen witnesses later.

The next day Reid would ask again, 'How many today Mel?'

'Twenty,' Mel would reply.

Heavy day today, the Australians would think and then discover that only one witness had been brought in.

Melnishan was present at all of the interviews during the SIU's stay in Ukraine. After each witness entered, he explained why the Australians were there and handed over the interview to the investigators and their interpreters, who were provided by the Australian and Soviet governments. Bruce Huggett usually started by explaining that allegations had been received in Australia about a man living in Australia. Then Reid would take over and ask the questions. At the end of the interview, or sometimes during it, Melnishan would interrupt to clarify some inconsistency between what the witness had said compared with a previous statement. Sometimes Reid would then reclarify Melnishan's clarification. The video camera recorded everything.

Reid was free to ask whatever he liked, but occasionally the procurators would try to speed things up, especially if it was late at night. Mrs Koleznekova was especially impatient. Reid argued with her nearly every day. She would say that he was asking the most ridiculous questions. Why, for instance, did he insist on asking the witnesses when the war had started? *Everyone* knew. Reid, however, had discovered that many of the witnesses didn't know. Certainly none of them had ever heard of the 'second world war'. It had even taken a while to establish that, in this part of the world, the conflict was called 'the great patriotic war'. Mrs Koleznekova would declare that, if they didn't hurry up, the Australians would be there at Christmas. 'You do want to be home for Christmas?' she would ask, fearing the answer.

But Reid was in no hurry. He could outlast Mrs Koleznekova. When she eventually went back to Moscow, it was a relief to everyone.

The SIU investigation team had believed that the 1987 statements provided by the Soviets had come from eyewitnesses. It soon became apparent that this was not always the case. Sometimes the witnesses hadn't actually seen what they were describing, but were relating information told to them by their parents, an aunt or a friend long since dead. The witnesses seemed to appreciate the difference between what they had seen and what someone else had told them, but not why they should be stopped from telling the dead relative's story. If they didn't tell the story, who would?

———

High above the square was a clock that gave the citizens of Rovno three vital pieces of information. Reid had worked out that the first figure was the time, although clearly it was wrong. The second reading appeared to be the temperature; he also doubted its accuracy. The third reading baffled him. As he and the other Australians walked through the square, he pointed up at the machine and asked the translator from Rovno, Stas Kostesky, what it meant. 'That's the radiation level,' Stas informed the group without halting his pace.

The Australians had been aware of the risk of radiation in Ukraine following the explosion at the Chernobyl nuclear power plant three years before. They had made enquiries with radiation experts in Sydney, and had been told merely to watch what they ate and drank. They'd brought about thirty kilograms of food with them, but now they wanted to know if the Ukrainians knew something that they should.

'When do we worry?' Reid asked.

'When the reading reaches twenty-five or twenty-six,' Kostesky answered. The reading appeared always to hover between about fifteen and eighteen.

They were making their way through the square again a few days later when Reid noticed the radiation reading. 'Stas, it's reading twenty-nine. Should we worry now?' he asked.

'No, it's never right anyway,' the translator answered without stopping.

————

Sometimes the Ukrainians wondered about the Australians. Reid had never seen snow before. When someone mentioned that it was snowing, he'd suddenly suspended the interviews. The Australians were soon outside. It didn't take very long for a snowball fight to start.

————

Anyone walking along the badly-maintained road would have heard laughter from the back of the van as it passed. It was a three- or four-hour journey from Rovno to Serniki and someone had suggested they tell jokes to pass the time. After nearly a month in the Soviet Union, the Australians had built up a lively friendship with their Soviet interpreters and the procurators who shared the van.

The investigators had been encouraged by the interviews in Rovno. Witnesses had given evidence about several suspects. The Polyukhovich case, however, had become the strongest. As well as those witnesses mentioned in the Soviet documents, the Australians had found others who claimed to have seen other events. They had decided to visit the village of Serniki, to find more witnesses and video the area.

Reid was satisfied by now that his case was not the product of a KGB plot. It was obvious to him that the people they had interviewed had not been coached or trained by some agency. It had become apparent after just a few witnesses that these people simply weren't sophisticated enough to stick to a bogus story. If there had been just one Soviet witness, then that person could have been explained away by some sinister government plan. But the SIU had interviewed dozens of people in Ukraine, Israel, the United States and Canada. If there was a conspiracy, it was an international one. Reid had feared that, after the first few witnesses had been instructed to talk only about what they had personally seen, word would get out and all the witnesses would claim to be eyewitnesses. The witnesses, however, continued to admit that sometimes they only knew what they had been told. There were inconsistencies among their stories and within the individual testimonies, but Reid and the others saw these as marks of authenticity. If all the Ukrainians had related exactly the same story more than forty years after the war, alarm bells would have rung.

The Australians were satisfied each of the witnesses had told their own stories. If the witnesses were KGB agents, they were the most brilliant KGB agents ever, and the Soviet Union had placed them all in a Ukrainian backwater in order to damn an old man living on the other side of the world.

Graham Blewitt had read about the Serniki region. He expected the van to drive into a ghostly terrain of marshes and forests. He realised, as the kilometres passed, that the land was not unlike rural Australia. The swamps had been drained long ago, and the flat land was devoted to agriculture. Except for the trees, they could have been in the Hay plains or Wagga.

As they approached Serniki, however, they returned to another world, rural Soviet Ukraine. Serniki was a primitive place. Homes had thatched roofs; there were no modern buildings. Most of the water was taken from wells. Motorised vehicles were rare and old, horse-drawn carts were common. Children and grey-haired peasants stared at them as they drove in. Blewitt had the impression the town was populated by the very old and young.

———

The Australians were staying a few kilometres from Serniki in a long, two-storey building, which they nicknamed the 'Zarechnye Hilton'. There were no showers and the water poured down the hotel's only toilet ended up in the back yard. The locals had been warned that the visitors would be arriving soon, and had painted the whole place. Floors, walls, doors and ceilings were all two tones of blue – light and dark. The smell of fresh paint was overwhelming.

The local procurator's wife, a slight woman in her forties, ran the hotel. She showed her delight at having such important and exotic guests as she took them to their rooms, all of which were upstairs off a corridor that ran the length of the hotel. Each small room faced the street and contained a bed, a small cabinet and a sink with a cold water tap in the corner. There were no curtains.

———

It was night, time to rest. While the Australians at times felt overwhelmed by the poverty around them, their confidence in what they were doing was growing daily. Blewitt mulled over the case. He had come to realise that there would actually be a prosecution. On his return, seventy-three-year-old Ivan Timofeyevich Polyukhovich would be charged with war crimes. It would be alleged that the pensioner had grown up in the region, worked as a forest warden during the German occupation and actively collaborated in the killing of Jews and partisans. My God, thought Blewitt, we've even found relatives of the old man prepared to give evidence against him. Blewitt was sure the witnesses would be up to the task.

A large light lit up the street in front of the Zarechnye Hilton. It poured through the curtainless window of his room as he lay on the bed, smelling the paint.

———

Investigators Bob Reid and Bruce Huggett and translator Rosa Leventhal walked up the driveway of the ordinary Adelaide home. It was just after nine in the morning of Thursday 25 January 1990. They knocked on the front door and an elderly woman appeared. Through the screen they met Maria Andreyevna Polyukhovich. Reid knew she had been ill. His information suggested she'd had open-heart surgery. He didn't want to upset her and asked simply whether Mr Polyukhovich was home.

'No, he isn't,' Maria replied. 'He's at the motor registration office.' She spoke with a heavy East European accent.

Since Reid had returned from Ukraine in early January the Director of Public Prosecutions had given him authority to lay the charges in his own name. Reid had also been told to use his discretion in carrying out the arrest. They had a search warrant, but Reid didn't want to wait with Maria Polyukhovich for as long as it took for her husband to come home. He decided to retreat gracefully, but Maria demanded an explanation.

'There's no problem at all,' Reid told her. 'Don't worry. There's nothing to worry about. We'd just like to have a bit of a talk to him, that's all.'

'What? What? I want to know what's happened!' she insisted.

'Nothing. Nothing's happened at all,' answered Reid. 'There are no problems. You don't have to worry about anything at all. He's quite safe as far as we're aware. There's nothing happened to him at all, okay?'

When Maria persisted in asking the reason for their visit, Reid and Huggett said they were from the government. Maria was still unsatisfied.

'It's just a routine thing,' Reid finally told her.

It was a lie but the investigator considered it a lie in her best interests. The last thing they wanted was for Maria to suffer a heart attack in front of them or after they left.

'Nah, nah, not routine,' said Maria through the screen door.

Reid explained again they didn't want to upset her and said goodbye. They'd come back tomorrow.

As they walked down the driveway Huggett spoke without looking at Reid. 'There was another woman in there.'

'Was there?' asked Reid. He'd been doing most of the talking and hadn't noticed. 'That's probably the daughter. Do you reckon he's there?'

Huggett kept walking. 'I think so.'

At midday, they received a call from the police officer who'd been left in Polyukhovich's street in an unmarked car. A man fitting Polyukhovich's description had been seen crossing the road. It had looked as though Polyukhovich might have been on his way to visit his daughter, who lived close by, but he'd turned around and gone home.

This time another SIU officer, Paul Malone, went with Reid, Huggett and Leventhal to the suspect's address.

Maria appeared at the screen door again. 'No, he's still not home,' she said.

Reid knew it was time to be firm. He explained that they had a search warrant, didn't want to upset her but did need to come inside and speak with Mr Polyukhovich.

Malone appeared behind the old woman and opened the door. He'd entered through the back.

———

Reid was trying to keep control. The elderly couple were speaking randomly, at times over each other, switching from English to Polish. Maria was looking ill.

Reid explained that they were investigating allegations that Mr Polyukhovich was involved in activities during the war in Ukraine. Polyukhovich exclaimed that he'd been in Germany from 1941 to 1943 and had never caused any trouble. He'd never been in the army or the police. The investigators told him to wait. He could explain things later at the police station.

Polyukhovich said he had some documentation and Reid was shown two faded documents, like passports. They had been kept in a purse in the bottom drawer of a dresser next to Polyukhovich's bed. They were second world war German work books, issued to foreigners; official documents of the Third Reich. One of them bore the name 'Johann Polichowicz'. It stated that the man pictured was born on 15 June 1916, in the town of Serniki in the Pinsk region. The other belonged to a 'Marie Polichowitsch', born on 10 May 1918. The workbook said she had two daughters: Anna, born in May 1938, and Luba, born in November 1941. Polyukhovich admitted ownership and explained that Maria had kept them as mementos.

Polyukhovich was struggling to control himself. He asked whether the police officers would like a drink of Coca-Cola or lemonade. They declined. Polyukhovich asked them where they were from. 'Sydney,' they told him.

Maria interrupted. 'Yeah, you want him dead,' she said.

'No, we don't want that at all,' Reid answered. He was sensitive to criticism that the Special Investigations Unit was persecuting old people.

'You want him dead,' Maria said again, convinced of their intentions.

'Mrs was sick. She has a stroke,' Polyukhovich said almost apologetically.

Reid asked if he wanted to get changed before they left.

'Do I have to change? Little bit better than something like this?' asked Polyukhovich.

'It's up to you, if you want to get changed,' Reid told him. He suggested that Polyukhovich might like to go to the bathroom.

Maria asked whether they would bring her husband back, and Reid promised that they'd look after him. She was becoming increasingly upset, and Polyukhovich was muttering words that were hard to understand.

'She'll be all right,' Reid told him.

Huggett was more formal. 'We will do everything within our power to offer any comfort we can to her,' he said.

Polyukhovich asked them not to take his wife, saying that she was too sick. 'Mrs stop home?'

'She'll be right. She's going to stay here all right,' Reid assured him. 'I'm sorry we've had to do it that way but it's the only way we could do it. We didn't want to upset her.'

'I know, I know, I know,' Polyukhovich answered.

'And we didn't want to upset you,' Reid said.

'You did your job,' Polyukhovich told him.

'That's right. That's all we're doing, our job.'

'My job different when I was working,' said Polyukhovich.

'That's right. You built houses; we investigate.'

Reid and Huggett were waiting for Malone and the other officers who had now arrived to finish their search of the house. Polyukhovich asked why they had to go to the police station.

'Oh we want to speak to you,' Reid told him. 'We want to try and get all this cleared up okay. And you're the only one that can help us clear it all up.'

Reid helped Maria to her bedroom. She needed to lie down, and he didn't want her to hear what would follow. He returned and explained slowly to Ivan that he had reason to believe he had been involved in the deaths of about 850 Jewish people from Serniki. He was now arresting him in relation to that matter. Polyukhovich said he understood. Reid read him his rights. By the time Reid had finished, the pensioner appeared confused, so Reid explained his rights again.

'Dear God, what are you arresting me for?' Polyukhovich cried out when Reid finished.

Polyukhovich said he had never been in Serniki. He'd stayed in Alexandrovo. He had never seen the killing. Was arresting him the same as putting him in gaol?

Reid gave Polyukhovich a card with the Australian Federal Police phone number printed on it and told him to give it to his wife. Again Polyukhovich told them he was not guilty. He'd made no trouble. 'Believe, believe me.'

———

Polyukhovich shifted himself into the middle of the back seat of the government car so that Reid and Leventhal could sit on either side. Huggett was driver. Looking out the window, Polyukhovich saw his son-in-law had arrived at the house and was standing in the garden.

They drove off. The investigators had no idea how to get to the Australian Federal Police headquarters. Reid offered directions from a street directory. Polyukhovich tried to help, until he also admitted that he didn't know where they were.

'You're as lost as me all right,' Reid said, looking back down at the directory.

———

At police headquarters Polyukhovich explained that he was born in Serniki but had moved to Alexandrovo, about seven kilometres away, when he was a small child. He had no memory of shifting. His father had died when he was nine, and at ten, after three years of school, he had begun to work full time on the family farm. At seventeen he had begun working in the forest for the Polish government. He'd stayed on in the job under the Russians and then for about two years under the Germans. His duties for the Germans had involved stopping people from stealing. If he caught anyone he was supposed to report them, but he hadn't reported many, because the fines were heavy.

Polyukhovich said he did visit Serniki. He was asked whether he could say anything about the deaths of 850 Jews in September 1942. No, he didn't know what happened there. 'Polish Jews, beautiful, good people,' he said.

'Okay, now did you have anything to do with the death of any of these Jewish people?' Reid asked.

'No, nothing.'

Polyukhovich said that Maria was his first and only wife and he was her first and only husband. Anna and Luba were his natural daughters. He said that he had never been known as 'Ivanechko' or 'Yanechko' and denied telling the *Advertiser* journalist in 1986 he'd been called 'Ivanechko'. Late in the interview he was told Maria had admitted to the investigators he'd had the nick-name 'Ivanechko'. 'I was never known as "Ivanechko". My wife is sick today and she doesn't know what she is saying,' he said.

Reid told him that Maria had also said that he was her second husband. 'Poor thing is sick today and cannot speak,' he explained.

The interview finished at 9.48 PM. Polyukhovich was taken away to be processed at the city watch-house.

Lawyers, magistrates
and judges

Lawyers, magistrates and judges

The next morning, Adelaide was preparing to celebrate Australia Day. One reporter had little interest in these activities. He left the large, impressive Samuel Way Building, which housed a small press room as well as most of Adelaide's Supreme and District Courts, and walked along the boundary of Victoria Square to the Magistrates Courts. He made this trip each morning to pick up a list of the matters to be heard that day. Always attached to the list were a few 'over-nighters' – people who had been arrested after the list was compiled the day before. On his way back to the press room he scanned the list and stopped smartly when he read: 'Polyukhovich, Ivan, also known as Ivanechko, also known as Jan Poluchowicz, also known as John Poluchowicz . . . War Crimes (9).'

The matter was listed for 9.40, which gave him about twenty-five minutes. First things first. Get a photographer down here fast, and keep the information away from the *Advertiser*'s other court reporter, who was older, had been at the paper longer, and would almost certainly try to pull rank and take the story. The reporter wasn't about to let that happen, but keeping the news to himself for nearly half an hour would be harder than getting a photographer here in time. At 9.30 he had somehow avoided his partner, and was waiting in courtroom one. Other reporters from radio, television and newspapers were waiting there as well. Lawyers Grant Niemann and David Stokes came in and took their places at the large wooden table situated in front of the magistrate's bench.

Stokes was a well-known criminal lawyer in Adelaide with his own small, busy practice based in the city. He was a former sprint champion, who was still involved in athletics as a senior coach. As of last night, he was Polyukhovich's lawyer. Stokes knew one of Polyukhovich's step-grandsons through his sporting contacts, and the family had turned to him for help a few hours after the arrest. By the time he'd arrived at Australian Federal Police headquarters on Greenhill Road, the interview had almost finished. Polyukhovich had greeted the lawyer with a nervous smile and explained that a 'nice lady' was helping him talk with the police. He was apparently referring to the translator, but Stokes had been concerned about how much Polyukhovich had in fact understood. He had advised him not to answer any more questions. Polyukhovich had indicated that he wanted to finish the interview.

When the interview had finished, Stokes was surprised to find that police bail was refused. Huggett had intercepted the old man walking in his back yard. This was considered a sign of flight. So if Polyukhovich wanted bail he would have to ask a magistrate in the morning. Stokes thought this was ludicrous. Where would Polyukhovich run? Both of his step-daughters lived in the same suburb and he was hardly quick on his feet.

Polyukhovich had spent the night in the city watch-house.

Grant Niemann had been in charge of the federal Office of the Director of Public Prosecutions in Adelaide for seven months. When he'd accepted the position he'd been only vaguely aware of the war crimes legislation, but he'd soon learnt that South Australia might be the first state to see a prosecution. He and Stokes had agreed this morning before coming to court that Polyukhovich could have bail. Stokes thought that the conditions Niemann demanded were too stringent, but the important thing was to get his client out of custody. The bail could always be re-negotiated.

Everyone stood as the magistrate, Grantley Harris, came in and sat down in a seat that looked more like a throne. It was framed by ornate white and gold plaster that continued along what appeared to be a white concrete canopy. This room had been used by the Supreme Court when South Australia was still a colony, and had been built to impress. Now it looked shabby. White paint was flaking away from the ceiling eight metres above the accused man, who had been led in by one of the cell officers.

Polyukhovich stood in the dock wearing trousers and a light blue shirt. Whatever thoughts were going through *his* mind, the lawyers knew they were taking part in Australian legal history. After this morning their names and pictures would be in newspapers and on television broadcasts around the world. Stokes had heard about the war crimes legislation, but had assumed that any prosecutions would be conducted in the larger cities of Sydney and Melbourne. Now, here in Adelaide, he would be representing the very first Australian European war crimes defendant

Investigator Bob Reid was sitting in the public gallery. His boss, SIU director Bob Greenwood, was there too.

Stokes told magistrate Harris that he was applying for bail, which wasn't opposed by the prosecution. He said he'd also be applying for a suppression order, but added that the application only related to publication of the defendant's address. Stokes didn't want some lunatic stalking the old man at his home.

Niemann outlined the bail conditions required by the prosecution. Polyukhovich was to live at his home address and not change that address without the court's permission. He was to report to Australian Federal Police headquarters at Unley each Saturday, Tuesday and Thursday. He was to surrender any passports in his possession, whether in his name or otherwise, and he was not to apply for any passport while on bail. He was not to approach any international departure point or leave the jurisdiction without the permission of the court and he was not to approach any prosecution witnesses. He must agree to forfeit the sum of twenty thousand dollars if he failed to keep this bail agreement without a proper excuse.

Stokes thought it worth mentioning that, while it had been agreed his client wouldn't approach any witnesses, it was necessary for the defence to know the identities of these people. Otherwise contact might be made unintentionally.

Niemann said that the prosecution simply wanted an undertaking that witnesses wouldn't be approached when they were known to the defence. He added that there were several matters relating to audio and video tapes which needed attention. He suggested the best course was to adjourn the matter until 2 March.

The magistrate ordered the bail agreement as requested and gave an order suppressing publication of Polyukhovich's address.

The more experienced reporters sitting in court were surprised that Stokes hadn't asked the court to suppress publication of Polyukhovich's name. Adelaide's judiciary had a national reputation for granting such orders. But South Australia's legislation had recently been changed to make it more difficult for people charged with offences to keep their identities from the public. Perhaps Stokes didn't believe an application could succeed. Nearly two years later defence lawyers for two other South Australian men charged with war crimes would try desperately without success to keep their names secret.

The hearing had taken only a few minutes. Before leaving the dock, Polyukhovich quietly said, 'Thank you very much.' It wasn't clear whether he was talking to the magistrate, the lawyers or the court in general. With a tight grip on Stokes's arm, Polyukhovich walked out of the court, into the sunshine and a group of television cameramen and newspaper photographers who'd been waiting for them in the street. Stokes said a few words while Polyukhovich, apparently not understanding what was going on, walked along with a nervous grin on his face, nodding to the cameras. He was plainly overawed by what was taking place. One television crew persisted in trying to get a response long after the others had given up. 'What did Polyukhovich have to say?' 'Why are you grinning, Mr Polyukhovich?'

Stokes had had enough but he chose his words carefully. 'Don't you realise this is an old man you're addressing?'

The television camera kept filming until they were about a block away from the court.

It was nearly ten. Apart from the label of 'war crimes', none of the media people had much idea what this man was accused of doing. The reporter obtained a copy of the charges. Each of them seemed to be long on legal jargon and short on detail. Many of them did not even identify the alleged victims by name.

Count one alleged that between about 1 August and 30 September 1941, Polyukhovich had murdered a woman 'described as Sercha, two other women whose names are not known but who are described as the daughters of the woman Sercha', and a male child believed to be Sercha's grandchild. These killings were alleged to have occurred near the village of Alexandrovo in the Rovno District of Ukraine.

Count two alleged that between 1 June and 30 September 1942, Polyukhovich had murdered a woman known as Tsalykha, her daughter and her grand-daughter near Alexandrovo.

Count three alleged that between 1 June and 30 September 1942, Polyukhovich had murdered one female person and two male persons described as having belonged to the Yankiber family near Alexandrovo.

Count four alleged that during September 1942 Polyukhovich had murdered one woman, two female children aged about fourteen and nine and one male child aged about one near the village of Serniki in the Rovno District. The names of the victims weren't known.

Count five alleged that during September 1942 Polyukhovich was knowingly concerned in the murder of about 850 people near Serniki 'whose names are not known but who are described as the Jews from the Serniki ghetto'.

Jackpot, thought the reporter. He continued reading.

Count six alleged that during September 1942 Polyukhovich had murdered an unnamed woman, described as 'the miller's daughter', and two male children, aged about seven and three, near Serniki.

Count seven alleged that during April 1943 Polyukhovich had murdered five people near the village of Brodnitsa in the Rovno District. They were Dmitry Kuzmich Turuk, Antonina Semyonovna Turuk, Kondrat Yefimovich Delidon, Alexei Kondratyevich Delidon and Lida Mesnikovich.

Count eight alleged that Polyukhovich had murdered a man called Pyotr Stephanovich Krupko near Alexandrovo between 1 April and 31 May 1943.

The last charge, count nine, alleged that between 1 April and 31 May 1943, Polyukhovich had murdered a woman described as Tsalykha's daughter near Serniki.

In all, twenty-four individual murders plus an alleged involvement in a mass killing.

As the reporter read the document a television journalist saw what he had in his hands. 'Have you got a copy of the charges?' she asked.

'Yes,' replied the reporter. 'I'll go and make a copy.'

'Is that the charges?' asked another television reporter.

'Er, yes. I'll make a few copies.'

There was no point in being difficult.

An hour later the charges had been handed out, the reporter's editor had been informed of the morning's events, and his partner was in a fury knowing that he had just missed out on the first appearance of the first Australian citizen charged with European war crimes.

Now, thought the reporter, where on earth's Serniki?

———

There was no way the South Australian Legal Services Commission was going to pay for Polyukhovich's defence. The commission was a government-funded organisation set up to provide legal aid. Certainly Polyukhovich qualified for assistance, but his case threatened to blow away the organisation's budget. Commission director, Lindy Powell, said it was impossible to predict how much Polyukhovich's case would cost but it was likely to be a six figure sum. The rejection, however, was merely a procedural matter that allowed Polyukhovich to apply for funding directly to the federal government under the War Crimes Act. If the government refused his request, both houses of parliament had to be told the reasons.

———

Within three weeks of Polyukhovich's arrest, investigators Bob Reid, Anne Dowd and Bruce Huggett were on a plane bound from Australia for Israel to interview witnesses again. Within two weeks of arriving, they were on their way once more to Ukraine. The Special Investigations Unit hoped to find still more witnesses not mentioned in the original Soviet statements. It was also looking for people who could verify times, dates and places, even if they were not eyewitnesses to crimes.

Reid called a public meeting at the Zarechnye school hall to appeal for any information whatsoever that could help the Australians. There were just a few thousand people living in several small villages in the immedi- ate area, and the Australians knew that there must have been talk about Ivanechko since the team's visit only three months ago. Nevertheless, Reid thought it important to keep the information he passed on at the meeting as vague as possible. He didn't want to be accused later of having put ideas into the heads of potential witnesses.

Reid stood at the front of the hall packed with about two hundred people, and explained through an interpreter that someone had been arrested in Australia for offences committed in and around the area. The accused person was said to have collaborated with the Germans and had been charged with a number of murders allegedly committed in about 1942. Reid said that the Australians were looking for anyone who might be able to help the investigators or exonerate the accused. He made it clear to Melnishan, the local official who oversaw the meeting, that they didn't simply want witnesses who would implicate Polyukhovich.

The investigators spoke with several witnesses over the next few days.

Some were helpful, but others were telling stories told to them by relatives long dead. While Reid was conducting the formal interviews, Huggett would mix with the villagers, looking for that person who might know something but was too shy or scared to come forward.

During this trip the Australians discovered Dmitry Ivanovich Kostyukhovich. Kostyukhovich was a decorated veteran of the great patriotic war and he would become the SIU's star witness. The sixty-six-year-old man told the Australians that he had lived on a farm next to Ivanechko's sister before the war started, and had seen Ivanechko frequently. When the war broke out, he'd joined the partisans. Kostyukhovich said that in the autumn of 1942 the partisans sent him to Serniki to gather information. Peering from a shed on a property on the outskirts of the town, he'd seen Ivanechko helping Ukrainian police officers force Jewish people out of their homes. As the column of Jews started to move forward he'd seen two young lads break away and run towards the River Stubla, which separated Kostyukhovich from the town. He'd seen Ivanechko shoot first one of the youths and then the other. Kostyukhovich thus provided the SIU with another two murders with which to charge Polyukhovich. More importantly, he could give further evidence that Polyukhovich had taken part in the liquidation of the ghetto from the very start of that terrible day.

———

Five days before Reid interviewed Kostyukhovich, on 16 March 1990, the defence in Adelaide had agreed that a South Australian magistrate should be allowed to take evidence overseas. Although Polyukhovich had been charged under federal legislation, the relevant rules of evidence were South Australian. The state's Justices Act required a defendant to be present at all times during the taking of evidence against him. This had presented the prosecution with a problem. They agreed that taking Polyukhovich to the witnesses would be far too onerous for a man in his seventies. It could also have been risky. It was always possible that if Polyukhovich stepped foot in Ukraine, the local authorities might arrest and try him on the spot. Bringing all the witnesses to Adelaide, however, was equally unattractive. They too were old, and a number of them were unwell. Only a small minority, if any, would ever have travelled by plane, and the prosecution didn't know whether they'd be prepared to travel to Australia. Somebody in the commonwealth government had worked out that taking the Australian court overseas would cost half as much as bringing the witnesses to Adelaide. The solution was to take the evidence 'on-commission'. Under this arrangement, Polyukhovich would be excused from attending hearings held overseas in the presence of a magistrate. The witnesses at these hearings would be examined and cross-examined just as they would be at a normal committal hearing. This evidence would be formally tendered, subject to arguments over its admissibility, at the start of Polyukhovich's committal in Adelaide.

The committal hearing was a legal filter. Rather than send an accused person directly to a jury a magistrate would first examine the evidence. Based on this the magistrate would decide if there was sufficient evidence to place Polyukhovich on trial in the Supreme Court. The committal system was based on the rationale that it was better to first test prosecutions before spending lots of time and money on them. In practice only the most outrageously bad prosecutions tended to be dismissed by magistrates. Still, defence lawyers found them extremely useful. They offered an opportunity to test the prosecution case without a jury watching. If a case was dismissed the prosecution had the option of relaying any charges directly in the Supreme Court, but it would inevitably have to convince the judge in pre-trial argument that the magistrate had been wrong.

The prosecution had been surprised when Stokes agreed to their proposal to take evidence on-commission. After all, every witness who was too ill or old to make the journey would be one less witness who could give evidence. But then, nothing like this had ever been done before. It was difficult to predict how the other side would react. The defence could think of reasons for going along with the prosecution. Hearing the witnesses in their own environment would mean that their appearance at the actual trial would be during their first visit to Australia. Better to have them fresh and nervous at the trial than allow them to get used to Australia with an earlier visit. Doing the work in Ukraine would also mean the defence would have immediate access to any other potential witnesses mentioned during the hearing.

Supervising Magistrate Peter Kelly had set aside the weeks between 2 July and 3 August 1990 for the overseas hearings and announced that he'd be the magistrate to hear the evidence.

The defence had warned they would be launching a challenge in the federal High Court to the validity of the war crimes legislation under which Polyukhovich had been charged. No date had been set, but most expected that the hearing would begin in mid-June. If the High Court decided that the legislation was invalid, the on-commission hearings would obviously be an expensive waste of time. The DPP was nevertheless keen to get under way, mindful of its ageing witnesses. The prosecution also believed that it had to assume the legislation it was enforcing was a valid act of parliament. If there was to be a challenge to the legislation, it certainly wasn't the prosecution's role to ask for a stay of proceedings. That was up to the defence.

The court had also been informed that queen's counsel Greg James would be heading the prosecution team and that Grant Niemann would be his junior. James had little experience as a prosecutor. He was a Sydney defence lawyer who specialised in high profile appeals. He had a remarkable mind for remembering cases, and a knack of not losing his grip on a piece of string while judges considered how long it was. He appeared each year in only a couple of criminal trials and Polyukhovich would be his first major prosecution. James had been consulted by the SIU and DPP since before Christmas. They knew that if anyone was going to recommend dropping the case, he would. He was also white, of British heritage, protestant, and did not belong to any political party.

The idea of exhuming the mass grave outside Serniki was raised at about the same time as the SIU was explaining to the Soviet authorities that an entire Australian court needed to spend a few weeks in Rovno. Before Mark Weinberg, the federal Director of Public Prosecutions, had allowed Polyukhovich to be charged, he'd required some proof of the grave's existence. The SIU had then asked the Soviets to carry out a preliminary exploration on the area, which had confirmed the existence of numerous human bones in a small area just outside the village. Weinberg had then allowed the laying of charges, but the prosecution believed more work was needed. The witnesses spoke of a massive pit containing hundreds of bodies. Only a closer examination would reveal precisely what lay outside Serniki. The prosecution approached the notion of a complete exhumation nervously. If no mass grave could be uncovered, or if what was uncovered didn't fit the descriptions given by the witnesses, the case was vulnerable. But they needed to know what was down there.

In Moscow, senior procurator, Mrs Koleznekova had not been enthusiastic about allowing an Australian court to sit on Soviet soil. When told that the Australians wanted to dig up the grave she was astonished.

'You want what?'

'We want to dig up the grave.'

'But it's there. We'll tell you it's there.'

'Yes, but we want to see it for ourselves.'

The answer came back after a week. The Australians could dig up the grave.

———

On 12 June 1990, the defence team, which now included former South Australian crown prosecutor Brenton Illingworth, failed in a bid to have the media banned from the pending overseas hearings. Illingworth and Stokes had argued that the on-commission sessions to be held in Rovno were a 'fact-finding' mission and that there was doubt about how much of the evidence given would find its way into Polyukhovich's committal.

If evidence tainted by innuendo, hearsay, the passage of time, or Soviet influence was published, potential witnesses or jurors might read it and become prejudiced.

Illingworth cited three examples of statements taken from witnesses that the defence claimed were obviously unreliable. Although Polyukhovich had been charged five months earlier, this was the first time any indication had been given publicly of the sort of evidence to be produced against him. Media reporters grabbed eagerly at these few crumbs that had fallen from the court's table. Their luck disappeared just as quickly when magistrate Kelly suppressed from publication those sections of the statements read out by Illingworth.

Kelly said, however, that he was not prepared to stop the media from attending those overseas hearings where the witnesses would give their evidence in person. Kelly preferred not to ban the media, but rather to hear any objections to evidence and its publication 'on the spot'. It would, he said, be a very radical thing to hold the Ukrainian hearings behind closed doors, given that they were dealing with a case of international significance. Prosecutor Niemann pointed out that it was not at all clear that Kelly would have the authority to close a court held inside the Soviet Union.

During this hearing, Niemann added the news that the prosecution now wanted the court to travel on from Ukraine to Israel and the United States, where more witnesses could give evidence. Stokes said he wasn't at all pleased about the prospects of taking evidence in Israel because of security problems. He'd heard that when the Israelis had tried John Demjanjuk for war crimes, a defence lawyer had acid thrown in his face and another defence lawyer died. The death had been declared a suicide, but Stokes had doubts. Nevertheless, the defence left the court prepared to negotiate over extending the hearings to Israel and North America. And they hadn't given up hope on the question of banning the media.

That same March day, on the other side of the world, Fyodor Grigoryevich Polyukhovich directed an Australian forensic team to a spot in a pine forest not far from his house on the outskirts of Serniki. Fyodor's jet black hair and beard were deceptive. He didn't look his sixty-four years. When interviewed by the SIU the previous December, he'd described how he'd been forced to help fill in the mass grave outside the village on the day the Jewish ghetto was liquidated. Nearly half a century later, but without hesitation, he pointed to the floor of the forest and told the team that they were standing on top of bodies that had been buried no deeper than three metres. He said they would find a ramp leading out of the grave.

Apart from a small hole which had been dug nearby, there appeared to be nothing which distinguished this place from any other. This was the hole through which Soviet investigators had retrieved human remains months before.

Among the Australians was Richard Wright, a professor of anthropology at the University of Sydney. As an archaeologist he'd carried out excavations in Africa, Europe and Australia. The Special Investigations Unit had turned to him when they decided to go looking for the remains of the mass grave. They'd also recruited Detective Sergeant David Hughes, a crime scene expert with the New South Wales Police Department, and Dr Godfrey Oettle, head of the forensic medicine division in Glebe, New South Wales. Oettle had brought Burt Bailey with him. Bailey had no formal qualifications, but was recognised as an Australian authority on anatomy. Now sixty-seven, he'd joined the University of Sydney in 1949 as an attendant in the anatomy department. He'd become expert over the years at identifying bones, and eventually he taught post-graduate students. Oettle had often brought specimens into the university for Bailey to examine. Now Hughes, Oettle, Bailey, Wright, and Wright's wife, Sonia, who would work as a field assistant, stood together in the forest. Investigators Reid and Dowd were also there, along with a team of Soviet forensic scientists, led by Dr Eduard Sharayev, and representatives from the procurator's office.

Professor Wright had been told in Sydney that the grave might be as long as sixty metres, as wide as five, as deep as two, and filled with bones. He'd told the SIU that it would take three months to examine such remains individually, and had suggested that they simply dig more sample holes at various points around the site, and estimate the number of corpses. It soon became apparent, however, that Dr Sharayev was eager for the grave to be exposed in its entirety. Sharayev had brought two bulldozers, a backhoe and a contingent of Soviet soldiers to perform the task.

They began their work the following day. The soldiers swept the forest floor with metal detectors, searching for any military hardware, or even unexploded ordnance. Then they felled more than a hundred trees.

Wright began to prepare for the digging of a series of shallow trenches about half a metre deep. These would determine the boundaries of the long-covered pit. The soil was made up of sands and some clay. Wright concluded these were late ice-age dunes, not unlike the large lineal dunes around Lake Eyre in Australia's Simpson Desert. Eighteen thousand years of weathering had carried the clay downwards while rising ground water had lifted bands of orange iron. In places his trenches revealed these ancient lines intact. Elsewhere they'd been blended into a iron-stained sandy blur, pocketed with lumps of clay instead of striations, indicating they'd been disturbed at some time. In this way the edges of a large rectangle running forty metres in a north-south direction were eventually revealed. The bulldozers and backhoe were used to remove the top layers of soil, and, on 27 June, soldiers with shovels began filling the bucket on the backhoe. The first bodies were discovered two metres down.

———

On 26 June 1990 Adelaide queen's counsel Michael Abbott told magistrate Kelly that the overseas hearings had nothing to do with the public. They were, he said, solely a matter between the prosecution, the defence, and the magistrate.

Abbott had been brought in to re-argue the defence application to ban the media from the on-commission hearings now due to start on 30 July. Stokes and Illingworth were in Europe, preparing for the hearings. They planned to make their own enquiries, then be in Serniki to view the opened grave, and finally to make their way back to Rovno where they would meet up with Kelly and the prosecution. Abbott argued that whatever the witnesses said to Kelly couldn't strictly be described as evidence because, at that point, it wouldn't have been admitted as evidence. He said the parties involved should first sort out the 'ground rules'. One rule should be to exclude the public. Kelly agreed that the information received would be better described as 'depositions', but he was still reluctant to hold the hearings in secret. He adjourned the court, promising to hear submissions from the media the next day.

On the next day, however, before the media's lawyers could speak, Abbott dropped a bombshell. There was no point in continuing to argue over who should be present at the on-commission hearings, he said, because there weren't going to be any. Polyukhovich had instructed him that he no longer consented to the taking of evidence overseas in his absence. 'If they make accusations against him he wants to see them face to face,' Abbott told the court.

Prosecutor Greg James was furious. Less than two weeks earlier defence lawyer Stokes had agreed to extend the on-commission hearings to Tel Aviv and Boston and now, one month before the first hearing was due to start in Rovno, the defence were pulling out. Three months of preparations, passports, visas, hundreds of phone calls, negotiations with witnesses and governments in North America, Israel and the Soviet Union, had all been wasted. Forty-one witnesses would now have to be brought to Adelaide at great personal inconvenience and cost. Most of them were very old and some might succumb to the pressures. But, James declared, 'the eyes of the world' were on Australia as it conducted its first European war crimes hearing and the prosecution would continue to do everything it could to help the defence. James almost demanded that

Kelly now begin the committal in Adelaide on 30 July. Another interruption, he said, would be devastating.

Kelly agreed, saying that an adjournment would only be given if there were extraordinary circumstances.

————

Investigators Bob Reid and Anne Dowd were in Germany when the SIU director, Bob Greenwood, told them to be back in Adelaide ready to start the committal in four weeks. After introducing the Australian forensic team to the Soviets and escorting them to Serniki, the pair had travelled to Germany hoping to locate former members of the German forces that had swept through the Serniki region. SIU historian, Professor Konrad Kwiet, from the University of New South Wales, had identified a German cavalry unit that had been in the area. Reid and Dowd had hoped that these investigations might find the people who had actually organised the liquidation, but they didn't. Despite all the war crimes investigations that had been conducted in Europe during the previous forty-five years, nothing had been found which mentioned the liquidation of the Serniki ghetto. Kwiet had given Reid and Dowd a list of Germans who might have been involved in the massacre of the one hundred Jewish men at the Serniki cemetery during 1941. The pair discovered that a number of the former soldiers had died, and others had been too ill to be interviewed. None of the old men they'd spoken to remembered, or were willing to remember, the events in Serniki. Reid also believed it unlikely that a cavalry unit would have taken part in a ghetto liquidation.

Reid and Dowd now had to leave Germany and get back to Rovno as quickly as possible. Two large QANTAS airline chests full of exhibits were sitting there. They'd believed that they'd be needed when the on-commission hearings began.

————

By 5 July soldiers using small trowels, brushes and buckets had removed all the soil from the top of the remains. That afternoon Sergeant Hughes took to the air in a helicopter. Through the eye-piece of his video camera he could see the River Stubla and the village below him. The pilot followed the line of Gregarin and Lenin Streets and Hughes recognised the church and the school building. They followed the road out of Serniki which led to Zarechnye and then Rovno. The lens showed the pine forest in the distance. Now Hughes was over trees, and suddenly the grave appeared below him like some huge open sore. Thin lines of white tape criss-crossed the dark pit at one-metre intervals. From this height he could not make out individuals, only the enormity of the massacre.

———

The outlines of the grave had been remarkably well preserved. It looked to be a deliberately designed rectangle, not a casually dug hole.

The sides, which were close to being parallel, sloped outwards at about ten degrees off the ninety-degree angle. As the sandy walls had dried out, clumps had collapsed into the pit. The team decided to bevel the sides. While this was being done, the ramp described by Fyodor Polyukhovich had been discovered at about the middle of the pit, rising from its base about a metre wide through the east wall to the forest floor. The middle of the pit was shallower than the end sections and contained fewer bodies, some of them still clothed. The Soviet team had worked on the northern end, where they'd uncovered naked bodies lying face down in row upon orderly row. The Australians, working in the southern section, had also found unclothed bodies, but these were twisted and intertwined with each other in disorganised agony. The precision of the liquidation had apparently ended in a hurried slaughter. In most cases, all that remained was a skeleton; some had ligaments and other soft tissue attached. The fat under the skin had been transformed through contact with water into a repulsive waxy material. Other skeletons still had hair quite clearly plaited and held in place with combs. Someone found an artificial leg. Many of the Jewish witnesses had remembered Yankel Kaz, a one-legged man who'd lived on the fringes of Serniki. The investigators took note.

Near the centre, the team found the body of a man still wearing boots. He had died carrying a pocket knife, a pair of glasses, and a purse containing a ten kopek coin dated 1939. Near him was a child also wearing boots. Still in the centre, just south-east of the ramp and lying close to each other, were the remains of a woman, a girl aged thirteen and a baby, probably a girl aged about six months. A handful of blue buttons were lying with the remains of the baby. The teenage girl's skull had been crushed; the fracture was consistent with the end of a rifle butt. Such injuries are well documented in forensic literature.

Within a week of the excavation starting, procurator Koleznekova had made it clear that she hoped the Australian forensic team wouldn't take long. She told the Australians that Soviet soldiers were not allowed to look at the same bodies for more than about five days. The Australians didn't believe this for a minute and continued to go about their work. They were encouraged by the enthusiasm the Soviet forensic team were showing for a complete exhumation.

On 6 July, however, the Australians decided that only the skulls would be examined. The intertwining of the bodies made full skeletal examinations difficult. At times it was hard to know where one set of bones finished and another began. The Australians believed that there was no real need to go beyond the skulls which, in most cases, revealed the information sought: the age, sex and cause of death. Just over half of the skulls showed bullet wounds through the back, most often at the base. Some showed fractures, while others had been completely smashed in. One person had been killed by a shot through the pallet; others showed entry holes through the side or front of the skull. Most of the bullet wounds matched up with 9 mm German ammunition found scattered throughout the pit. As well as these bullets, which the forensic team knew were general issue to the German forces during the second world war, they found 7.62 carbine Soviet bullets. Cartridge cases were uncovered which, when the sand was scraped away, revealed they'd been manufactured between 1938 and 1941. The Australians also agreed that there was no need to go deeper into the pit, although it was obvious the layers continued further down. Professor Wright said it was 'too unpleasant' in the summer heat and flies to continue downwards, particularly in the southern end where many of the bodies still retained some flesh.

Sonia Wright worked as a removalist while her husband, Oettle and Bailey examined the skulls, which were then returned to the grave. Wright acted as scribe for Oettle, later transferring their findings onto a computer. The artificial leg was put back in the grave, but items such as the watch, coin and a pink comb found pinned to hair attached to a skull, were tagged and placed in a tent under constant Soviet guard. The Australians were allowed to enter the tent at any time without appointment.

At the end of the exhumation 553 bodies had been examined. The forensic teams were satisfied that 407 were female and 98 male. Decomposition and injuries made it impossible to know the sex of the remaining 48. The bodies were categorised by age. The investigators were confident that 63 of the bodies had belonged to females aged from birth to nine. A total of 134 bodies were grouped in the ten to nineteen bracket. The remaining bodies were divided fairly evenly into ten year groups. The single oldest occupant of the grave had died aged somewhere between eighty and eighty-nine. A total of 410 had suffered bullet wounds to the head, and ten had depressed fractures of the skull. In 133 cases the cause of death wasn't clear.

———

An American rabbi staying in Pinsk had agreed to officiate at the funeral service, which was held at one on Sunday 13 July 1990. A large crowd gathered for the ceremony – the forensic teams, representatives from the procurator's office, and the local villagers, many of whom had visited the site during the last six weeks and watched the work from a distance.

A breeze swayed the tops of the tall pines peering down into the pit. Tears rolled down Burt Bailey's face as the rabbi spoke. He watched as the old men from the village walked to the edge of the grave on unsteady legs. They grasped shovels in their shaky hands, and tipped the first dirt back on the remains.

———

Although it was Sunday night, investigators Reid, Dowd, Blewitt and prosecutor James were working at the public prosecutions office in Adelaide. They had been frustrated by the defence decision to call off the overseas hearings, but were determined to show they could mount their case anywhere, anytime. Tomorrow morning, 30 July 1990, the committal would begin, and they were making sure that every detail was in order. It was after nine, time to start packing up, when Reid's phone rang.

It was Chief Inspector Rob Maggs from the South Australian Police Department. Maggs was one of the officers Reid had liaised with about holding the war crimes hearing in Adelaide. That weekend Reid had shifted from his city hotel in Hindley Street to an apartment in the eastern suburbs. Reid had intended to tell Maggs his new contact number, but he'd left it for Monday morning. Maggs, however, had been trying to get hold of Reid for some time. He'd rung the DPP office in desperation, hoping that someone from the Special Investigations Unit would be there late on a Sunday night.

Maggs told Reid there'd been a shooting at West Lakes. A fellow by the name of Polyukhovich had been injured, and Maggs thought he might be Reid's man.

'Rob, it's the night before the committal. Don't joke about it,' Reid said.

Maggs wasn't joking. He said he'd pick Reid up from the DPP office in ten minutes.

By the time they arrived at the scene of the shooting, Polyukhovich had been taken to the Queen Elizabeth Hospital to have a single bullet removed from his chest. A teenager on roller skates had found Polyukhovich shortly after seven that evening, lying on the side of a road near a bridge over a stormwater drain. The teenager had flagged down a motorist. Polyukhovich had cried out that he'd been shot, but the truth of this hadn't been obvious until they'd lifted his jumper to reveal a blood-soaked shirt.

Reid hadn't spent much time in Adelaide and, after rushing through the western suburbs in the dark, had no idea where they were. Road blocks had been set up. The lights on top of emergency vehicles rotated, sending blue and red flashing all over the area. Police were rushing everywhere and a communications bus had been parked near the scene. Reid, who'd just spent six years in a homicide squad, was frustrated to be out of his jurisdiction.

———

Reid walked into the hospital ward, where the old man was lying on a movable bed. He was grey, but recognisable as Polyukhovich. Reid had seen a few bodies during his years as a police officer, and doubted whether this one would make it through the night. He walked downstairs and confirmed the injured man's identity to the waiting detectives, who wanted to know the nature of the case against the pensioner and where proceedings stood. Reid was taken to the Port Adelaide police station and then back to South Australian Police headquarters in the city.

Sometime during the night Reid rang Blewitt, who was still at the DPP office waiting for word. Blewitt said that a meeting had been arranged for seven thirty in Niemann's office. By now it was Monday. Before the night finished, Reid paid a visit to defence lawyer Stokes's home. Stokes had been in contact with Polyukhovich's family and the police and had fielded numerous phone calls from the media wanting information he wasn't prepared to give them. The lawyer and the investigator talked for a while and Reid went back to his apartment to get an hour's sleep. During the night Stokes noticed police patrol cars driving past his house.

———

The phone rang in Blewitt's room at about 5 AM. It was his boss, Bob Greenwood, in London. Blewitt was still numb, but forced himself to wake up. After the shooting had been confirmed, Blewitt's first concern had been to contact Greenwood, who was overseas on SIU business. He'd been unable to reach him and left messages at his hotel. Greenwood explained that he'd learnt some of the details from the Australian High Commission in London. Blewitt filled in the gaps and promised to keep him informed.

———

The hearing in front of magistrate Kelly lasted only a few minutes. There wasn't much anyone could say. Stokes formally told the court that Polyukhovich was in a critical but stable condition. No one knew when he would be able to attend court. Kelly adjourned the hearing for a week, giving each party leave to call it back sooner.

The prosecution lawyers and investigators walked out of the court to a barrage of questions from journalists. Why hadn't the SIU and DPP foreseen that someone could shoot Polyukhovich? What measures had they put in place to prevent this? Didn't they owe him that duty? The prosecution were surprised by the journalists' vehemence. They felt besieged as they explained that they were under no obligation to provide the defendant with protection. They'd received no indication that anyone had planned to attack him, and no protection had been requested. They were annoyed by the accusing tone of the journalists. Polyukhovich was, after all, on bail, not in protective custody.

———

To Stokes, Polyukhovich appeared to have shrunk. Not physically, but emotionally, psychologically. His client, lying on his hospital bed, looked more than just old and frail. Over the last few months he had seemed increasingly bewildered. His immediate family had rallied around him, but Polyukhovich – who had always been very quiet – appeared more and more isolated from the rest of the community. Stokes knew that the case was placing enormous strains on the family and now his client was recovering from a gunshot wound.

———

Within a few days the South Australian police were satisfied that Polyukhovich had shot himself. No official announcement would ever be made, but Reid asked Chief Inspector Denis Edmonds from the major crime section to attend the court appearances that followed, in case the defence made allegations about the shooting. The defence never conceded that their client had tried to take his own life, but they didn't push the issue either.

Reid never believed there was some mad assassin running around Adelaide shooting war crimes suspects. Each time he had to refer to the shooting in an affidavit, he described it as a self-inflicted firearm wound, and was never challenged. But Reid also rejected the notion that the shooting was some sign of guilt on Polyukhovich's part. Reid knew the pensioner was under enormous pressure. The self-inflicted wound could be explained as the action of a man who, on the eve of his committal hearing, wanted to protect his family from the pain of the courtroom.

———

On 8 August 1990, prosecutor James demanded that the court be given more information about Polyukhovich's health, including his psychiatric condition. James said that people around the world were speculating on whether the defendant had shot himself or been attacked. To protect him from himself or others, he shouldn't be allowed simply to walk out of the Queen Elizabeth Hospital. James asked for Polyukhovich's bail conditions to be altered, requiring him to undergo psychiatric assessment and be subjected to security arrangements. Magistrate Kelly refused to alter the bail and adjourned the court for another week.

Although the state of Polyukhovich's health meant all bets were off for at least the time being, the prosecution went through the motions of informing the court of another development. It had new charges to lay. These were the product of the work carried out during the past six months, a more considered view of the evidence, and a defence challenge to the original charges in the federal court. The challenge, which was to have begun on the same day as the committal, attacked the charges on the basis that they did not set out sufficient information. It claimed that Kelly had no jurisdiction to hear the case. The new set of charges answered this by narrowing down the dates when offences were alleged to have occurred and by naming victims more specifically. As well, the wording was altered to make sure it complied absolutely with the War Crimes Act.

More importantly, however, the prosecution had decided to drop one of its original charges and add several new ones. The first charge laid against Polyukhovich in January had alleged that he'd murdered a woman called Sercha, Sercha's two daughters whose names weren't known, and Sercha's grandson. These killings were supposed to have taken place near Alexandrovo during August–September 1941. The alleged circumstances were similar to many of the other counts – a woman and her family discovered in the forest and then shot. While the details of the killings fitted together to the SIU's satisfaction, the dates had begun to trouble them. From other witnesses they knew that the first German sweep through Serniki occurred in about July 1941, when about a hundred Jewish men were killed at the cemetery. But from then until the ghetto was liquidated in the autumn of 1942, Serniki was, apart from the constant harassment of Jews, relatively peaceful. The murder of Sercha's family didn't appear to fit in with this pattern of killings. The witness who'd testified about Sercha's death, however, couldn't have said autumn 1941 when he'd meant autumn 1942. He'd produced partisan documentation which showed he'd been transferred in about May 1942 out of the Serniki region to another part of Ukraine hundreds of kilometres away. The prosecution thought it prudent to drop the count.

Added to the charges was Dmitry Kostyukhovich's allegation that he'd seen Polyukhovich murder two Jewish youths trying to escape the round-up. Another new count alleged that Polyukhovich had killed Alter Botvinik. Botvinik had been a friend of the Kaz family in Serniki. Sonja and Pepe Kaz had survived the war and were expected to give evidence at the committal hearing, should it ever begin. A third charge alleged that Polyukhovich had killed a man called Roman Kolb in January 1943. The prosecution also made an amendment to the charge involving the killing of the Turuks and Delidons in the forest during April 1943. These people were now described as having been suspected partisans or communists. One more death, that of Nadezhda Turuk, was added to their number. Polyukhovich now faced twenty-five individual murder counts instead of twenty-four. The central charge, that of the pit killing, remained. It had been altered only in a minor way to match the evidence uncovered at the exhumation. It now claimed that Polyukhovich had been party to the murders of about 850 and not less than 553 Jewish people.

———

Back in court on 13 August 1990, a picture emerged of a demented and depressed old man who had tried to take his own life while in a confused and frightened state. Prosecutor James told the magistrate that, since the shooting, Polyukhovich had twice tried to rip away the medical equipment attached to him at the Queen Elizabeth Hospital. James claimed that the day before the shooting Polyukhovich had been examined by a senior psychiatrist who had found the defendant was 'grossly depressed and confused'. The South Australian police had concluded that there had been no assassin, and had decided to stop providing security because if Polyukhovich was a 'threat to himself that was no concern of the police'. The Director of Public Prosecutions had arranged for the federal police to take over the security arrangements. James stressed, however, that it was not up to them or the DPP to ensure that Polyukhovich was safe from his own hand.

The latest addition to the defence team, Adelaide queen's counsel Malcolm Gray, conceded none of this. Gray said that there was nothing in the hospital reports to suggest Polyukhovich might harm himself. He said, however, that it was time for everyone to consider the possibility of the case simply never getting to trial. There was evidence the pensioner was suffering from dementia and depression, making it impossible for him to instruct his lawyers. Polyukhovich would need to stay in hospital for at least another month, and would then need time to convalesce. Magistrate Kelly altered the bail conditions so that they required Polyukhovich to receive medical treatment and submit himself to any recommended psychiatric treatment. He also had to give the federal police forty-eight hours notice before leaving the hospital and had to allow present security arrangements to continue.

——

By late August the prosecution of Ivan Polyukhovich had degenerated into a legal tug-of-war over the pensioner's mind.

Frustrated by the course of events, the DPP decided to force the issue by formally raising the question of Polyukhovich's fitness to plead. It argued that under the Commonwealth Crimes Act magistrate Kelly had no choice but to immediately send the case to the Supreme Court, where a jury would be empanelled to decide the state of Polyukhovich's mental condition. If the jury found that Polyukhovich was fit to plead to the charges, the case would be sent back to the Magistrates Court as soon as Polyukhovich could attend. If, however, the jury found that Polyukhovich was unfit to plead, a Supreme Court judge would have to decide whether there was a *prima facie* case against him. If that could be established, recent changes to the Crimes Act offered a series of options. The court could dismiss the charges because of Polyukhovich's condition, or decide whether he would be fit to stand trial within the next twelve months. During that period the court could order the accused to be detained. If Polyukhovich's mental condition was not expected to improve, but the judge believed a case existed, he could order that Polyukhovich be held in a hospital or gaol. The law dictated that this detention last no longer than the maximum sentence the accused would have received had he been found guilty of the charged offences. Because this maze of options was only open to the prosecution due to amendments which had come into force within recent weeks, they did not apply to the charges laid in January. James asked for the original charges to be dismissed. He said that he wasn't playing tactics; he simply wanted the matter dealt with as quickly and humanely as possible.

Defence QC Malcolm Gray had to tread a fine line. One way to conclude the case was to convince the court that his client was too old and sick to survive it. If Gray argued the mental illness case too strongly, however, Polyukhovich would come before the Supreme Court sooner than anyone had expected. Gray said that he wasn't suggesting Polyukhovich was unfit to be tried; he was simply warning that continued court proceedings could have a deleterious, if not fatal, effect on the defendant.

Magistrate Kelly agreed with James, dismissed the old charges and sent the matter to the Supreme Court.

The following day, 28 August 1990, the DPP kept up the pressure, asking Justice Duggan in the Supreme Court to set dates for a fitness-to-plead hearing. The defence countered by saying that Kelly had been wrong to let the case leave the Magistrates Court. The pros and cons of this increasingly complicated wrangle could not be settled in an afternoon, so Duggan set aside four days in September for the defence to argue against the fitness-to-plead hearing. If they failed, a jury would be empanelled on 22 October to decide the state of Polyukhovich's mind.

––––

The tangled legal proceedings in Adelaide's state courts were eventually overtaken by the High Court in Canberra. On 3 September its seven judges began hearing the defence challenge to the constitutional validity of the War Crimes Act. After three days the High Court still hadn't heard all the arguments, so the case was adjourned until November. The first session had gone so well, however, that the defence decided in mid-October to ask the High Court to stay the other proceedings back in South Australia pending the outcome of the challenge. The application was heard by Justice Mary Gaudron, who agreed with the defence.

A few days later, Polyukhovich returned home, having made a steady recovery during almost three months at the Queen Elizabeth Hospital.

The constitutional challenge focused on the retrospectivity of the legislation, an aspect which many in the legal profession found distasteful. The defence claimed that federal parliament didn't have the power to make the law, and that the passage of time meant a fair trial was impossible. While the government might argue that there was an international trend towards prosecuting war crimes suspects, it couldn't be said that there was an overwhelming concern about such offences.

In turn, the government's lawyers relied on the external affairs powers contained in the Australian Constitution. The High Court, in judgments dating back to the mid-1970s, had endorsed the federal government's power to control activities within Australia on the grounds of meeting international obligations. The best known case had involved the Franklin Dam in Tasmania, when the federal government had used its signing of a World Heritage agreement to stop an area of wilderness from being flooded despite protests from the Tasmanian state government. In the case of war crimes, the federal government argued that Australia was again meeting its international obligations and that any problems with retrospectivity had to be seen in this context. The crimes created by the legislation were crimes against all humanity. Those crimes had been committed against Australia and Australians just as they had been committed against the victims of the Holocaust. The atrocities had violated international law, and international law was itself part of the regime of Australian law. Therefore the government was entitled, indeed obliged, to act.

Late in 1990, Bob Greenwood told his deputy Graham Blewitt he would soon resign as head of the Special Investigations Unit. Greenwood had often talked about going back to private practice, but now he'd made up his mind. He'd go as soon as the right chambers were available. He wanted Blewitt then to take over the running of the unit.

Blewitt's first reaction was disbelief. The unit had been Greenwood's creation and it was difficult to imagine it without him at its helm. Greenwood assured him that he would be available to give advice at any time. Besides, hadn't Blewitt run the office many times when Greenwood had been away? It would be like a protracted absence.

By the time Blewitt formally took over as director in April 1991, the SIU had worked under a cloud for nearly half a year. The High Court challenge had finished four months earlier, but there was still no sign of a decision from the country's top judges. It had been hard to maintain morale. The defence attack on the legislation had sounded effective and it became difficult to keep staff at the SIU when everyone knew their jobs could be lost after a decision that could be handed down any day. This might be the case in which the High Court began to draw boundaries around the federal government's external affairs powers.

Combined with the uncertainty was the knowledge that funding for the unit would cease on 30 June 1992. Greenwood had told the government several months earlier that, provided no new allegations or evidence emerged, all of the SIU's investigations should be finished by that date. Blewitt believed he could probably get extra funding, but the deadline made it difficult to replace senior people. At that time about eleven million dollars had been spent investigating 813 different suspects.

The SIU had been working hard on about a dozen other cases while Polyukhovich's lay in limbo. Two more cases, involving South Australian men Heinrich Wagner and Mikolay Berezowsky, looked particularly strong. Blewitt was becoming increasingly confident that charges would be laid against the pair if only the legislation could get through the High Court. He believed, in fact, that it was likely at least six, and as many as twelve, people would be charged with war crimes within a year of the legislation being endorsed. All of these suspects were men aged in their seventies who had migrated to Australia from eastern Europe.

———

On 14 August 1991 Australia's amended War Crimes Act survived the High Court. It was endorsed by four judges and rejected as invalid by three.

For Chief Justice Mason the case had ultimately been a simple one. In his sixteen-page judgement he reasoned that the court didn't need to be satisfied that Australia had an interest in war crimes in order for the act to be valid. 'It is enough that parliament's judgement is that Australia has an interest or concern,' he said. 'It is inconceivable that the court could overrule parliament's decision on that question.' It made no difference, Mason found, whether the law created a criminal liability by reference to past or future conduct, so long as the conduct was external to Australia.

Justices Dawson, Toohey and McHugh also endorsed the act, although Toohey did so with reservations. While he found that the legislation was constitutional, he said that there was insufficient evidence of any international obligation to investigate and prosecute war crime suspects as an exercise of the external affairs powers. Likewise, there was insufficient evidence of any international concern that war criminals should be tried in countries other than those in which the crimes had been committed.

The slimness of the victory couldn't take away Blewitt's smile as he walked down the long steps away from the court into the bright Canberra morning. After waiting anxiously for months, now was not the time to ponder legal niceties. All that mattered was that the highest court in the land had found that the act was valid. New prosecutions would be set in motion soon, and at last the way was clear for the case against Polyukhovich to resume.

———

On paper the case against Ivan Polyukhovich looked very convincing and that was worrying for Michael David QC. David was one of Adelaide's best criminal lawyers, who'd been enlisted as a replacement for Malcolm Gray within a month of the High Court decision. Gray had appeared briefly as senior counsel just before the case had been suspended nearly twelve months earlier, but had since taken up a position heading the National Crime Authority's new Adelaide office. Defence lawyer Stokes had turned to David knowing that, while there are queen's counsels who are best left to talk with judges, there are also QCs who are made for juries, and that Michael David was one these. He could be stern in court and yet he always seemed like a reasonable, at times long-suffering, man.

David would be ideal, but he had only a few weeks to prepare for the start of Polyukhovich's committal on 28 October 1991. The case had been left in confusion over Polyukhovich's health. Now, however, the defence decided that Polyukhovich was able to resume the proceedings, even though they believed that he was an old, frail and sick man.

David had realised he'd need help and insisted that Lindy Powell become his junior. Powell had recently resigned as the director of South Australia's Legal Services Commission, a position she'd held since November 1987, and was free to return to private practice. She'd been asked to represent Mikolay Berezowsky, who was expecting to be charged with war crimes after being interviewed by the SIU in July.

David and Powell would become authorities on Australia's war crimes prosecutions. Together they would defend the only three people ever charged under the amended act – Polyukhovich, Berezowsky and Heinrich Wagner. In September 1991, however, they couldn't be sure what was and wasn't important. The uniqueness and complexity of the case frightened them. So many witnesses and so much history. The lawyers needed to keep as many options open as possible while they waited for the prosecution case to unfold at the committal hearing.

On 18 October Michael David put the prosecution on notice that the defence intended to challenge the crown case on all fronts. He gave the warning while applying to magistrate Peter Kelly for a suppression order that would stop the media publishing the prosecution's opening address. David said the defence planned to challenge the admissibility of statements made by Polyukhovich to the authorities on the day he was arrested. They would also challenge identification evidence, 'expert' witnesses – particularly an historian the prosecution said it intended calling – documents tendered by the prosecution, and the accounts of so-called eyewitnesses. David said the defence would argue that much of this was inadmissible evidence. It would be prejudicial for the media to report on the prosecution's address before a decision was made on the status of much that would be in it.

Magistrate Kelly said he thought that the application was premature. Anyway, he said, he wasn't going to hear the committal. He'd decided that as the supervising magistrate in charge of the Adelaide Magistrates Court administration he wouldn't have time to sit on such a long, demanding case. Another magistrate, Kelvyn Prescott, would hear the committal. Prescott, Kelly said, would be in the best situation to know what should be published after he heard the opening on 28 October.

The whole of that day had been set aside for prosecutor James to outline his case against Polyukhovich. It was eagerly awaited by the reporters who'd been following the case. After twenty-one months, precisely what Polyukhovich was alleged to have done would be revealed for the first time.

It was planned that, after the opening, the hearing would adjourn and reconvene about two weeks later, when the exhumation team would be called to give evidence. The court would have to wait until the following March for the first of the overseas witnesses.

———

David and Powell hadn't been working on the defence case long when Stokes informed them that a war crimes lawyer from Canada, Doug Christie, was in Adelaide and wanted to see them. They were to meet him for lunch at a motel on South Terrace. Christie had earlier in the year successfully represented Canada's first war crimes defendant, Imre Finta, who had been tried for atrocities against Jews in Nazi-occupied Hungary. David and Powell had never heard of Christie, but were reluctant to pass up any opportunity. The fear that they might miss some important point would stay with them for several months, but the visit with Christie would last only a few minutes.

They arrived at the motel to find that a couple of other Adelaide lawyers had been invited to make up the numbers. The conversation began with a discussion of the differences between the war crimes legislation in Canada and Australia, but moved quickly on to the historical truth of the Holocaust and Christie's advice that documents found in Soviet archives were invariably forged. After just a few minutes, David and Powell politely said they had to leave. While the defence team were keeping their options open, they weren't about to adopt such tactics. Stokes was later instructed that the defence should have nothing to do with Christie.

A case to answer

A case to answer

The interior of the Sturt Street Magistrates Courts was designed when people thought red went well with off-white. The building began its life as a soap factory and warehouse. In the 1970s the South Australian government decided to lease the eastern half of this long, boring, red-brick structure and build inside it the prototype of the courtroom of the future. The result was quite roomy. The seats were red and so was the carpet, which reached halfway up the wall. The fittings were black or white. From the angular ceiling protruded a dozen large, rectangular boxes containing rows of fluorescent lights concealed by long strips of white metal. At the time it was modern, but soon it looked silly and dated. So the government built another one in the same style alongside the first. The courtrooms had been used by various jurisdictions, and even as the set of a film starring Richard Chamberlain, but today one of them would be used for the start of Australia's first European war crimes hearing.

A few protesters were gathered outside. They stood next to the building's featureless brick wall holding large white placards with messages neatly printed on them in capital letters. These signs declared that it was wrong to spend taxpayers' money on 'this witch hunt'. Another read, 'War crimes legislation contrary to our tradition of common law.' A third said, 'War crimes trials are selective. Is Hawke going to charge Japanese war criminals?' The person carrying this last card, which referred to Prime Minister Bob Hawke, didn't seem to know that Australia had prosecuted more than nine hundred Japanese war crimes suspects after the second world war. Of the 644 Japanese defendants convicted by Australian military tribunals, 148 had been sentenced to death and executed. Those trials had been the result of the original War Crimes Act passed in 1945.

The prosecution team was used to this sort of attack and to claims that the war crimes investigations were the result of some world-wide Jewish conspiracy. They seemed to encounter such opposition wherever they went; at parties, in taxis, opening a newspaper. Some of the investigators admitted they honestly didn't know what had motivated the politicians who created the legislation and didn't really care. The investigators had their own motives. They believed that what they were doing was not only lawful, but morally correct. The time that had passed since the war was not an issue for them. If someone had today found the killer of Adelaide's Beaumont children, who had mysteriously disappeared thirty years ago, no one would suggest letting the matter rest. Everyone within the prosecution seemed to agree that the legislation was flawed because it was strictly limited to second world war Europe. But in a 'normal' Australian case, if just one of several killers could be arrested no one would suggest that he or she shouldn't be tried because some of the offenders escaped justice. The solution would be to extend the legislation so that any war criminal, from any conflict, could be prosecuted if found living in Australia.

Defence lawyers Michael David and Lindy Powell took a similarly pragmatic approach. If someone asked David whether the legislation was right or wrong he'd say he simply didn't know. The question was interesting but he and Powell were not interested in giving philosophical lectures. They didn't have time. They viewed themselves as a pair of barristers who'd been given the job of defending a client. No, don't ask them whether the prosecution of war criminals decades after the war is right or wrong, ask them how good or bad the prosecution case is.

No one from the defence or the prosecution stopped to argue these issues as they passed the demonstrators and bored television camera crews. It was very hard to find pictures to accompany television reports of court proceedings and the crews gratefully filmed the demonstrators for the evening news.

Inside, Greg James prepared to start his opening address for the prosecution. But first there was a preliminary matter. Time had been no friend to the prosecution. Two witnesses had died since the laying of the latest charges, which meant that the prosecution couldn't proceed with count eight, the murder of Roman Kolb in January 1943. The tally dropped back to twenty-four murders and the pit killing. There was a quick discussion about suppression orders, which magistrate Kelvyn Prescott didn't seem keen to impose, and then all was quiet. At last James could begin.

The essence of the proceedings, he said, was the allegation that Polyukhovich had collaborated with an execution squad or squads operating in German-occupied Ukraine between 1941 and 1943. The War Crimes Act required the prosecution to prove that offences committed by Polyukhovich during this period were performed while implementing the Nazi policy of exterminating the Jewish population and local dissidents. It was therefore necessary, James explained, to put the historical background in place.

James said it was a notorious fact that, during the years 1939 to 1945, the Nazi government of Germany waged war in Europe and from 1941 against the USSR. Early in the war the Nazis had considered deporting Jews to the island of Madagascar off the African continent, but the capture of Poland and other eastern territories brought another two million Jews under German control. Shifting this huge population was out of the question. In early 1941, the Nazis adopted an alternative solution – mobile execution squads. These squads would follow close behind the army. At first they killed Jewish community leaders. The killings were sporadic, as the squads had to move fast to keep up with the advancing German lines. Those Jews who remained were resettled in ghettos where they could be dealt with more conveniently later.

James said he would call as one of his witnesses Professor Raul

Hilberg from the University of Vermont in the USA. Hilberg, an international authority on the topic, would testify that Hitler's Third Reich and its allies and collaborators had generated a flow of several million pieces of paper during the course of the war. While systematic efforts were made by the retreating Germans to destroy these records, many of which detailed the killing of Jews and partisans, many orders, letters and reports had survived. If necessary, the prosecution would seek to tender some of these salvaged documents to prove that a policy of annihilation could be traced from Adolf Hitler and his deputy Heinrich Himmler down to those Germans operating in the Alexandrovo and Serniki area.

A special order had appeared on 28 July 1941 over the typed signature of Himmler, the chief of the police and the SS – Hitler's elite bodyguard which had grown into a huge complex organisation used to annihilate the Jews. Trusted locals were to assist the units that were combing swamp areas where Jews and partisans often escaped. Four days later an explicit order from Himmler had required that all Jews be shot and all Jewish women driven into the swamps. James stressed that the unauthorised killing of Jews, however, was illegal and subject to punishment.

'The extermination was to be a disciplined and controlled exercise,' continued James. 'A line was drawn between organised killing operations and unauthorised wanton killings motivated by lust or robbery or some other failing of character. Civilians, including German and non-German public and private employees, were sometimes permitted to assist in massacres but such participation did not, however, confirm licence upon them to kill individuals at other times or locations.' SS men and policemen could be tried by the SS in police courts, soldiers could be court-martialled and civilians prosecuted in ordinary criminal courts for unauthorised killing.

James explained that the Germans established and rapidly expanded an indigenous police force. Recruitment was based on political reliability and physical fitness. By 1942, these police units contained tens of thousands of men and far outnumbered the occupying German forces. Marshes and forests were of special concern to the Germans. Professional foresters were armed with machine guns, rifles, grenades and issued with olive-brown uniforms. Their numbers were augmented by native militias.

In the eastern territories, German and Ukrainian employees were subject to a decree dated 12 September 1942. It allowed them to shoot in self-defence or overcome physical resistance to official acts or, upon warning, prevent a person found in the forests from fleeing. In a closed forest they were allowed to shoot without warning if they found any armed person or groups of four or more committing an offence.

James said that Professor Hilberg would give evidence that the Volhynian region, which included Serniki, was effectively by-passed during 1941, but that this respite ended in a wave of killings between August and November 1942. The Germans had poured all available forces into the operation and Himmler was presented with the results: more than 1300 partisans killed in battle; more than 8500 partisans and partisan suspects killed after capture; a total of 363,211 Jews killed.

James was not merely providing historical background. One of the prosecution's lines of attack was to show that a strictly regulated regime was imposed in Ukraine during the war, under which specific groups of local people were given powers that could be used only at specific times and for specific reasons. If the prosecution could prove that Polyukhovich had held some official 'police-type' position under the German regime, they would go a considerable way to showing that he had a case to answer.

The prosecutor now began to narrow the focus of his address. He told the court that a larger percentage of people had apparently survived the killings in the Serniki region than elsewhere in the occupied territories. He said evidence would be given that local villagers had been conscripted to dig a large pit in the nearby forest just before the liquidation of the Serniki ghetto. Many villagers had warned the Jews who had been settled in the ghetto that a massacre was impending. Consequently, many of the Jews had escaped and survived to give evidence in these proceedings.

James said that it was not alleged Polyukhovich had taken part in the first German sweep through Serniki in 1941, when about a hundred Jewish men were killed. Instead the charges fell into two groups: those involving the September 1942 liquidation of the ghetto and the subsequent clean-up operation, and a series of killings in April–May 1943.

Many of the witnesses were not, by themselves, threatening to the defence. They merely confirmed the establishment of the ghetto, the visits of Germans to the village, the digging of the pit and the filling of the pit with Jewish bodies. Others would go further, James continued. They had identified Polyukhovich from Special Investigations Unit photo-boards as 'Ivanechko', a local official. And then, James said, there were about a dozen crucial witnesses who would testify that they had seen the defendant actually take part in war crimes. At least one witness would give evidence that materially supported more than one charge. He was Dmitry Kostyukhovich, the war veteran discovered by the SIU on its return visit to Ukraine in 1990. He claimed to have seen Polyukhovich shoot two youths and to have seen Polyukhovich take part in the ghetto round-up.

Collectively and specifically, James promised, the witnesses would claim to have seen the defendant, along with two policemen, escort the local miller's daughter and her two children down into the pit. Shots had been heard and Polyukhovich and his two colleagues had left the grave without the woman and children. Around the time of the massacre the defendant was also seen leading, at gunpoint, the Jewish woman Tsalykha, her daughter and grand-daughter. The defendant had forced them to strip to their petticoats and shot them. On another occasion a local Ukrainian youth had seen the defendant escorting two Jewish men and a Jewish woman out of the forest. Polyukhovich had made them stand in a line and fired a single shot from his gun. When only two of the prisoners had fallen to the ground Polyukhovich was alleged to have rushed at the remaining man and crushed his skull with the butt of his rifle.

Perhaps the most dramatic of the promised testimonies would come from an eighty-year-old man now living in Israel. James said that Ze'ev

Erdman would say that, on the day after the liquidation, he had met the defendant in the forest and saw him shoot a woman, bash one of her daughters to death, skewer a second daughter with a bayonet, then throw a one-year-old boy into the river.

Another Israeli witness would tell how he'd seen Polyukhovich leading Ze'ev Erdman and Alter Botvinik at gunpoint. Botvinik had wrestled with the defendant and, in the confusion, Erdman had escaped. The witness would say the struggle ended with Polyukhovich shooting Botvinik dead.

Shifting to April 1943, James said that a witness would claim to have seen the defendant and another man leading a Jewish woman at gunpoint. Although this witness hadn't seen what followed, he had heard a shot soon after and later saw her body.

At this point Michael David interrupted. 'There's no name for the deceased in this matter, I take it? It says "unknown". We haven't got a name?'

'If I had a name, I would have given it to you,' James replied curtly.

'I ask that that be provided, if this is "Tsalykha's daughter" mentioned in count four. I would want to make sure this isn't the same person,' David said.

James was clearly annoyed at the interruption and for the moment the matter went no further. The defence kept it for later. From the statements they'd read, it appeared that the death of Tsalykha's daughter had been witnessed by more than one person in more than one place. Indeed, when the charges had been originally laid, count one and count nine had both referred to a person described as 'Tsalykha's daughter'.

James went on. In April 1943 the village of Brodnitsa, not far from Serniki, was burned to the ground in the wake of partisan activity. Among those who fled to the forest were the Turuk family. A few days after Easter, they had run from their camp upon hearing shots. They collided with a group of policemen, including the defendant, who were escorting neighbours of the Turuks, the Delidon family. Three witnesses would be called to say that they saw the defendant fire his gun during these events in the forest. One of the witnesses would describe how his brother had cursed the defendant and asked to be put out of his misery. The defendant took a rifle from one of the other policeman and shot the wounded man in the back of the head.

Only one charge remained to be explained, but James hesitated. It was nearly lunchtime, and there were circumstances surrounding the last charge which required discussion. The court adjourned.

An hour later James told the court that the prosecution planned to call two witnesses to support count eleven, which alleged that Polyukhovich had murdered Pyotr Krupko. One of the witnesses was Krupko's fifty-seven-year-old grandson, Vasily, who claimed he saw the shooting. The other was seventy-seven-year-old woman Tatyana Ulitko, who said that she discovered Pyotr Krupko's body and at one time saw the defendant help burn down a village. James had to explain that both of these people were ill. The prosecution could not guarantee that they could make the journey to Adelaide.

James continued outlining the evidence to be called from the rest of the overseas witnesses for another half hour. These were the background people, the supporting cast. Then he described the exhumation evidence and the work done by the investigators. He didn't finish until four.

James had said many of the witnesses would describe Polyukhovich as having been a local policeman while others would say he'd been a forester. Exactly what the prosecution alleged his status had been wasn't clear, and some journalists settled for the general term 'local official' when reporting James's address.

It seemed that Polyukhovich had also been seen wearing an extensive wardrobe while working for the Germans. Some of the witnesses said that he'd worn civilian clothes with an arm-band. Others had him wearing a green German uniform. One witness said he'd worn several different outfits.

The defence also noticed that, apart from the pit killing and the shooting of the Delidons and Turuks, each of the charges had only one eyewitness. James had sought to cover this by saying that the acts of the defendant could be explained only on the basis that he was following a policy. There was, in other words, a course of conduct and each charge supported the others. This was not, he had said, a case of homicidal mania.

When James had finished, magistrate Prescott turned to the defence. Michael David told him that, after hearing the marathon address, several matters had fallen by the wayside. But David said the defence still intended to challenge two key areas: the extent of Professor Hilberg's evidence and the admissibility of the photo-board identification. David explained he was not talking about general matters such as whether the Holocaust had occurred. He meant the defence would challenge whether Hilberg should be allowed to give evidence regarding very specific matters, such as whether Ukrainians were recruited for killing Jews or fighting partisans.

'We might start off with the fairly simple proposition that a document speaks for itself,' David said. 'You don't really need Professor Hilberg to speak about it.'

David said that he understood the crown was relying on a combination of factors to prove the defendant was the person who committed the offences, but the photo-boards which the Special Investigations Unit had shown to the witnesses would be most rigorously challenged. There were many problems with them, not least that the journalist Mark Aarons had shown some of the witnesses a photo of Polyukhovich before the SIU arrived in Ukraine.

None of this came as a surprise to the prosecution, and the day finally closed at 4.45 PM after a lengthy argument over suppression orders requested by the defence. Magistrate Prescott refused the request.

———

There were two surprise additions to the scene when the committal resumed two weeks later. Ninety-year-old Sir Walter Crocker, a former South Australian Lieutenant-Governor, had joined the ranks of the few protesters outside the court. Behind him, roughly painted on the court's brick wall, was a swastika, followed by the words, 'ss Kill Jews', followed by another swastika.

During the next three days forensic experts Hughes, Wright and Oettle described the exhumation they had conducted in Ukraine more than a year ago. This evidence would ultimately remain virtually uncontested, but for now the defence junior, Lindy Powell, scrutinised it closely for flaws. She spent hours cross-examining each of the experts, covering the same themes with each of them: the role of the Soviet procurators and the pressure they had exerted to finish the work as quickly as possible; who had controlled the exhibits; and countless questions about the uncovered ammunition and cartridges.

Sergeant Hughes explained that, despite pressure from the senior procurator, Mrs Koleznekova, the Australians had been satisfied with the amount of time they'd spent at the grave. He said that as objects were found they were given to the Soviets, but the Australians had been allowed to see the exhibits whenever they liked and without appointment. Several days after they'd left the grave site, and when he was about to board the train at Rovno, one of the procurator's staff had given Hughes twelve bags. They contained the exhibits: a ten kopek coin; a watch, chain and brooch; bullets; cartridge cases; a rubber boot; blue buttons; a pink comb; dentures; and some clothing and hair samples. Hughes said that he found nothing to suggest that the Soviets had tampered with the exhibits. He based this satisfaction on X-rays taken of the exhibits as they were recovered and on notes, photographs and plaster castings he'd taken at the scene. But Powell pursued the issue and eventually put it to Hughes that the Australians had effectively lost control of at least some of the exhibits. Hughes agreed that this was a fair comment, but continued to say he trusted the Soviet authorities.

Among Professor Wright's contribution to the proceedings was an attempt to work out scientifically the age of the grave. After all, who was to say it was a second world war grave? Serniki's part of the world had suffered under various autocratic regimes. Wright said that the seasonal rings exposed when the trees were cut down showed they'd been planted about 1960, while the cartridges found in the pit had been stamped 1941. The forensic team had even gone to the trouble of sending a sample of hair taken from the pit to laboratories in Canberra and California for carbon-dating. That work had narrowed the period by another five years. Wright concluded that the grave had been filled between 1941 and 1955.

———

The proceedings stalled for several days, during which the defence said that Polyukhovich was too sick to attend court. They resumed on 20 November with investigator Reid in the stand. Polyukhovich's arrest and interview were the main topics. Reid said that after arriving at Polyukhovich's house about midday, it had taken fifteen or twenty minutes to establish that Polyukhovich was the man they intended to arrest. Defence QC Michael David focused on the warnings that Reid had given his client. Reid explained that the scene had been very emotional. He'd wanted the Polyukhovichs' assistance in making the ordeal as 'least upsetting' as possible.

'His wife was crying, he was upset, and I was just getting control or trying to get control of the situation where we could just sit down and, once everybody was better in control of their emotions, we could talk,' Reid said.

'What assistance were you looking for? What was he supposed to do to assist?' David asked.

'Nothing. The whole idea was to calm the situation down,' Reid replied.

David knew what he was after and that wasn't it. 'What were you going to do to make it as "least upsetting" for him. I mean what were you trying to tell him?'

'It wasn't intended as a threat,' Reid said. 'It was intended, as I have said, to calm the situation down.'

'Of course, at that stage, you didn't tell him he didn't have to answer any questions at all did you?'

'I had given the caution that I was advised to give.'

'That warning doesn't incorporate the fact that he doesn't have to answer any questions?'

'Not at that stage, no.'

Reid repeated that he'd tried hard to control the encounter at the house. Maria had cried from the start and talked over her husband. Reid hadn't even had a chance to explain the search warrant before Polyukhovich had begun protesting that he'd done nothing wrong. He'd told the defendant to wait and that later, at the police station, he could tell 'the whole story'.

'Would you agree with me that you held out to him that it would be an advantage to speak to you?' David asked.

'No, I never said that at all and I don't think I gave that impression,' Reid replied.

'Don't you think this might have that impression?'

'If him telling a story is an advantage, well, yes, but I wasn't going to put words in his mouth. He could tell his version of the story. I don't feel that that was holding anything out to him or an advantage or anything like that, no.'

Reid said that both the Polyukhovichs understood some English, and often would begin to answer his questions before they'd been translated by the interpreter. 'I had to force the conversation back into Polish as opposed to letting it flow.'

At one point Reid had told Polyukhovich that they wanted to 'get all of this cleared up, okay, and you're the only one that can help us clear it all up'. 'What did you mean by the words "cleared up"?' David asked.

'Basically to get a story from him to find out what he wanted to say or what he was going to say in answer to the allegations,' Reid answered.

'So what you meant to convey to him was "we want to hear what you've got to say".'

'Basically yes.'

'That was different than getting the matter cleared up wasn't it?' David asked.

'Yes, I agree with that now. Yes,' Reid conceded.

The investigator told David that he'd believed Polyukhovich had understood his right not to answer questions when he was first cautioned after they entered the house.

'You thought he understood that he didn't have to answer any questions?' David asked.

'Yes.'

'Could you please dig up that question and answer which led you to that state of mind.'

Reid found the section and read it. 'I said, "Okay, Mr Huggett and myself are going to ask you some questions shortly, but I must warn you that anything you say may be taken down and used in evidence. Do you understand that?" He said, "Yeah, yeah, yeah." '

'That's not enough is it?' David asked.

'It's not to the extent that you're asking, no. It doesn't go as far.'

At Australian Federal Police headquarters Reid had cautioned Polyukhovich repeatedly regarding his rights throughout the rest of the interview. Huggett had told Polyukhovich he should not answer any questions unless he wanted to 'freely and voluntarily'. Each time Reid had put a new allegation to Polyukhovich, he had repeated that the pensioner had a right to remain silent. After one of these cautions, Polyukhovich had said in English, 'Yeah, I understand nothing to talk more. I not talk more.' Reid had asked if this meant Polyukhovich didn't want to answer any more questions. Through the interpreter Polyukhovich had said, 'What else can I say? I've already answered all those questions. I was never anywhere and I haven't seen anything. I was never in Germany organisation or police or Ukrainian police. We didn't have any Ukrainians there, we had white Russians there.'

Michael David had reached the heart of the matter. 'Did you think at that stage that was a clear message from him to you that he didn't want to answer any more questions?' he asked Reid.

'No that's why I asked him that question: Did he want to answer any more questions? If he said, No, I don't want to answer any more questions, I would have completed the interview there.'

'But read it as a whole,' said David. 'He says, "What else can I say. I've already answered all those questions." Now that's a clear message to you that he doesn't want to answer any questions, surely.'

Reid explained that, at the time, he was putting specific allegations to Polyukhovich and he'd believed the fair thing to do was to put every allegation to him, each time warning him that he wasn't required to answer.

'That's fine,' said David. 'But were you trying to tell him that it was for his benefit to continue with the conversation?'

'No, not for his benefit,' Reid replied.

'What's the difference?' asked the lawyer.

'In fairness to him,' said Reid.

'In fairness to him or for his benefit?'

'I was giving him the benefit of knowing what the allegations were.'

David came to a point in the record of interview where Polyukhovich had said that, if he said nothing, it might be thought he was guilty. Polyukhovich had clearly misunderstood the legal situation, in which no inference could have been drawn from a refusal to answer questions. Why, David asked, didn't Reid explain this to Polyukhovich? 'He is continuing on, on what he says, because he thinks there might be a disadvantage in concluding it,' David said.

'Yes, in hindsight I agree, yes,' Reid conceded. 'Perhaps I should have clarified it.'

After two days in the witness box Reid was nearly finished, but David asked that Reid simply be stood down, rather than dismissed. The defence might want to ask him more questions after the overseas witnesses had given their evidence next year.

Prosecutor James then called in turn investigator Bruce Huggett, interpreter Rosa Leventhal and journalist Mark Aarons. None of these took long and, just before three on Thursday 21 November 1991, the first session ended with magistrate Prescott adjourning the court until 9 March.

The defence had begun to expose weaknesses in the record of interview, which would be used later to have some material ruled inadmissible. But the prosecution had also made gains. Despite the problems with the interview, Reid could handle the rigours of cross-examination. He emerged looking as though he'd done his best under extremely difficult circumstances. And the exhumation evidence had been compelling.

Everyone felt tired and the main event was still three months away.

———

Within days of the court adjourning, Lindy Powell was in a dirty little room at the L'vov airport banging on a locked door and screaming to be let out. Next to her was Gabby Brown, another Adelaide lawyer helping with the war crimes defence. The pair had flown to Ukraine to gather evidence that could be used to defend Polyukhovich and Mikolay Berezowsky. They'd deliberately decided not to ask for official assistance while in Ukraine, fearing that their work might be hindered in some way.

Now, however, they were too much on their own. They'd been promised that a guide, who would double as a translator and driver, would meet them as they got off the plane. After struggling through the customs section, where the word 'queue' was meaningless, Powell and Brown had hoped to see this man standing with a sign carrying their names. All they'd found was a terminus filled with uniforms. One of them had peremptorily picked up their bags and headed for a small room. The Australians had chased after him, demanding an explanation. The uniform had replied by placing the bags in the room, walking out and closing the door. When the women had gone to open the door, they'd found it locked.

Someone who couldn't speak English finally had let them out, but the terminus seemed as unfriendly as before. After two hours of standing there – where else could they go? – their guide had appeared. He was extremely sorry and said something about having been given the wrong flight information. They should have lunch, he suggested, and they left to find a hotel, where the women's alienation was enhanced by the chipped crockery and customers' stares.

From L'vov, Powell and Brown were driven to Rovno, where they stayed the night. The next day they went straight to Serniki. Their first task was to locate Ivan Polyukhovich's sister, Olga. Locals directed them to a home in Alexandrovo where, in a barn not far from the house, they found a small, ruddy-faced woman.

Olga used her large, gnarled hands to encourage the women into her tiny wooden home, which had been painted blue. Powell was struck by how closely Olga resembled her brother. The lawyer recoiled at the smell of the household. Before her eyes could adjust to the darkness, she felt the ground give way beneath her. Her right arm slammed onto the ground, stopping her from falling into a potato pit just inside the door. Olga apologised as Brown and the translator rushed to help her out. Powell wore a bruise under her armpit for days.

After her nerves had settled, she and Brown asked Olga who in the area would be able to give them information about the war. Olga suggested a list of people, which included a number of prosecution witnesses. The defence believed it wouldn't be appropriate to approach them. Powell and Brown visited the others on Olga's list over the next few days, shocked by the sights and smells of Serniki in winter. Each of the houses in this poor village was shut up to keep out the bitter cold. The odour in most was terrible, but one old man lived in a lovely house, clean and painted, with a warm stove heating the rooms. He gave them what appeared to be very favourable evidence. It seemed he'd seen everything, and that their client wasn't there. Powell hadn't realised how difficult it would be to interview the witnesses and they were having trouble with their video camera. That was all right, said the old man, they could return later and interview him again. Powell and Brown returned three days later but the man began telling a quite different story. Powell stopped the interview. 'Hang on, this isn't what you told me on Monday,' she said.

'Oh no, but you've come back again.'

'Yes,' said Powell, not seeing the significance.

'Well you can't have liked what I said the first time,' the man replied.

———

The two lawyers left Ukraine in early December with the view that witnesses from the Soviet Union were inherently untrustworthy. They hadn't
uncovered a conspiracy. Rather, they'd discovered a people who, in their
view, had been so oppressed by an authoritarian government and fed
propaganda for so long they couldn't be used in an Australian court.
Many of the villagers were generous and kind, but their age, language
and culture made it difficult to converse with them, or know what motivated them when they spoke. The villagers had been too compliant, too
eager to know what the Australians wanted. On the other hand, the
defence lawyers had spoken to those people rejected by the prosecution
as unreliable or irrelevant. Perhaps Powell and Brown had gained a distorted impression by avoiding the prosecution witnesses. They'd have to
wait for the case to resume in March to find out.

The pair made two other discoveries during their trip. From prosecutor James's opening, the defence team had expected some witnesses to
say that Polyukhovich had been a police officer. But Powell and Brown
had found many people who described him simply as a forest warden. If
the case turned on his official job, they felt sure that they could produce
as many witnesses to say he was not a policeman as the crown apparently could produce to say he was. The second discovery related to
Dmitry Kostyukhovich's evidence. Powell had made Brown stand four
times in the spot where it was alleged the two youths had been shot by
Polyukhovich, while Powell stood where Dmitry said he'd been that
morning. Powell was convinced that identification was not possible from
such a distance.

———

No one had expected Walt Disney's Goofy to make an appearance at the resumption of the committal. But there he was, displayed on each of the five television sets placed around courtroom eleven. The junior prosecution and defence solicitors were using a cartoon to test the equipment. Goofy strained to lift a barbell, collapsed under it, then became entangled in some piece of equipment meant to build up his two-dimensional chest.

Ivan Polyukhovich sat next to Maria in the front row of the public gallery. What they made of all this wasn't clear.

A television set pointed towards the witness box on the northern side of the room. There was another at the right end of the wooden bar table for the prosecution, one at the opposite end for the defence, and a fourth pointed towards the jury box. The fifth set was perched high above all the rest, next to where magistrate Kelvyn Prescott would shortly take his seat.

This room was much larger than the Sturt Street court used four months earlier. It was actually a Supreme Court room, part of the old Supreme Court complex in Victoria Square built decades ago, with high ceilings, white walls and ornate plaster, especially around the judge's seat. The room was used only for Supreme Court civil cases, but the Court Services Department had agreed to hand it over to the Magistrates Court for the war crimes hearing after Prescott had complained that Sturt Street didn't have a library. Reporters, wanting the best vantage point, sat where juries had once deliberated, and Goofy played to an empty chair where once solemn judges had presided.

Just before ten the television sets were switched off, and a few moments later magistrate Prescott walked in. Defence leader Michael David rose to his feet, explaining that his client couldn't see the televisions properly from where he sat and that the interpreters might have trouble hearing the evidence from the gallery.

The solution was obvious. The reporters and sketch artists in the front row of the jury box would have to shift. They hesitated, but quickly realised that Prescott wasn't about to brook any argument. They searched for seats in the packed gallery, leaving the back row filled with luckier journalists. Ivan and Maria Polyukhovich and two interpreters took over the vacated seats. From here Polyukhovich would spend the next three months staring across ten metres of courtroom into the faces of his accusers directly opposite.

————

'I call Abraham Dinerman,' prosecutor Greg James said.

A tallish, balding man, wearing a light grey suit, white shirt and a large, silvery-grey tie was led from the entrance at the back of the court, through the gallery aisle and into the witness box. He looked up at Polyukhovich as he walked in, then back at where he was walking.

Frank Owen, the orderly, asked him if he swore to tell to the truth. The man said something to Owen that others couldn't hear.

'This is the Old Testament,' said Frank. 'The book of Genesis.'

The man placed a skull cap on his head, Frank read the oath again and the man said, 'I do.'

'My name is Abraham Dinerman,' he told the court in answer to Frank's question. 'My occupation used to be a poultry farmer.'

Dinerman explained that he'd been born on 5 May 1927 into a Jewish family in the village of Serniki, which was then part of Poland, but that he'd lived in the United States for many years. In Serniki he'd lived with his brother, who was one year his senior, and his mother and father who'd run a small grocery store. He said that there had been about nine hundred Jewish people living in Serniki in 1941, the year the Russians left. A local Ukrainian police force had then taken control.

Dinerman paused.

'Would you like a glass of water?' James asked.

'No, I'm okay. They used to rob, kill and rape families,' Dinerman said slowly.

'Was there a point of time, after the Russians had gone, when other people, not Ukrainian, came to Serniki?' James continued.

'The Germans came in on horses . . . that was summer time. I remember it was nice and warm outside.'

He described how the German soldiers had rounded up a group of Jews and marched them past his home towards the new school in Serniki. He said that he never saw those people again, but heard the sounds of machine guns and rifles the next morning coming from the Jewish cemetery.

'Did that shooting continue for some time?' James asked.

'No, not – not like – the second time was longer,' Dinerman said.

He spoke as if he meant what he said, as if he remembered the events quite clearly and as if his heart was pounding. Every now and then he'd look across at Polyukhovich and then back to James.

The reporters in court sat up. After more than two years, this was the start of the emotional evidence the case had always promised.

James asked whether the witness could remember the names of the police who stayed in Serniki after the German departure. When Dinerman began to explain that his father had known two police officers from a place called Svaritsevichi, Michael David stood up and objected. The witness, he argued, was giving hearsay evidence.

'Did your father tell you the names of two of the policemen that he knew?' James asked.

'Right, he knew them,' Dinerman replied nodding his head. He clearly didn't understand the problem.

'What were the names of those two persons?'

Again David objected. There was, he said, a difference between what the witness knew and what he'd been told by someone else.

'I press it,' said James. 'The only way one ever knows a person's name is that others have told you the name of that person or that person has told you the name of themself. Indeed, a name is a description by which one is known.'

Dinerman had only been in the court thirty minutes, but magistrate Prescott decided that the witness should leave the room while the issue was sorted out.

'We might as well have this argument now,' David said. 'This obviously is a problem that is raised because of the nature of this case, bearing in mind we are fifty years down the track. Normally speaking, in a normal criminal trial, the actual name of a person isn't subject to an objection but here we have a situation which in my submission your honour is going to have to rule on . . . It's a straight application of hearsay. They are not here, I am unable to cross-examine that person who gives him that information. He might be wrong.'

James was ready for this. He declared that the prosecution wasn't tendering this evidence as proof of the truth of its contents – the fact Dinerman said that his father had told him x, y or z was a policeman didn't mean x, y or z *was* a policeman. The prosecution was merely trying to get the labels this witness had used in his own mind to identify people.

David understood and said that, so long as the prosecution took it no further, the objection was withdrawn.

Dinerman returned, again stealing a look at Polyukhovich as he entered. He began naming and describing police officers he remembered from Serniki. Then James asked him about the ghetto in Serniki which Dinerman said was set up in late 1941 or early 1942.

Dinerman described how more Jewish people from surrounding towns had been brought to Serniki, how they had been made to wear yellow patches and ask for permission to travel. Dinerman said he'd only stayed in the ghetto a couple of weeks before fleeing to a farm run by a Ukrainian, Jan Hryn. Hryn had known Dinerman was Jewish, but had given him a job looking after his cows.

Just before the Jewish festival of Rosh Hashona in 1942, Hryn had told Dinerman that ditches had been dug outside Serniki. He'd given the boy a bag with bread in it and Dinerman had spent that night in Hryn's barn. Dinerman said that the next day he'd heard shooting coming from Serniki as he sought refuge in another barn about four miles away. He'd spent the night there, and early the next morning had heard trucks. He'd peered out of the barn and seen trucks, local police officers and Germans in the distance. The uniforms worn by these Germans had been darker than those worn by the invaders months before. These men, Dinerman said, were chasing Jewish people. For a time they'd been obscured by trees and then he'd seen the Jews brought out into a clearing.

'They all lined them up,' Dinerman said slowly. 'About ten, fifteen, twenty in a line, and they were shooting with a machine gun and rifles. They had no clothes on.' He took a large white handkerchief from his pocket and wiped his brow, wet eyes and red face. 'They were naked, no clothes,' he repeated.

'Could you recognise any of the Germans or Ukrainians?' James asked.

'No,' Dinerman managed to say.

'How long did these shootings take?'

'For half a day.'

Dinerman said that when it became dark, he'd left the barn, but had to pass by the place where the shootings had occurred. He paused, still crying.

'And what did you see?' James asked.

Dinerman used his handkerchief again, then stopped to drink from the glass of water Frank Owen had poured. 'All the ground was covered with blood,' he said. He didn't look at James.

'What did you do?'

'The ground kept moving, kept moving back and forth,' Dinerman continued, ignoring the question.

'The ground was moving?'

'Yes.'

'What did you do?'

'I walked up the side, and I ran for the woods . . . I ran in the woods and I cursed. I cursed everywhere.'

Dinerman was shaking, sweating and kept glancing back at Poly-ukhovich as he spoke.

He said that he'd met up with Pepe Kaz's first husband, Motl Bobrov, and later had found his own parents and brother. They had stayed in the forest and survived with the help of people from a nearby town who'd given them food until the Russians returned in 1944. No, they hadn't joined the partisans.

'To come back to the time before the Germans came, before the war,' James asked, 'did you ever meet anyone who was nicknamed Ivanechko?'

'He used to stop in the store. He came, I used to see him on the bicycle with a rifle,' Dinerman replied. 'He used to go in civil clothes when I was taking care of the cows.'

Ivanechko, Dinerman said, had lived about ten kilometres from Serniki on the left-hand side of the road. He'd had two brothers and two sisters as well, Dinerman thought, one of whom still lived in the town of Zelin, in Ukraine. Ivanechko's older brother was called Cirillo. This man had a German wife but wasn't involved in killing Jews. Ivanechko had worked as a game warden under the Polish government and had taken care of the woods.

Then James asked the witness to look at a document. Dinerman identified it as a map of Serniki that he'd drawn. 'I get up at three o'clock in the morning and I took some papers, I just took a pen, and everything I had in my mind I put down.'

There were no measurements, he said, but he'd marked his family's house with the initials 'A.D.'.

'Did you yourself ever see – just yourself – Ivanechko either kill or beat anyone?' James asked.

'No,' answered the witness.

James asked whether Dinerman recalled speaking with SIU investigator Bob Reid in April 1990 (four months after Polyukhovich was charged). Dinerman remembered. That was in Miami. Reid had shown him photographs.

'Would you have a look at what you are now shown?' James said, in the way lawyers ask questions when they want to direct a witness. The court orderly placed a cardboard sheet in front of Dinerman. On it were twelve black-and-white photographs of different men. The photos were hinged to the cardboard at their top so that, if the sheet was held upside down, they fell over revealing their backs and anything that was written on them. This was one of the photo-boards – a crucial part of the SIU's identification procedure.

'Do you recognise those pictures?'

'I would recognise them in the dark,' Dinerman replied.

'Was that the photograph spread shown to you by Mr Reid?'

'He showed me a lot of pictures.'

'Were these the pictures?'

'These are. This is the one,' Dinerman said pointing with his finger at one of the photographs.

'Are you now pointing to a particular picture?'

'Yes.'

'Which picture?'

'Number nine.'

'Would you have a look at the back of picture number nine? Is that your signature and date there?'

'Right. I put – on the other pictures – my initials and date.'

'I think we'll take the break there, Mr James,' the magistrate inter-rupted, and the court was adjourned.

When it resumed, the video of the interview between Dinerman and Reid, made in April 1990, was played to the court simultaneously on the five television sets. They showed Dinerman sitting at a table, casually dressed and looking more relaxed than he now was as he sat in court watching himself. But even then, he'd looked wary. Reid could be heard but not seen on the video as he asked Dinerman whether he recognised anyone in the photo-board before him. The Dinerman in the video pointed to photograph number nine and said, 'His looks are heavier.' The television sets showed Dinerman pause. He was clearly upset. Photographs eleven and twelve also looked familiar, he said, but number nine was Ivanechko.

The real Dinerman sitting in court looked across at Polyukhovich sitting opposite, back at the video, then back at Polyukhovich.

After the video finished, Dinerman said that it had correctly recorded what he and Reid had done with the photographs. Defence lawyer David said that he had no objection to it being admitted at this stage.

James resumed his questioning. 'Except on the occasion in which Mr Reid referred you to the photograph, after you left the town of Serniki, have you ever seen the person known to you as Ivanechko, since?'

'I have heard his voice,' Dinerman answered.

'Have you ever seen him?'

'No.'

'Would you look around the courtroom?'

'If I had seen him, I wouldn't be here today,' Dinerman continued, apparently thinking it necessary to finish answering one question before following any direction.

'Would you look around the courtroom and tell me if there is any person you recognise in the courtroom?' James repeated.

'I can close my eyes and can point him right there,' Dinerman said. His voice was raised and so was his finger, which now pointed at Polyukhovich sitting silently opposite.

David leapt to his feet to object. He wasn't going to let an in-court identification get past without a fight, not fifty years after the event when there was one isolated old man sitting opposite the witness.

James responded by saying that the prosecution had asked for the defendant to take part in a line-up, and the request had been rejected. The in-court identification was therefore entirely appropriate.

Dinerman was stood down again to allow argument between the lawyers.

The issue, James said, was the weight to be given to such in-court identification, not whether or not it was admissible. It might be that, when the case got to trial, the trial judge would exclude the photo-board and the video from evidence. In that case, the prosecution would need the in-court identification. On 5 March, only four days earlier, the prosecution had put a request to the defence for Polyukhovich to take part in a line-up but they'd refused.

David stood up again. He said that a line-up would plainly have been unreliable after such a long period, especially since Dinerman had also been shown a photograph that the prosecution said was Polyukhovich. His advice, not to take part in a line-up, could be seen in his written reply to the DPP.

James saw he needed to continue. He said that whether a trial judge would find Dinerman's evidence tainted was not for the court to decide here. The witness hadn't identified Polyukhovich as an assailant or as a person who'd committed any crimes. He'd simply identified him as a person who had been in a particular place at a particular time. Further, the prosecution planned to ask Dinerman to identify photos seized from Polyukhovich's home at the time of the arrest.

David said that the crown's position was absurd. 'We are asking for an in-dock identification when the last time this person saw the defendant or suspect was fifty years ago. In between time he has seen a photo the crown has shown him. Your honour, with respect, can't shy away from this.'

Magistrate Prescott, however, was satisfied that the issue was what weight the in-court identification should carry, not whether it was admissible. Dinerman would be allowed to point his finger again. Before he was brought back, David asked for all reference to Polyukhovich's refusal to take part in a line-up to be suppressed from publication. Members of the public, he said, might reason that an innocent man would have nothing to lose by taking part in a line-up and infer that Polyukhovich's refusal meant some measure of guilt.

Prescott agreed. The suppression order was made and Dinerman was asked to return.

'Prior to the legal matter that arose, I asked you the question, "Can you see in court that person?" Can you see that person in court?' James asked.

'The person in court, yes. Right there the person in the dark glasses, Ivanechko,' Dinerman said.

'That's Ivanechko in the dark glasses?'

'Right.'

'Are you now pointing – '

Dinerman intercepted James. 'It's the man from right, and he's the second one on the left.' He pointed across the courtroom.

'Is that person sitting in the jury box with fourteen other people, some men, some women?' James asked.

'Yeah, I don't know the other people,' Dinerman said, looking at the journalists and sketch artists who filled the back of the jury box.

'This is their line-up,' David said sarcastically to his defence partner Powell in a voice that wasn't meant to be hushed. The queen's counsel glanced at the reporters and rolled his eyes.

James ignored him and began questioning the witness about Yankel Kaz, whom Dinerman remembered as a man in Serniki with a wooden leg.

James then asked Dinerman to look one by one at a series of old photographs, and say whether or not he recognised anyone. Each time, Dinerman quickly pointed to the photograph and said, 'That's Ivanechko.' If it was a group picture, he scanned it for a moment, pointed out one of the figures and declared, 'That's Ivanechko.'

David objected to the procedure, but magistrate Prescott said that this ground had already been covered. The evidence would be received. David asked for Dinerman's identification of the accused to be suppressed from publication but Prescott refused him that as well. The court rose for lunch.

———

Dinerman was brought back in by SIU investigator Bob Reid, who had his hand on the shoulder of another, smaller man who looked up at Polyukhovich and stared as they walked through the court. He was taken to a room just outside the court where he would wait to be called.

James resumed his questioning and returned to the topic of the pit killing. This lasted only a few minutes. Dinerman couldn't say how many Jews had been at the pit. It could have been a couple of thousand. He wasn't sure, but there were a lot of children.

Then Michael David stood up to question Dinerman on Polyukhovich's behalf.

'Mr Dinerman, you lived in the ghetto, is that right?'

'Not too long.'

'Your house, where you normally lived, was that in the ghetto area, or did you shift house?'

'No, not at all,' Dinerman answered.

'You shifted houses to go into the ghetto?'

'I don't understand. My house where I lived, that is, probably from the ghetto, a couple of thousand feet.'

'Then you moved houses, and went into the ghetto?'

'I didn't move, they moved me.'

'The ghetto itself was not surrounded by fences or barbed wire, was it?'

'I left the ghetto.'

David repeated the question.

'I left the ghetto, so I cannot tell you what is what.'

'When you were living in the ghetto, was it surrounded by fences or barbed wire, to keep you in?'

'The ghetto, when I moved in, wasn't a ghetto for a couple of weeks.'

Witness and lawyer were talking at cross purposes. Dinerman was becoming unsettled and David impatient. His questions seemed reasonable, even obvious, but this old man, whose native language was not English, seemed to be stumbling over them. Perhaps he was speaking too firmly and quickly. David asked for an interpreter but the magistrate wasn't convinced that one was needed.

David then questioned the witness about his description of Serniki, which he'd recalled in so much detail. It was detail, David was to learn, that would be confirmed by each of the Jewish witnesses. They remembered the town with remarkable uniformity.

David changed tack. 'You saw the Ukrainian police often?' he asked.

'I never was in the police station. I saw them on the way to take care of the cows ... How do you think I remembered his face?' Dinerman was pointing at Polyukhovich again. 'I see him with the rifle there, on a bicycle.'

David decided to run with this statement. 'You do not say he was a policeman. Was he?'

'No, he was a volunteer.'

'He was a warden,' David said, rather than asked.

'A game warden,' Dinerman confirmed, nodding his head.

'He was not a policeman,' repeated David.

'He was a volunteer. He volunteered to kill Jews.'

'This is ridiculous,' David declared angrily. But it was lawyer's anger, nothing deep. The last comment must be struck out, he said, and magistrate Prescott agreed. Clearly, Dinerman was not in a position to say that the defendant had volunteered to kill Jews.

'Was he a policeman, or was he not a policeman?' David asked.

'No, he was a volunteer.'

'Was he a warden, who worked in the forest?'

Dinerman explained that Polyukhovich's family had worked as wardens for the Poles, then the Russians and the Germans and that ... he volunteered to kill Jews.

David demanded that the last part of the answer be struck out and Prescott agreed once more.

Dinerman told the court that he had seen Polyukhovich many times while he was looking after the cows for Jan Hryn. He apparently couldn't help adding that, if he'd got too close, he wouldn't have been around long. This comment was struck out. Dinerman repeated that he'd never seen Polyukhovich shoot anyone and said that no, Polyukhovich hadn't worn a uniform.

David was interested in the activities of the Ukrainian police in the ghetto, but Dinerman couldn't see what they had to do with him. He had only ever been in the ghetto for a couple of weeks. Dinerman said that he'd seen Ukrainian police killing people from the barn.

'You saw them, I think you said, beating people in the forest. Is that right?' David asked, as if he were a long-suffering parent dealing with a child's confused story.

'They beat me up,' Dinerman answered.

'Beat you in the forest?'

'No, before the ghetto they did it.'

The recollections appeared to be falling into one another.

'You never saw Ivanechko do anything – '

Dinerman cut him off. 'Excuse me – '

'I insist the witness answer the question.'

But Dinerman continued 'The first time they were killing the Jews they were not involved. After, he became a volunteer to do it to the Jews.'

'I insist on an answer,' David repeated.

'Put it again,' Prescott said quietly from high above.

'From what you saw, you never saw Ivanechko ever do anything like that, did you?' David asked patiently.

'I saw him with a rifle. An honest man was not wearing a rifle to walk around.'

The rest of the afternoon continued in a similar vein. Dinerman showed the strain of being questioned in such detail. It seemed he would burst at one point, when he said, 'I was able to see – I would be able to recognise, I was able to see it. The machine gun was shooting, the machine gun was shooting, they were falling in the ditches.'

David returned to the topic of the photographs, and Dinerman cried as he explained that he 'only saw' the Ivanechko photo. The others were meaningless to him. But David wanted to know whether or not he'd seen all of the pictures shown to him in court before his court appearance, or only the photo-board shown to him by investigator Reid in Florida. Dinerman had trouble understanding and eventually turned to Magistrate Prescott for help. Pointing at the prosecution, he said that they'd shown him photographs but were also trying to confuse him. Prescott told him to wait until a question had finished before responding.

The questioning resumed, back and forth.

'Who showed you the photographs?'

'I don't pay attention . . . I just pick him out . . . You can show me ten pictures right now and I look at his face and I get nerved up.'

'I'm not concerned as to whose face you saw. I want to know who showed you those pictures in Australia.'

'Who show me pictures?'

'Yes.'

'You show me pictures like this – '

Prescott managed to establish that Dinerman had been shown some photographs about four days earlier.

Eventually, to everyone's relief, they left the topic of the photographs and moved back on to the ghetto. No, Dinerman had never seen Ivanechko in the ghetto. Ivanechko was not a policeman, he said. He remembered Ivanechko from when Ivanechko would visit his father's store, but Ivanechko would not have remembered him. At other times, his father would point out Ivanechko's home.

David had had enough. Prosecutor James asked a few more questions and showed Dinerman a bundle of photographs. The witness confirmed that they were the photographs shown to him a week earlier. His evidence was finished. It was past four when an exhausted Dinerman made his way out of the court.

He had said nothing to link Polyukhovich with any specific crime, but James was happy enough. The witness had identified Polyukhovich in court and on the photographs as Ivanechko, the warden who lived near Serniki. On that he hadn't been shaken.

———

Although it was late, there was still time to introduce another witness. The man Bob Reid had earlier led through the court was brought in and identified as Nathan Dinerman. Nathan was smaller than his brother and looked much younger, although he was a year older. He gave his hat to Reid, entered the dock, put on his skull cap and took the oath. He was, he said, a postal clerk living in the United States. Between 1936 and 1942 he and his family had lived in Serniki.

Prosecutor Grant Niemann asked him to describe the towns which surrounded Serniki. Nathan responded in a confident Massachusetts' accent. 'Sure, which side shall I start from?'

Niemann asked him how far Alexandrovo was from Serniki.

'Between five and seven miles I would say, something like that. It's a lot of sand there. It was all farms. In Russian they say "chutor".'

Nathan smiled at the sound of this last word. Perhaps he was pleased by his pronunciation or memory.

Niemann was pleased that Nathan's evidence flowed so easily. Nathan Dinerman, it seemed, had no doubts about himself or the world around him. He smiled a lot, except when he looked across at the defendant. Then his face became serious. Niemann would ask another question and Nathan's attention would return and so would the smile. His alertness, however, never left him.

He named more towns. Asked if he remembered any others, he replied, 'Sure,' and rattled off another half dozen. He could remember that the Germans first came in summer but not the date they arrived.

It was half past four and time to end the first day of overseas witnesses.

Next morning Bob Reid knew that Nathan Dinerman would complete his evidence in an hour or two and that Pepe Cohen needed to be ready. The investigator made his way to the Hilton hotel where Pepe was staying with the other witnesses. He would accompany her to the court.

After escaping from Serniki with her sister Sonja, Pepe Kaz had married a man from the area, Motl 'Max' Bobrov. After surviving the war, the couple had migrated to the United States, where they had run a farm in Massachusetts. After Max died, Pepe's friends had managed to persuade her to move to the city, where she met and married David Cohen.

The decision to come to Australia to give evidence had been difficult. Pepe was now seventy-five. Each year she'd managed to visit Sonja in Israel, but that was a familiar journey which ended with friends and family. What would she find in Adelaide? When she had finally arrived in Australia, Reid had taken her aside and thanked her. Pepe had told him that she'd spent her life serving others. Now it was time to do something for herself. This man had been charged with murdering her mother, sister and niece.

Reid walked into Pepe's room to find her in a terrible state. Fellow SIU officer, Anne Dowd, was standing with her.

'Pepe, what's the matter?' Reid asked.

'I haven't got a black dress,' Pepe answered. She was looking at a perfectly good dark blue dress that she obviously believed was inadequate.

Mystified, Reid tried to encourage her. 'You look beautiful. The blue dress looks lovely.'

'I forgot my black dress. I left it at home,' Pepe repeated, obviously very upset.

Reid turned to Dowd and said quietly, 'Come on, quick. Let's get in the car. We'll go and buy her a black dress.'

'Oh, I suppose it's dark,' Pepe murmured, still looking at the blue dress and speaking more to herself than to Reid or Dowd.

'No, don't worry Bob. We'll go like this,' Pepe said and paused. 'Today's the day I bury my mother.'

———

Nathan Dinerman returned to the stand showing the same confidence as he had on the day before.

In answer to prosecutor Niemann's questions he described how, when the Germans first entered Serniki, he'd sought refuge in a Jewish woman's house and had hidden for two days above her large brick oven.

The next day he'd heard rifle shots coming from the cemetery. Nathan remembered the names of some of the Ukrainian police who'd patrolled the village after the Germans had gone. He had vivid memories of two officers severely beating a Jewish woman. She had lain on the ground for perhaps an hour and then crawled away on all fours. Nathan said that she'd never walked upright again, and had needed a stool to support herself. In Alexandrovo, the Ukrainian officer Doroctuiks had struck Nathan's mother in the head with a rifle 'just because we were Jewish'. Nathan and his father had escaped from Serniki in 1942, a few days before Rosh Hashona, and had stayed in the woods until 1943.

Niemann wanted to know whether Nathan remembered a person called 'Ivanechko'. Nathan said that of course he did. If you were travelling from Alexandrovo to Serniki, Ivanechko lived on the left hand side. Nathan said that he had seen Ivanechko often as a youngster, but not since 1942. Niemann asked him to look around the courtroom and say whether the person he had described as Ivanechko was there.

'Of course I see him,' Nathan said.

David rose to object but magistrate Prescott overruled him.

'Here's Ivanechko,' Nathan continued.

'Would you point to him?'

'In the glasses. White hair, combed back. But when I knew him his hair was black. As soon as I walked in yesterday I saw him. Can I add something else or not?'

'Yes,' Niemann said.

'If I didn't see the pictures, I would recognise him too without the pictures. I am so sure of myself.'

Niemann produced a photo-board and Nathan immediately pointed to one photo, saying, 'Yes, I see him already, right here. This is the man. This is Ivanechko.' Nathan had signed the back of the photo during his interview in the United States with the Special Investigations Unit. Eight individual photographs were put in front of him; each time he pointed straight to a man, saying that he was Ivanechko.

Niemann asked whether Nathan remembered any Jew in Serniki who had a wooden leg. Nathan mentioned Yanek Kaz, who had lived in the new village next to Serniki.

For the defence, Michael David approached Nathan cautiously. This witness was sure of his testimony. David asked him how long he had lived in the ghetto. Several months but less than a year. He was guarded by Ukrainian police? Yes. How many were there? Twenty or thirty.

'And if they caught anyone escaping what would happen?'

'Give them a bullet.'

'They used to tell you that, the Ukrainian guards?'

Nathan frowned. 'I don't understand you.'

'They used to tell you that. They used to say, "Look, if you escape you get shot," ' David said by way of explanation.

'They didn't have to say it, we knew it,' Nathan answered, still frowning.

'Did they say things like that? Did they threaten you?'

'I'm sorry?'

'Did they say anything else to you?'

Nathan decided to interrupt the questioning. 'It's hard for me to understand your English because I speak American English. It's a different English. I want to make sure I know what you are saying. I got used to his and Bob's English already.' Nathan pointed at Niemann, who sat grinning at the bar table, and Reid, who was in the front row of the gallery. 'I got to listen carefully. If I don't understand you I'm not going to answer. If you talk slow I'll understand you,' Nathan concluded.

David didn't enjoy being lectured by a witness about his Australian accent, but he could only do as he was told. He asked his next question slowly.

Nathan said that Ivanechko hadn't worked as a policeman. Ivanechko was a forest warden who'd carried a rifle and, yes, he'd seen Ivanechko carrying a gun in the ghetto.

'But not as a policeman?' asked David.

'Not that I know of. Can I say something else?' Nathan asked innocently.

'Please.' David encouraged him.

'When I was in the wood the people in Zelin told me that he joined the police,' Nathan said.

If something inside David tightened he didn't let it show. 'I don't mean to be rude,' he said politely, 'but you can't tell us what other people said.'

'I asked your permission, didn't I? And you said yes so I told you. I didn't jump the gun. I didn't volunteer. I asked your permission.'

The gallery was enjoying the sport. David knew that he'd been outsmarted, a rare experience. He conceded graciously to the clever little man. 'You won. That was good,' he said.

The rest of the cross-examination was taken up with questions about the police station, the layout of the ghetto and the village, relations with the police, and the police uniforms and weapons. By the time David had finished, Nathan had corrected his pronunciation a couple more times. 'Oh you say "nimes", you mean "naymes".' The QC was glad to sit down.

Prosecutor Niemann stood up to re-examine the witness. He had enjoyed Nathan Dinerman's testimony, especially since the defence had managed to draw out that the witness believed Ivanechko had wandered through the ghetto carrying a gun.

'How soon before Rosh Hashona in 1942 did you see Ivanechko in the ghetto?' he asked Nathan.

'Probably I would say June or July I saw him. I think so, in summer time.'

'Was he carrying a gun at that time?'

'He was carrying a gun.'

'No further questions.'

———

'I'm a housewife,' Pepe Cohen told the court. 'My maiden name was Kaz.'

Pepe explained that she was born in the city of Pinsk on 15 December 1916, and her family had moved to Serniki when she was a baby.

Prosecutor Greg James asked Pepe about the members of her immediate family in Serniki, then showed her a series of photographs, some of
them taken before the war. These included photos saved decades earlier
on the night she had fled Serniki with Moyshe Kriniuk. They had been
in the bag that she had dropped, which Moyshe later insisted they must
find because it contained food. Pepe displayed a remarkable memory for
the time, place and circumstances of each of the precious pictures. 'This
is my mother, this picture was made in 1936. My mother was a widow at
that time. She didn't want the picture . . . That is children from my sister's
class, Sonja. There are three girls, Ukrainian. They didn't want to come to
school in uniform like it was required . . . This is my teacher Rovinsky . . .
This is Batushka, a priest.'

Pepe gave her evidence methodically, even stopping to spell a name
in two languages without being asked. She was instantly likeable; there
was a terrible contrast between her grandmotherly manner and what she
had lived through. She was an emotionally powerful witness for the
prosecution and one for the defence to fear.

Prosecutor James wanted to know the location of her house in Serniki
and the names of other people living in the area. Pepe named without
hesitation the Bobrov family, Pinchos Turkienicz, Zilberfarb, Galandski
and Feldman. James asked her about her brother-in-law's murder during
the hiatus between the Russian withdrawal and the German occupation.
Then Pepe described how her family had left Serniki and stayed at a
friendly farm near Alexandrovo, before being forced back to the Serniki
ghetto. She detailed the restrictions placed on the Jews living in the
ghetto. Asked about the Ukrainian police, she said that they 'used to do
their work at night'.

'They used to come and knock on our Jewish homes and look for the
girls. It doesn't matter how old. Ten, twelve, fifteen . . . That was against
the law by the Germans. They were not allowed to go to rape girls, but
they did.'

Pepe described her first attempt to escape from Serniki with her sister

Sonja, how she and Sonja had eventually escaped with Moyshe Kriniuk's family, and how her mother Tsalykha, sister Luba and Luba's baby had fallen behind in the forest. She described those first few days hiding in the woods and her eventual return to the ruined ghetto and the discovery of the grave site.

When asked if she remembered a man called Ivanechko, she said she had seen him twice, but had not got too close. She had, however, a clear memory of his appearance.

'He was exceptional, because he was dark skinned,' Pepe said. 'The Christians or Gentiles, they were fair faced, and he was exceptionally dark faced. Shaped a little bit like oval and pointy, and his mouth was exceptionally visible, because he had teeth that he couldn't close his mouth over too well. Or maybe he was talking and that is just the way it is.'

Pepe said that Ivanechko hadn't worn a uniform and she couldn't remember if he'd carried a rifle. She'd never seen him in the ghetto.

James asked a few questions about the registration of the Serniki Jews at Vysotsk, the SIU photo-board used by Bob Reid when she was first interviewed in September 1989 in the US and her discovery of the site of the grave where her mother, Luba and the baby had been buried a few months after their deaths. Pepe said she didn't want to mention the name of the family which had taken her to her mother's grave. She did not want to 'jeopardise' them. It became clear that Pepe had kept their identity secret for fifty years.

James decided to return to the topic of Ivanechko. He asked Pepe to look around the court and see if that person was present.

'He didn't see me. He doesn't know me, because I was a young girl, and he didn't pay attention,' Pepe said. 'Because he was Alter's friend, I paid attention when I saw him.' Pepe was referring to Alter Botvinik, one of the alleged victims. 'When I saw him I know nothing about him and I would never think that he could do a thing like this.'

Could Pepe be avoiding the question? James prompted her. 'Look around the courtroom,' he said gently.

'I saw him, and I will point him to you, because even he has changed,' Pepe answered. 'He has lost weight, and he is greyish, or maybe he got a little bit of a job on his teeth, because they are not so full as when he was young. He had a full face, pinkish, good looking. Now he is a little like me. I am old, and I don't look like I looked when I was young.'

'Could you point him out please?' James asked.

'Yes, he is next to the blue shirt and the pink blouse.'

Finally, Pepe had identified Polyukhovich as Ivanechko.

———

During what was left of the afternoon, David confirmed that Pepe had only ever seen Ivanechko twice and that the last time had been in 1942 just before the ghetto was liquidated. But she could not incriminate Ivanechko.

———

Wednesday was a rest day but on Thursday Pepe was back in the witness box. David spent some time questioning her about the layout of the village, particularly the area near the bridge. He was especially interested in what could be seen from the Kaz and Kriniuk properties near the river. The reason for his interest hadn't emerged, but it would become an important part of the defence attack on Dmitry Kostyukhovich's evidence. Pepe told the court that, from her family's house, you could see the whole bridge and all of the street which led away from the river on the other side until it turned towards the market place. Much time was then taken up trying to determine the boundaries of the ghetto. Pepe described where her mother, sister and niece had been buried.

At one point in all of this Pepe asked if she could say more than the question required.

'Oh no,' said David. 'I got caught out like that the other day.'

Pepe might not have been told of Nathan Dinerman's exploits, but the rest of the courtroom appreciated the humour.

Prosecutor James took only a few moments to close Pepe's testimony. He finished by returning to her mother's grave. 'Before you saw your mother's grave, you spoke to a girl from a good family?' he asked.

'Yes.'

'Do you know the name Ekaterina Bogatko?'

'I know the name Bogatko.'

'Do you want to tell us the name of the girl that you spoke to?'

'Do I have to?' Pepe asked.

'Yes.'

'It was Vera Bilko. And her father, his name was, I think, Pravlo. I am not sure. It is possible I could remind myself exactly. I think it is Pravlo and the mother was Anna.'

It had taken nearly a whole day's testimony spread over three days but finally Pepe had buried her mother, sister and baby niece.

———

The next witness called was Jack Kriniuk. The boy who had escaped Serniki with his family had become a tall, distinguished-looking man, who looked like he was used to being in control. Even now, taken out of his home environment, he gave the impression that he was only here because he wanted to be. He put on his skull cap and took the oath. When asked his occupation, the millionaire modestly replied, 'Self-employed garment manufacturer in New York City'.

Niemann was asking the questions for the prosecution. What was Serniki like before the war? How many Jewish people lived there? What did they do for a living? What were relations like between the Jewish and Ukrainian people?

'Can you recall what happened at that time when the Germans occupied the region?'

Kriniuk, speaking slowly and carefully in a broad New York accent, remembered that the Germans were on horseback the first time they entered Serniki. 'The first time we saw Germans they rounded up mostly men, only men, and they took them to the cemetery and they killed them there.'

'Did you see this?'

'The killing? No. I saw them coming in and rounding up the men.'

'Just tell us what you can remember seeing yourself.'

Kriniuk described how he, his father and uncle escaped the execution in the cemetery by running to the forest; how after a few days some Ukrainian police caught up with them and shot his uncle dead. He described how the chief of police recognised his father, how his father had dreamt of a rabbi while they slept in the cell, and how the police chief had freed them. Then Niemann wanted to know about the ghetto, how it was formed, its boundaries, the role of the Ukrainian police. Although he hadn't shown it, Kriniuk was nervous when he took the stand, and he wasn't becoming calmer.

'The Ukrainian police, did they wear a uniform?' Niemann asked.

'I would say most of them did not, maybe some. I just can't recall clearly.'

'Were they armed?'

'Yes. They had revolvers and some of them had rifles.'

'Do you recall any of the Ukrainian police at the time?'

'Yes. By their name, no.' Kriniuk paused. 'I recall an incident when they came to my house and took me and my father, and beat us a few times.'

He paused again, as if he'd travelled a long way and was resting, but still had a steep hill to climb.

'And one night I remember, I will never forget all my life, they came into my house and raped my sister and made me watch.'

Kriniuk was crying. It was only 11.15, but Niemann asked for an adjournment.

———

Kriniuk was still wiping away tears as he stood in the small waiting room just inside the entrance to the building.

Pepe Cohen, who was there to sign her evidence, got to her feet. This matriarch of the Jewish survivors from Serniki, a dwarf standing next to Kriniuk, scolded him gently. 'Now Jack Kriniuk, you've got to do this. I didn't cry in the witness box. Now you've got to be strong.'

———

Fifteen minutes later the court resumed.

'They came into our house at night,' Kriniuk began. 'We were sleeping and they woke us up and they took my older sister and they raped her and made us all watch. I turned away my face, and they turned me and hit me, made sure I watched it. And I was crying. I was only thirteen. And they finished whatever they had to do. They left. My sister walked over to me and said, "Don't cry, don't cry. I'll be all right, I'll be all right."'

Kriniuk's wife, Rae, was sitting in the gallery. Nearly every night for the last forty years her husband's sleep had been broken by nightmares. Rae was a survivor of the Holocaust herself, but Jack had never told her about his sister's rape. Tears were falling down her face.

Kriniuk paused and then said, 'If I may, I would just like to speak a little about the Jewish and Ukrainian people and the relations we had.'

The court was hushed. He could have said whatever he liked.

'I think it is important to explain the life we had with the Ukrainian people. We had an excellent relation. We were friends. We were trading, we were going to school together. We shared food. We went on hikes and the River Stubla we were bathing in. And I think the majority of the people from Serniki, Ukrainian people, were sorry what happened. They tried to hide Jewish people. They tried to make sure as many as they could survived. And they gave us food and they explained their feelings – how much they are hurting about what is happening. And if there wasn't a war I'm sure we would still be there and be a happy family.'

'Approximately how old was your sister at the time?' asked Niemann.

'My sister was twenty-one years old.'

—

During the rest of his evidence, Kriniuk went on to explain that his mother and four sisters had been killed during attacks on Jews living in the forests. He said that those in the forest had known that Ivanechko was coming. This was obvious hearsay evidence and the magistrate struck it out. The witness was asked not to say things he hadn't seen.

Kriniuk said that he had known Ivanechko. He was a forest ranger from Alexandrovo who used to visit Moyshe Kriniuk's store. 'I saw him a few times and he was riding a bicycle with a rifle. Especially for the German times he was always with a rifle.'

Niemann asked if Kriniuk had known where Ivanechko was going when he'd seen him on his bike. 'No. I couldn't ask questions where he was going. We didn't want to come close to him.'

David objected and Prescott agreed the answer was inadmissible. It was struck out.

Kriniuk was asked to identify a number of photographs of people who'd lived in the village during the war, but the prosecution didn't ask whether he recognised anyone in court.

—

Investigator Reid walked into the Hilton hotel the next morning while Jack Kriniuk and his wife were having their breakfast. Rae saw him and came running up to him. Reid had a special affection for the spouses of his witnesses. He had to be rather detached with the witnesses, but with their husbands or wives he could afford to be more like family. He could gauge from them how the witnesses were coping.

Rae cared deeply for Jack. Reid remembered how she had answered the phone in New York after the first interview. 'He never slept last night,' she'd said, and Reid had started to doubt whether it was worth putting these people back through it all again. When Reid got to know the Kriniuks better, however, Rae had told him Jack very rarely slept restfully on any night. Now, Reid wondered what had been the effect of yesterday's evidence.

Rae seemed excited. 'The most marvellous thing's happened,' she said.

'What's that?'

'I never slept a wink last night.'

Reid believed her. He thought that Jack must have had awful nightmares and that Rae was being sarcastic when she'd used the word 'marvellous'.

'I'm really sorry about that Rae, I was hoping that that wouldn't happen.'

'He kept me awake *all* night. Snoring.'

———

Milton Turk was another of the Serniki boys who had made good after fleeing Europe. He was now a very wealthy builder living in Toronto, Canada. He'd grown up with Jack Kriniuk and his evidence was similar. Like Kriniuk, Turk was not asked if he recognised anyone sitting in court. He said he could remember that the Germans had first arrived in Serniki during the Jewish month of Av in 1941, because that was when they'd killed his father. The local Ukrainian police had carried rifles, he said, but only one of the local policemen had worn a uniform, a long shabby German army overcoat. Turk said he remembered Ivanechko but had never seen him injure anyone.

'Was there more than one person by the name of Ivanechko or just one?' prosecutor James asked.

'To the best of my knowledge there was one Ivanechko and there was one Janechko,' Turk answered carefully. Ivanechko, he said, was a forester from Alexandrovo, aged in his twenties. He couldn't recall him wearing a uniform, but he had carried a rifle. Janechko was a farmer aged in his forties who had lived between Vichevka and Brodnitsa. Turk had never seen this man carrying a gun.

———

Whether it was real or imagined, defence lawyers David and Powell felt enormous hostility from the Jewish witnesses. What, for instance, had been behind the episode where Nathan Dinerman had made a fool of David? Before the committal had resumed the defence had asked for an opportunity to speak with the Jewish witnesses in the presence of the prosecution. Only Jack Kriniuk and Milton Turk had agreed to meet them. These two men had seemed suspicious of Powell's questions and surprised when she'd not asked many. Perhaps they'd expected the defence lawyers to question the very fact the Holocaust had occurred, or claim that their families had never been killed. The witnesses were unaware that the defence team was only interested in those people who might be able to incriminate Polyukhovich, not in debating the Holocaust.

———

The next scheduled witness, Nathan Bobrov, was eagerly awaited. He was the first person the prosecution had promised would give evidence of actually seeing the accused commit an offence. On 13 March, however, David told the court that his client had suffered gastroenteritis and couldn't attend. The court remained adjourned until Thursday 19 March, when Polyukhovich was well enough to return.

The prosecution team were angered meanwhile by an article in Adelaide's afternoon paper the *News*. The tabloid claimed that war crimes investigations had cost the federal government thirty million dollars but that 'little expense has been outlaid for the comfort of overseas witnesses called to give evidence in the Polyukhovich committal'. The article said that elderly witnesses at the hearing had been distressed by 'uncomfortable and stifling' conditions outside the court, referring to the small room where the witnesses sat while they waited before giving their evidence.

In fact, none of the witnesses had complained about the waiting room and none would stand for any criticism of Reid. The SIU officers in Adelaide for the committal had organised day trips to keep the witnesses occupied, taken them to dinner and made sure they had medication they needed. Reid had even spent a night beside Pepe Cohen after she'd become ill. The witnesses and their spouses, in turn, treated Reid like he was family. Niemann declared that it was nonsense to suggest the cost of the investigation had reached $30 million. The SIU's total budget since its inception would not reach $16 million by the end of the financial year.

———

The committal had been progressing smoothly for the prosecution when fifty-nine-year-old Nathan Bobrov walked into the court to give his evidence. Bobrov a tall, handsome man who spoke Hebrew in a soft voice, was the sole witness to count seven, the killing of Alter Botvinik. His interpreter, a middle-aged woman, sat next to him. She was the first interpreter to appear in court.

Bobrov told prosecutor James that he'd been born in Serniki, but his family had owned a farm near Alexandrovo not far from a property where Ivanechko's family had lived. As a young boy he'd often accompanied his father to the farm. Sometimes he'd visited the Ivanechko property, where he'd known he could get a drink of water. In about May 1942, after the ghetto's establishment, he'd gone to live with a friendly Ukrainian farmer near Alexandrovo, but the nine-year-old would sometimes return to Serniki to visit his family. The last time he'd made this trip he'd heard strange noises coming from the village. Bobrov had asked a Ukrainian man what the sounds meant, and he'd been told the Jews were being killed. Later Bobrov had learnt that the noise was automatic gunfire, the sound of the ghetto being liquidated.

Bobrov told the court through his interpreter that it had been too dangerous to stay with the farmer in Alexandrovo. He'd left, but remained in the region. One or two days later he'd encountered Ivanechko, who was carrying a rifle and wearing a dark, high-collared jacket with pockets down the front and sides and shiny brass buttons. Ivanechko had told young Bobrov to find his father. Sometime later, still in the same area and from a distance of about forty metres, Bobrov had seen Ivanechko escorting two local Jewish men at gun point. They were Alter Botvinik and Ze'ev Erdman. Botvinik and Ivanechko had begun to fight, and Erdman had run off. Ivanechko had fired a shot and Botvinik had fallen to the ground dead. Bobrov had seen Ivanechko again within twenty-four hours, this time escorting about eight Jewish men through the countryside at gun point. Ivanechko had told him to join the group, but Bobrov had escaped behind some bushes. Not long after, he'd heard shots and screams.

Bobrov said that Reid had shown him a selection of photographs in September 1989 and again at a second interview in February 1990. He'd not been able to recognise anyone. Since arriving in Australia, however, he'd been shown a photograph of two men on bicycles and had recognised one of them as Ivanechko. This was one of the photographs seized by the SIU from Polyukhovich's home on the day of his arrest.

David started the defence cross-examination shortly before lunch. He would spend the next two sitting days grilling Bobrov over and over again about his earlier statement to the SIU. In this statement he'd stopped short of accusing Ivanechko of any crime.

Bobrov said that when Reid had interviewed him in September 1989, he'd known Ivanechko was responsible for Alter's death, but there had been a reason for his silence. 'Throughout the years I carried it as a heavy burden that perhaps if I had intervened, Alter would not have been killed,' he said. 'And in the second interview I said exactly what had happened.'

Bobrov said that in that part of the world, at that time, children were educated to be courageous and help others in trouble. For nearly fifty years he'd been too ashamed to tell anyone except his cousin what he'd witnessed and that he'd done nothing to save Alter.

'How old were you when you saw this happen?' David asked.

'Nine and three quarters,' Bobrov answered.

———

During the rest of the day David focused on a meeting between Bobrov and Pepe Cohen's sister Sonja in Israel in December 1989. This meeting had fallen between the first and second interviews with Reid. The Serniki survivors had kept in touch with each other and met each year for a memorial. So it wasn't unusual for Bobrov to see Sonja. Nor would it have been surprising if they'd discussed the war and Alter's death. Alter had been Sonja's boyfriend. But David wanted to know whether Bobrov had told Sonja he'd seen Alter being killed. The interpreter said that Bobrov denied having told Sonja this, but it was obvious that Bobrov and the interpreter weren't getting on very well. The SIU's Hebrew interpreter, Edytta Super, and Israeli consultant, Miri Drucker, sat in the public gallery frowning and shaking their heads as the evidence was interpreted. They were plainly upset about the presentation of Bobrov's story.

———

The next morning the woman interpreter's place had been taken by a short man with dark curly hair. He smiled a lot but seemed nervous sitting next to Bobrov.

Defence QC David returned to the topic of Bobrov's conversation with Sonja. 'You never spoke about Alter's death, is that right?'

'No.' Bobrov said, however, that Sonja had told him Alter was her friend.

'So you spoke about Alter to her?'

'I haven't spoken to her. She told me.'

'How did it come to be that she told you about Alter? What happened?'

'I don't know. They were talking about different things and she also mentioned Alter to us.'

'And you never said anything to her about the incident where you saw Alter killed?'

'No.'

David pressed the issue. 'Did you speak about the death of Alter?'

'No, I haven't spoken about the death of Alter. However, she said that what is past is past. We cannot return the incidents.'

Bobrov said that Sonja had told him Ivanechko was responsible for killing her family. David put it to Bobrov that in February 1990 he'd made a statement in which he'd said that he'd told Sonja he'd been present at Alter's death. Bobrov denied telling Sonja he was there. Again and again the trio – David, Bobrov and the translator – went over this issue. Either he had or hadn't told Sonja that he'd been there. Bobrov's credibility was in jeopardy.

Bobrov said that in 1989 he'd thought Ivanechko would never be tried but later 'saw that the matter was coming about'.

'Then you changed your story,' David challenged.

'I didn't change anything, I just said the whole truth,' Bobrov answered.

'You changed your story about seeing Ivanechko kill Alter, didn't you?'

'Yes.'

As the day progressed the relations between both the witness and the translator and the witness and the lawyer became more strained as variations emerged in Bobrov's evidence. The SIU's Hebrew interpreter and Israeli consultant were still shaking their heads.

David played the video from the 1990 interview many times. After one showing, David asked Bobrov if he still maintained that he'd never spoken to Sonja about being present at Alter's death. Bobrov replied that on the video he'd used the words 'I think that I had been present'. 'I didn't say to her that I had actually been there,' Bobrov said.

'Let me get this clear,' said David, 'Are you now saying that you said to Sonja that you thought you were present at the death of Alter?'

'Truth,' Bobrov answered.

'At that time you were speaking to Sonja, were you sure that you had seen someone killing Alter?'

'I was very sure.'

Asked why he'd told Sonja that he believed he'd been present at the death of Alter, the witness said he'd wanted to see her response.

If a jury had heard all of this, they would have been very confused and, since the prosecution must prove everything and the defence prove nothing, confusion invariably works for the defence.

———

Boris Teribilov told the court that he was fifteen when the Germans first came to Serniki. He'd avoided capture by pretending he was bed-ridden with typhus. Two days later he'd heard shooting. In September 1942 he and four other children had been shot at while trying to escape by swimming across the River Stubla. Local police had taken him back to Serniki. He said that when the Germans finally came to his home, his mother and brothers had hidden under the house, but they'd been discovered. Teribilov himself had escaped detection by hiding beneath the oven. He still remembered the sound of one of his brothers crying as they were led away.

Teribilov wasn't asked if he could identify anyone in court and wasn't shown a photo-board. But he could identify a photograph of the 'miller's daughter', Perl Fischman. She was Teribilov's aunt and the victim named in count three.

———

Nathan Bobrov senior looked sterner than the cousin with whom he shared a name. From the way he stated his occupation as 'motor mechanic' it appeared the sixty-two-year-old was not someone to trifle with. This man's mother, sister and two brothers had been killed in the ghetto's liquidation.

Prosecutor James asked the witness about topics that were becoming familiar to everyone: the layout of Serniki where Bobrov senior had grown up, and the people who had lived in the region. Within minutes, however, it was obvious that Bobrov was becoming annoyed with the translator, the small man with the curly hair who'd translated much of his cousin's evidence. Bobrov senior could speak Hebrew, Yiddish, and some Russian. Now, in quite good English, he accused the interpreter of not doing his job properly.

'You don't translate exactly what he is asking,' Bobrov said loudly.

'Is that right?' James asked the embarrassed interpreter, who was looking more and more uncomfortable.

'It's a matter of verbs. In English there are sixteen and in Hebrew there are only three. So that's the problem probably but I have tried honestly to translate the right words,' said the interpreter. Reporters looked at each other and shrugged.

The hearing moved on and Bobrov reverted to Hebrew. He explained that his family had worked on a farm near Alexandrovo that had shared a boundary with Ivanechko's property. He said that Ivanechko's family name was Polyukhovich, and the witness had often visited his neighbours who'd given him drink and food. He'd spoken sometimes with Ivanechko, who was then about twenty-four and working as a forester.

'Do you know whether at that time he carried a gun?' James asked.

'At that time, he did not have a gun,' Bobrov senior answered with a frown. He was watching both James and the interpreter closely.

'When you went to the house did you see any gun?'

'A gun?' Bobrov senior asked through the interpreter. 'Do you mean a pistol?'

'No, I said a gun,' James replied.

Bobrov now spoke angrily in English. 'I am asking you please to correct my testimony before, because there was a mistake, which the interpreter committed. Your question was about a pistol. A gun or a pistol?'

James tried the question again using the word 'firearm', but it was too late. At this point the transcript would say 'Witness addresses interpreter at length.' In fact, Bobrov was shouting at the little man in Hebrew.

James stepped in. 'I ask for a short adjournment. I think I can understand the tenor of what the witness is putting to the interpreter.'

Bobrov senior left the box in fury. A few minutes later magistrate

Prescott called the lawyers into his chambers. Half an hour later the court resumed.

The witness said that before the Germans arrived, Ivanechko had carried a shotgun but had behaved like a friend. The forester used to leave his bicycle at Bobrov's family property at least twice a week. After the occupation, Bobrov had stopped going to the Polyukhovich home. He'd seen Ivanechko carrying a rifle and wearing a black uniform with bright buttons.

In September 1989 Bobrov senior had picked out one of the photographs shown to him by Reid, and in court he quickly identified a series of pictures shown to him by James as including Ivanechko.

'When you came into court and were giving your evidence, did you see any person in court that you recognised?' James asked.

'Yes.'

'Who was it?'

Bobrov pointed across the room without looking at Polyukhovich. David objected on cue and was overruled. James asked Bobrov to name the person.

'Ivanechko.'

The next day Bobrov senior told the court that one night, about a month after the liquidation, he and his father had encountered Ivanechko in Alexandrovo. They'd walked towards him until they were about five metres apart. Bobrov said that Ivanechko had fired two shots into the air and run away.

'Was that the last time you saw him?' James asked.

'Yes.'

'As at October 1942 were you and your father in the partisans?'

'At that time we started to organise ourselves.'

Bobrov senior said that he had returned to Serniki a few months later; there had been no sign of his home. The village was overgrown with weeds.

———

Witness Zalman Kaz said that he used to play with Ivanechko as a child. Kaz, seventy, described himself as a Jewish coffee bar operator from Israel. He said that 'Ivanechko' was a nickname. He didn't know the man's real name. Kaz recalled that one day he and the girl who later became his wife had been 'doubling' on a bike. They'd collided with Ivanechko, who'd been riding from the other direction.

'And you received an injury to your right shoulder?' James asked.

'Yes, this one,' Kaz answered, pointing to his shoulder. 'He didn't do it purposefully,' he added quickly.

Kaz said that about the time the Germans invaded, three Ukrainian men had come to Serniki and told a meeting of people that they should 'kill the Jews, kill the Poles and kill the communists'.

———

'It appears there has been a break down in relations at the bar table,' prosecutor James told magistrate Prescott. The queen's counsel was referring to the transcript of Bobrov junior's evidence. The witness had read the transcript and rejected it. The defence lawyers weren't about to let him rewrite it. James suggested that they might hold a 'mini-trial', calling the witness and the interpreter to give evidence on what had actually been said by the witness.

'Surely that's not about to occur,' Prescott said, clearly pained.

For the defence, David said that it would be appalling if the witness was misrepresented, but that there were fundamental problems with the evidence. In some places Bobrov junior wanted the transcript to show something opposite to what the court had heard translated. The whole of the cross-examination had been based on interpreted words. For the prosecution, James argued that 'one can't say that's what the witness said unless the witness agrees'. Prescott wanted to know what the law was on this issue. David said he didn't have a clue.

The court was adjourned. Prosecutor Niemann returned nearly an hour later carrying an armful of books. There seemed to be very little law on the issue, although the prosecution found that reference to a similar situation had been reported in the *Sydney Morning Herald* in 1889. There was more discussion, but the problem hadn't been solved at the end of the day.

Next morning magistrate Prescott was pleasantly surprised when Niemann told him that the prosecution and defence had reached agreement on Bobrov's evidence.

'We have been very, very good,' David said.

Prescott didn't enquire into the nature of the agreement. All the Jewish witnesses had given their evidence and the magistrate was happy to let the committal move on to the next, most crucial stage – the Ukrainians.

———

The jet-lagged women were crying while the men tried hard not to show how nervous they were. The first group of Ukrainian witnesses had arrived. In a matter of days they'd travelled through time and space from Eastern European villages to late-twentieth-century Australia. At their motel in the seaside suburb of Glenelg, investigator Reid had found the women in panic. Their rooms were near a road filled with speeding cars and some menace which Reid couldn't fathom, but which apparently was going to abduct them. The only solution was to abandon the allocated rooms and shift them to the back of the motel.

Reid was grateful the committal was being held in Adelaide and not the larger eastern cities of Sydney or Melbourne. While most of the Jewish witnesses saw Adelaide as a slow-moving, polite, little city, to the Ukrainians it was chaos and paradise combined. They were struck by the abundance of food, clothes and cars; especially the cars. They were so modern, and there were so many of them, travelling so fast and being driven by women! The streets and houses were so clean. Their rooms were clean, too, and filled with gadgets like light switches and indoor toilets.

The SIU organised day trips to help the Ukrainians settle in and keep them occupied while they waited to be called to court. At first they would gather in one of their rooms and wait for Reid to drive up to the motel courtyard. Then they'd walk out in a huddle. Within a few days, however, they had become more confident and would wait for him outside. The Ukrainian officials travelling with the group were more independent than the villagers, who would stare while the officials went off to the beach without escort and return unharmed. This helped reassure the villagers, but they still always stayed together. If one went to the pool or the beach, they all did.

Reid became brave after a few days and decided that a reunion should be arranged between the Ukrainians and the Jewish witnesses. The idea had been discussed among the SIU ranks. The Jewish witnesses, particularly the North Americans, had often paid tribute to the Ukrainians and said that had it not been for them, many of the Jews wouldn't have survived. Prosecutors Niemann and James agreed to the reunion on the condition that everyone promise not to talk about the case. The North American witnesses had unfortunately left Adelaide, but the Israelis were eager to meet the villagers, and took it on themselves to host the evening in a city steak-house.

———

It would be either one of Reid's greatest achievements or worst disasters. He began the night by welcoming everyone and reminding them that they couldn't talk about the case. It appeared that this was well understood. Then an uncomfortable silence settled in. The Ukrainians, sitting along one side of the upstairs function room, showed all the wear and tear of village life; the Israelis sat on the other side looking smart, modern and affluent.

Just when Reid was certain the evening would be a disaster, one of the Ukrainians, Ivan Mikhailovich, got up and quietly walked across to Zamal Kaz. The pair began talking. Suddenly, they burst into tears and threw their arms around each other; they remembered that they had sat next to each other in school. Kaz and Mikhailovich were inseparable for the rest of the night, tightly holding each other's hand. Soon the room was alive with talk about the old days. Everyone remembered the Bobrovs' parents and Jack Kriniuk's father, the generous wholesaler who used to extend credit that wasn't always repaid.

———

The first Ukrainian gave his evidence on Thursday 26 March 1992, eight days after the group arrived. Sixty-six-year-old Fyodor Grigoryevich Polyukhovich had been left an invalid after serving in the Red Army during the great patriotic war. His nerves were bad, but his evidence was translated smoothly by the Ukrainian interpreter, a tall, well-built, middle-aged man who carried himself with pride. The interpreter's confidence showed in the way he imitated the tones used by the witness and, after the trauma of the Hebrew translations, was welcomed by the court. At least this interpreter sounded the same as the witnesses.

Fyodor claimed to have seen the events alleged in count three: the killing of 'the miller's daughter' and two children at the pit. During the morning session he managed only to recount how he'd lived his life in his father's home on the outskirts of Serniki. The town, he explained, was full of people named 'Polyukhovich', so it was necessary to use 'street names'. Fyodor had known one man named Ivan Timofeyevich Polyukhovich, whose street name was Ivanechko. He'd known Ivanechko since 1940, when Fyodor's sister had moved to the Alexandrovo area. He also remembered a Jewish woman named Tsalykha.

———

Fyodor was standing outside the court looking worried. Magistrate Prescott had said that the court would reconvene after lunch at 2.15. It was now 2.15, and Fyodor was insisting that they should go in. Reid explained that the magistrate was busy considering some corrections to the transcript and that they'd have to wait, but Fyodor wouldn't listen. 'The judge told me to be back at 2.15 and I'm here at 2.15 and I should go and tell him that it's 2.15,' he said through his interpreter. 'Otherwise he might send me to gaol.'

Reid said that he would go in and tell the magistrate. This wasn't any good because Fyodor knew that he himself had to do it. Eventually Reid convinced Fyodor that he was in no peril.

———

Fyodor told the court that about five days before the Jews were killed, a pit had been dug no more than five hundred metres from his home. On the morning of the massacre, he'd seen a column of Jews being led from Serniki toward the grave. The line of men, women and children had stretched perhaps three or four hundred metres and took half an hour – maybe an hour – to pass. Germans alternated with local police along the column's length. They were carrying guns.

'Were you able to recognise any of the police that were guarding the Jews in the column?' Greg James asked for the prosecution.

'I have been too far away. I was myself frightened,' replied Fyodor through the interpreter.

There was a problem here. In his opening, James had promised that Fyodor would place Ivanechko in the column escorting the Jews out of Serniki. Now he was saying that he was too far away to recognise any of the police.

The prosecutor moved on. The witness said he'd later heard the sounds of automatic gunfire. It lasted from about eight in the morning until two or three in the afternoon. That afternoon Fyodor had been tending his father's cows in a field when a German and a policeman had told him to help fill in the grave. They'd threatened to burn down his home if he refused. Fyodor had seen at the pit between fifty and a hundred men burying Jewish bodies, which were covered already with a layer of sand. As Fyodor worked alongside them, he'd seen a cart pull up carrying three men, a woman and two children.

'That is Polivnyk, Martochyn, Ivanechko,' Fyodor said. 'Upon the cart there's a Jewess and two youngsters, two children. And they take off the cart and lead them into the pit, but we all who were burying, we hid. And they led into the pit, that Jewess with the young, and they shot them. Well, we heard the shots.'

'Polivnyk, Martochyn and Ivanechko – when they arrived at the pit with the Jewess – did all three of them have guns?' James asked.

'They did have.'

Fyodor said that he recognised the Jewess as the local miller's daughter. Later in the afternoon, he said that the woman and the children had been escorted into the pit down an incline.

James wanted to know if each of the three men had been policemen.

'The policemen was Polivnyk, Martochyn but I do not know whether Ivanechko was a policeman or not. I do not know,' Fyodor said.

James showed Fyodor the photo-board Reid had used in December 1989 when Fyodor had identified one of the photos as Ivanechko. The prosecutor asked if Fyodor recognised Ivanechko in court today.

'He sitteth there,' was the translated answer. Fyodor was pointing to Polyukhovich opposite. Prescott overruled David's objection.

The next day James continued with Fyodor for a while, and then asked permission to interpose another witness and return to Fyodor later. After the recent trouble with translations, the prosecution wanted a definitive translation of Fyodor's evidence before he was cross-examined.

———

Stepan Sidorovich Polyukhovich had been a month away from his twentieth birthday when he'd been ordered to throw sand on the Jewish bodies lying in the grave. At sixty-nine, sitting in the Adelaide Magistrates Court, holding one hand with the other, he seemed a small, quiet, thoughtful man. When he'd arrived at the grave under the orders of a Ukrainian policeman, the Jews were still being killed. He said that he remembered seeing Martochyn, Polivnyk, Doroctuiks, Yulov and Ivanechko there. Then

Below: This photograph was attached to an International Refugee Organisation Resettlement Medical Examination form bearing the name Jan Poluchowicz. The SIU placed this photo among eleven others chosen randomly from the post-war IRO selection documents kept at the Australian Archives. The photos were then shown to witnesses who were asked if they could identify any person. This identification method was later ruled inadmissible.

DEUTSCHE FORSTVERWALTUNG UKRAINE
FORSTDIREKTION LUCK — AUSSENSTELLE PINSK
NIEMIECKI   ГЕРМАНСКОЕ
Zarząd Lasów Ukraina | Лесное Управление Украина
Dyrekcja Łuck - Oddz. Pińsk | Дирекция Луцк - Отд. в Пинске

DIENSTAUSWEIS
LEGITYMACJA - УДОСТОВЕРЕНИЕ

Persoenliche Unterschrift — Własnoręczny podpis
Собственноручная подпись

Above: This document was found in Ivan Polyukhovich's home by investigators on 25 January 1990, the day he was arrested. It was issued to a Johann Polyuchowitsch by the Forestry Department in Pinsk and was dated 4 March 1943.

Right: These work books were found in Ivan Polyukhovich's home on the day he was arrested. They carried the names Johann Polichowicz and Marie Polichowitsch.

Above: Luba Botvinik nee Kaz.

Below: Luba's daughter, Tzila Botvinik

Above: The Kaz family. *Bottom row, left to right:* Leah known as Tsalykha, Tsalykha's daughter, Sonja. *Top row, left to right:* Tsalykha's children Pepe, Shana, and Luba.

Ivan Polyukhovich was alleged to have murdered Tsalykha, Luba and Tzila in September 1942. The photographs on this page were carried by Pepe Kaz as she escaped from Serniki shortly before the ghetto was liquidated and were tendered by the prosecution in the case against Polyukhovich.

Above: An aerial view of the open grave not far from Serniki, taken during the exhumation in mid-1990.

Above: A scene from the base of the exhumed grave outside Serniki.

Below: Australian members of the forensic team which exhumed the grave outside Serniki in mid-1990. *From the left,* Dr Godfrey Oettle, head of the forensic medicine division at Glebe in New South Wales, Burt Bailey an Australian authority on anatomy, and Richard Wright, professor of anthropology at the University of Sydney.

Below: SIU investigator and director, Graham Blewitt

Above: SIU investigator, Bob Reid

Below: Deputy Director of Public Prosecutions in Adelaide, Grant Niemann

Above: Senior war crimes prosecutor, Greg James QC

Below: Ivan Polyukhovich's senior defence lawyer, Michael David QC

Below: Polyukhovich's solicitor, David Stokes

Above: Polyukhovich's junior defence lawyer, Lindy Powell

Above: Magistrate Kelvyn Prescott

Below: Polyukhovich's trial judge, Justice Brian Cox

Below: Ivan Polyukhovich, taken during 1990. *Advertiser*

Above: Defence lawyer David Stokes (left) accompanies Ivan Polyukhovich away from the Adelaide Magistrates Court after he received bail on 26 January 1990. *Advertiser*

Right: Ivan Polyukhovich leaving the Adelaide Magistrates Court on 5 June 1992, the last day of his committal hearing. *Advertiser*

Above: Prosecutor Greg James QC (left) escorts Ukrainian witness Dmitry Kostyukhovich to the
Adelaide Magistrates Court on 24 April 1992. *Advertiser*

Above: Fyodor Grigoryevich Polyukhovich *Advertiser*

Left: Sergei Potapovich Polyukhovich *Advertiser*

Above: Ivan Polyukhovich and his wife Maria outside the Supreme Court, 18 May 1993, the day the jury returned unanimous verdicts of not guilty. *Advertiser*

Above: Heinrich Wagner, charged with having murdered nineteen children and a railway construction worker and with being involved in the murder of 104 people in Ukraine between 1942 and 1943. The DPP eventually dropped the case, citing Wagner's poor health as the reason. *Advertiser*

Left: Mikolay Berezowsky, charged with being involved in the murder of 102 Jewish people in Ukraine in 1942. A magistrate later dismissed the prosecution. *Advertiser*

he quickly corrected himself. He hadn't seen Ivanechko at the pit. He said that three carts had been used to carry the bodies that day from Serniki to the grave.

Stepan recalled that the Germans had ordered a woman who lived only a short distance from the grave to fetch them some milk. 'Soon after she brought the milk, the German drank the milk and she says to him, "Mister, how does it sit on your soul that there are so many bodies lying, and you drink milk?" And he went over, cleaned the sand, and wrote the number "575" upon the sand with a finger.'

Stepan said that he knew Ivan Timofeyevich who had worked in the forest, carried a gun and was known as Ivanechko. Stepan identified him from a series of photographs. Then James asked if Stepan knew anyone in the court from those Serniki days. Stepan said he recognised Ivan Timofeyevich and his wife and pointed at the couple sitting opposite. He said that he'd seen Ivanechko many times walking with armed police through Serniki. A few months after the liquidation he'd seen Ivanechko arrive in Serniki with a large detachment of men. Soon afterward, the remaining Jewish homes had been burned. About this time Ivanechko had worn a 'military' uniform and carried a gun. But Stepan had never seen Ivanechko kill anyone.

'You did not see Ivanechko hurt anyone?' James asked.

'I did not see such.'

'Was there any other person named Ivanechko or Yanechko or anything like Ivanechko who you knew in the area?'

'No, there was not.'

———

During the next two days a quick succession of witnesses gave their accounts of the village during the occupation. The defence had settled by now on a strategy of cross-examining each witness very tightly. Whereas committal hearings are sometimes treated as 'fishing expeditions' by defence lawyers, David and Powell had decided to keep out any extraneous testimony. They were treating the committal as if it were a jury trial, with the objective of asking magistrate Prescott to find that there was no case to answer. They believed that it was too dangerous to allow the witnesses to 'wander'. It was hard work getting evidence out of these people. Any loose questioning might backfire and help the prosecution.

————

Among those who gave evidence at this time was sixty-one-year-old Vera Grigoryevna Kheskovets. In answer to questions from Grant Niemann she recalled how as a child she had grown up with her brother Fyodor Polyukhovich and her sister Anna in their family home just outside Serniki. She recalled how during one summer a large pit was dug not far from where they lived and how later she'd grazed her sheep there and played among the piles of sand. Kheskovets said that the open pit may have stood there for five days but she remembered that one morning, while she was grazing her sheep, she'd seen a column of people coming towards her. Asked whether anyone was guarding the column, Kheskovets said she remembered a small dark vehicle was driven in front of the group but she could not see the sides of the column. She said she had been frightened, so she had chased her sheep away and stayed away from the area for the rest of the day.

'What happened at that time, towards the evening?' Niemann asked.

'I stood there with the sheep and cried up until towards evening.'

Kheskovets said her father found her and told her: 'All have been killed, there is no one remaining, but do not cry.'

————

The next witness to give evidence was sixty-six-year-old Ivan Mikhailo-vich Kostyukhovich from Serniki. He recalled that Yankel Kaz, or 'crooked Kaz', the man with the wooden leg, had lived only two hundred metres from his home. One of Ivanechko's sisters had also lived nearby, and Mikhailovich remembered seeing Ivanechko visiting her. After the Germans had taken over, he'd seen Ivanechko wearing a police uniform. Prosecutor Niemann asked Ivan Mikhailovich to describe the uniforms worn by police in as much detail as possible. Then he asked Mikhailovich again if he'd seen Ivanechko wearing such an outfit. In an apparent back flip Mikhailovich replied, 'No.' He also said that he'd never seen Ivanechko carrying a gun.

Only one of the seven people who gave evidence during the Monday and Tuesday could identify the accused and his wife in court. Ivan Ivanovich Bogatko said that 'Ivanechko, Polyukhovich Timofeyevich' was sitting opposite him and that next to Ivanechko was Maria, Ivanechko's second wife. Ivan Bogatko said that Ivanechko had lived about half a kilometre from his home near Alexandrovo. He'd seen him once a week, maybe more, for several years. The witness recalled how, in the summer of 1942, the village elder had told him to take a spade and go to a spot about four hundred metres from his home. There Ivan Bogatko had found the local Jewess Tsalykha, her daughter and grand-daughter. They were dead, covered in blood. Ivan gave no evidence about who'd been responsible for the killings, but said that he'd dug the grave into which their bodies had been placed.

When Bogatko's evidence was finished defence lawyer David stood and said that the next two witnesses for the prosecution were relevant to the question of the German policy of exterminating the Jewish race. The queen's counsel had no questions to ask them, but whether or not their evidence was admissible would have to be sorted out later.

Ignas Steinkalk, a grey-haired man from Victoria, walked in and took the oath. He identified a document shown to him as his statement. He stared viciously at Polyukhovich as he walked out. He didn't say a word, but the intensity of his emotion was plain as he glared over his shoulder at the defendant. Investigator Reid followed behind Steinkalk and touched his shoulder as if to guide him out of the court. Perhaps it wasn't necessary. The moment passed and Steinkalk was out of the court, but he'd left behind him an impression of deep hatred.

Jacob Raykin from New South Wales was brought in to identify a document as his statement.

Both these men looked as if they were aged in their seventies.

The rest of the day was taken up with Eduard Sharayev, the head of the Soviet exhumation team. None of the media people were interested in him. They waited impatiently for the next adjournment, when they could ask to see the mysterious statements of Steinkalk and Raykin.

It turned out that Steinkalk was born in Warsaw, Poland, and had escaped to Lithuania when the Germans had invaded. The Third Reich had soon overrun Lithuania as well, however, and Steinkalk had been put in a Jewish ghetto in Vilno. In 1942, the ghetto's Jewish commander had called for volunteers to do a 'good deed for the Jewish people'. Steinkalk and about thirty other men had been driven about fifteen kilometres from the ghetto to a place where four or five large pits had been dug. They'd been filled with the naked bodies of men, women and children.

'Around the top edge of the pits there were machine guns,' Steinkalk's statement read. 'I also saw pieces of skull, skin and hair all around the pits. There were also other bodies outside the pits. One of the jobs we had to do was take the bodies and put them in the pits.'

Steinkalk and the others had been ordered to load trucks with nearby piles of clothing. While he'd been doing this, he'd found a girl of about twelve, a boy about ten, and an elderly man. All of them were wounded and hiding. The conscripted workers had hidden these people under the clothing and taken them back to the ghetto.

Raykin's statement was even more horrific. He had also been trapped in one of the Lithuanian ghettos. At about Easter 1942, he and the other Jews had been marched several kilometres to large pits, where they'd been forced to undress. Raykin remembered standing in line around the edge of one of the pits. 'When I stood at the edge of the pit I saw the naked bodies of men, women and children in the bottom . . . I also saw several machine guns pointing at us from the small trees around us . . . I fainted and fell into the pit on top of the other bodies. I eventually regained consciousness. I felt blood over me and there were bodies on top of me and around me.

'I couldn't get out. I struggled there a long time. One of my feet was tangled amongst the bodies . . . When I got out it was raining. The pit I climbed from was half full of bodies and there was a white powder spread over the bodies . . . I saw a pile of clothing and I searched through it looking for my own clothes. I couldn't find them so I took other clothing.'

The journalists left the court in a sombre mood as the orderly put the statements back in their plastic covers.

———

The only person who claimed to have seen the Jewess Tsalykha, Pepe Cohen's mother, die was Ekaterina Bogatko, Ivan Bogatko's sister.

She said that it had been during the summer of 1942. Ekaterina had been ten at the time. She had been standing in a field of buckwheat, minding her three-year-old niece, while her older sister had been harvesting the cereal. She said that Ivanechko had appeared from the nearby forest with an automatic weapon slung over his shoulder. He was pointing the gun at two women, one of whom was carrying a baby girl. The group had walked a distance until they were only about fifty metres away from Ekaterina, then the women had been made to strip to their underwear. Ivanechko had fired a burst of shots into their backs. The women and baby had fallen to the ground and the baby had rolled there, crying and waving its hands. After a while Ivanechko had walked off towards his home.

Not too long after this a woman, either Ivanechko's sister or mother, had arrived, picked up the dead women's clothing and walked away in the same direction as Ivanechko. Ekaterina and her sister had walked over to the blood-soaked bodies and seen that all three were dead. Her sister had identified the corpses, saying, 'These are of Tsalykha.'

The next time Ekaterina had seen Ivanechko was during March 1943. Ivanechko and another man had escorted her mother, father, herself and two other men to a cottage near Svaritsevichi, not far from Alexandrovo.

Ivanechko had ridden a white horse. As they'd passed a column of Germans, he'd shouted the words 'partisans, partisans'. He'd beaten her father along the way. Ekaterina said she'd seen her father and two other men placed in the cottage along with a family of five people. The building had then been set on fire.

The woman began crying. Prosecutor Niemann, who'd drawn this evidence from her, asked for an adjournment.

She regained her composure five minutes later and went on to explain that she had seen the cottage being torched while hiding with her mother in some bushes. 'Upon that day, they burnt everything in the world,' she told Niemann. Ekaterina and her family had lived outdoors until the end of the war.

Towards the end of his questioning, Niemann took Ekaterina through the identification process. In 1989 she had picked out Ivanechko from a photo-board. When Niemann asked whether she saw anyone in the court whom she recognised, she pointed to Polyukhovich and said that he was Ivan Timofeyevich, the man she had earlier referred to as Ivanechko.

During cross-examination, David gestured at Polyukhovich and asked if the witness was positive that Polyukhovich had killed Tsalykha.

'Yes, he is remembered unto me from my childhood,' answered Ekaterina through the interpreter.

'You last saw this man when you were ten years old?'

'Yes, up until the time as I die, I will know him and I will know him in the earth.'

Ekaterina told the defence lawyer that she'd seen the woman pick up the clothing after Tsalykha had been killed, but it had been her older sister who'd recognised this woman. Yes, she'd known Ivanechko's mother and sister but, at the time, she'd been too small and frightened to recognise who it was. Yes, Ekaterina's sister had also named Ivanechko, but Ekaterina herself had recognised him. These sorts of admissions opened a clear avenue of attack for the defence. Her testimony appeared to be a mixture of what she'd seen or known and hearsay.

After lunch, David questioned her about Ivanechko's clothes. Ekaterina said that he'd been wearing a blue or green uniform similar to what the police had worn. In December 1989, however, she'd told investigator Reid that she couldn't remember what Ivanechko was wearing when he killed Tsalykha. Why the change? Ekaterina said that she still couldn't remember what the uniform had looked like. She only remembered the colour. Did the witness perceive a difference between the questions David was asking and the question Reid had asked her three years earlier?

'What clothing was he wearing in March 1943?' David asked.

'In uniform . . . that same, bluish with green, neither blue nor green.'

'Was it black?'

'No, not black.'

But Ekaterina had told Reid in 1989 that Ivanechko had worn black during the 1943 murders. The witness was clearly distressed. She wiped away tears while David played the SIU interview to her on the television screens. She said that she'd meant Ivanechko's clothes were dark, not black. David played another part of the video. It showed Ekaterina telling Reid through an interpreter that she'd not seen the men herded into the cottage.

'I did not consider it necessary that I had to say that,' Ekaterina explained.

'Irrespective of the reason, did you say to Mr Reid that you did not see the men herded into the house?'

'I simply did not consider it necessary . . . Now I am standing by the Bible to tell the truth, that which I saw.'

David hadn't finished yet. In May 1987 the witness had told the Soviet procurator Melnishan that both Ivanechko's sister and mother had picked up Tsalykha's clothing. She'd repeated this to the procurator three months later. She had also told journalist Mark Aarons in January 1987 that both women had picked up the clothes. Why was she now saying that only one of the women had gone to the scene?

Next morning Ekaterina returned to the witness box for a few minutes.

'Did you know the woman Tsalykha?' David asked her.

'I did not know. The sister knew. I was too little to know them.'

'Did you know it was Tsalykha who was killed from what your sister said?'

'I knew.'

'Because of what your sister said?'

'Yes. The sister approached me. She said that Tsalykha was killed with the daughter and the grand-daughter.'

'Had you seen Tsalykha before that afternoon on any occasion?'

'Did not see.'

———

The next witness was 'Big Ivan'. That was the name Reid and the others at the SIU had given him, and it had been adopted by everyone, just as everyone was calling the accused 'Polly' instead of Polyukhovich.

Big Ivan's real name was the same as the accused's, Ivan Timofeyevich Polyukhovich. There was also a link between the two men through marriage. For nearly ten years Big Ivan had lived with his grandfather, uncle and aunt. His aunt was none other than Maria Andreyevna, the defendant's present wife. Soon after war had broken out between Germany and Poland, Big Ivan's uncle had been captured by the Germans and put in a prisoner-of-war camp. About this time the accused Polyukhovich had left his first wife, Maria Stepanovna, and begun visiting Maria Andreyevna. Big Ivan claimed that in 1943 his aunt and her two daughters had moved to Serniki with Polyukhovich. Eventually she'd left Ukraine with him and after the war she and her children had migrated with him to Adelaide.

Big Ivan's smooth, ruddy face and shock of black hair made him look much younger than his sixty-three years. A reporter thought that he saw Polyukhovich nod at Big Ivan as he took his place in the witness box. Big Ivan said that he knew the person Ivanechko well. As a child he'd passed

Ivanechko's house on the way to school and, after his uncle had become a prisoner of war, Ivanechko had frequently visited his aunt Maria. By the time Ivanechko and Maria had shifted to Serniki, Ivanechko had been carrying an automatic gun. Big Ivan said he remembered an occasion around September 1942, however, when he'd seen Ivanechko armed simply with a rifle.

The witness and another youth had been grazing cattle not far from Alexandrovo. Across the River Stubla, from the direction of the forest, Big Ivan had seen Ivanechko escorting a girl of about fifteen, a man aged about twenty and another man about thirty. The group had walked to near the river's edge and then the three Jews had stood in a line. The girl had been closest to Ivanechko, who'd walked back three or four metres and fired his rifle, hitting her between the shoulders. She and the first man had fallen to the ground, but the man furthest from Ivanechko had remained standing. Big Ivan said that Ivanechko had then struck this man repeatedly with the butt of his gun until his head had been 'completely hammered'.

Big Ivan alleged that several months later, in 1943, he'd seen Ivanechko and three other men set fire to Big Ivan's grandfather's house. That night there'd been many fires in Alexandrovo.

When asked if he recognised anyone in court, Big Ivan had no trouble identifying the accused and Maria sitting opposite.

Michael David began his cross-examination early on Monday 6 April 1992. The queen's counsel concentrated on only a few issues, asking the same questions again and again. He began with the cows that Ivan had been tending at the time of the killings. Who owned them? On whose land were they grazing? Who did they belong to? They were your grandfather's cows, were they? Where were you? Whose cows were they? What were they doing on someone else's land?

'What sort of question? The cows were not dancing. They were eating.' Big Ivan clearly wondered what sort of a fool would ask such nonsense.

'How did they get there?' David asked.

'With their feet.'

Big Ivan said that he remembered the murders clearly, because he'd been only fourteen at the time and it was the first time he'd seen a person killed. Despite the defence lawyer's efforts, the witness was remarkably consistent.

David started asking Big Ivan precisely where he'd seen the bullet enter. In the SIU interview he'd said that the woman had been shot in the back of the head. In court, he'd said that it was just below the head, between the shoulder blades.

Big Ivan was not impressed. He obviously couldn't see much point in being so concerned about the exact point of entry. Through his inter-preter he answered David, 'How many times ought I say it? I said it was hit in the back; two fell and the third remained ... Fifty years have passed. I am not a forensic doctor to register the bodies, to look at the wounds. We looked in fear and instantly ran away.'

After lunch David returned to the topic. He got the same answer: It was a long time ago, I was frightened, but I saw the wound just below the head.

David moved to the topic of the clothes Ivanechko had been wearing at the time. What had been the colour of his cap?

Ivan was finding this extraordinary. 'Who can remember after fifty years what colour it was?' he shouted. 'Whether it was black, green or blue?'

David later tried to explore why, if Big Ivan had seen Ivanechko kill three people, he hadn't said something to Maria. If Big Ivan's allegations were true, then Maria, his aunt, was being courted by a murderer?

Big Ivan said that he was too young to complain to Maria, but believed his grandfather would have been upset that she was seeing Ivanechko. 'We were frightened then to say anything against him. If you say so then he would kill straight away.'

'Did you get on well with Maria at this time?' David asked.

'In good,' Big Ivan replied.

'Did you used to say to her, "You are seeing a murderer?" '

'I did not say anything.'

'When you were alone with Maria did you say anything about that?'

'No.'

'You would see her daily.'

'Naturally.'

'Did you ever talk to her about the fact that she was seeing a murderer?'

Grant Niemann objected. The defence, he said, was badgering the witness by continually asking the same questions. The witness wasn't avoiding the issue. It seemed that Michael David just wasn't happy with the answer.

'Can I conduct my cross-examination in the manner I wish?' David asked firmly. 'The answer is not clear.'

'What's not clear?' Niemann asked.

'We don't know whether he's spoken to Maria in private,' David retorted.

Magistrate Prescott allowed David to continue, but it made no difference. Big Ivan stuck to his story: he hadn't spoken to Maria.

All that remained was for David to work on the 1943 burning of the grandfather's house. Big Ivan had told Reid in the 1989 SIU interview that he'd seen a shed burnt. In court he was claiming he'd seen the house burnt. Big Ivan answered this by saying that he believed Ivanechko was responsible for the shed fire but, no, he hadn't seen him do that.

'I suggest that you didn't see him kill anybody in the field either,' David said, coming full circle.

'I saw,' Big Ivan answered.

'Same as you saw him burn the shed. You didn't see that at all, did you?'

'I am here on the spot, and here you know better than I do, or what?' the witness retorted.

Big Ivan's evidence spilled over to the next day, when he recounted how his two cousins – Polyukhovich's step-daughters Luba and Anna – had visited Rovno in the mid-1980s. Big Ivan said that he'd met the women and had wanted to tell them Polyukhovich was a murderer, but couldn't. The pair had not wanted to listen. They had given him a photograph of their step-father and sometime later a local KGB officer had seen this. Big Ivan couldn't remember whether or not the officer had taken the photograph away.

Big Ivan left the court as the strongest witness the prosecution had produced so far.

———

Four weeks had now passed since the resumption of the committal on 9 March, and about half the Ukrainian witnesses had given their evidence. The defence team was anxiously waiting for Dmitry Kostyukhovich to appear, but there was no sign of him. Although he'd been a late addition, Kostyukhovich was clearly a pillar in the prosecution case. He must be in the batch of witnesses expected to arrive from Ukraine in the next few days.

Defence lawyer David braced himself for another tiring session. Big Ivan had been replaced in the witness box by Fyodor Polyukhovich. It had been nearly two weeks since Fyodor had given his evidence-in-chief, in which he'd described the deaths of the miller's daughter and the two children at the grave site. Now it was the defence's turn to question Fyodor.

The cross-examination began slowly. Fyodor said he wasn't sure whether the children with the miller's daughter had been girls or boys. The youngest had been two or three years old; the older child had been six or seven. They'd been wearing pants. Fyodor said he'd known Ivanechko from 1940 onwards. Ivanechko's first wife had been a neighbour and he'd seen part of their wedding.

Marking points in time seemed to be a constant problem with the Ukrainians. Fyodor was no exception.

'So you had seen him before that day that you say you saw him at the pit?' David asked.

'No, I did not see.'

'But you've told us you saw him at his wedding?'

'That was in 1940 as he was getting married.'

'I'm not talking about on that day,' David explained. 'Have you ever spoken to him?'

'No, I met him rarely. In passing several times I saw.'

'Are you sure that it was Ivanechko who was at the pit on that occasion with the two policeman?'

'Naturally I'm sure.'

David pointed out to Fyodor that in 1989 he'd told Reid that the cart carrying the miller's daughter and the children was manned by Ivanechko, Polivnyk and another policeman who hadn't been a local. In court Fyodor had named the third officer as being Martochyn, a policeman from Serniki. Fyodor's response to this apparent inconsistency was to say that it had happened a long time ago. 'I thought over that it is Martochyn.'

'Did someone tell you Martochyn was there?' David asked.

'I saw.'

'Did someone tell you Ivanechko was there?'

'I saw with my own eyes myself.'

After lunch David put it to Fyodor that he'd given a statement in 1989 saying that he'd seen Ivanechko walking with the column of Jews leaving Serniki. Fyodor said that perhaps Ivanechko was on the other side of the column, but he hadn't seen him. The witness didn't seem to understand that the lawyer was not interested in what he had or had not seen in 1942. The lawyer was interested in what he'd said to an investigator three years ago. David played the video of the interview with Reid five times, but it didn't make any difference. Fyodor either couldn't or wouldn't understand the distinction, that David was asking him about the version of events he'd given in 1989 and not what had taken place in 1942.

They'd been going for only twenty minutes but David asked for an adjournment. Ten minutes later they tried again, but the stalemate remained. David tried another part of the interview, where Fyodor could be heard talking to Reid through an interpreter about the clothes Ivanechko had worn on the day of the round-up.

'Did you tell Mr Reid that Ivanechko was wearing civilian clothes?' David asked patiently.

'I did not say anything like it because I did not see Ivanechko then when they were being led.'

'Rewind the video,' David demanded.

It was played again.

'What did you say just then?'

'I was being asked what generally he wears, not when they were leading the Jews,' Fyodor answered.

Referring to the video, David asked, 'When you said there "civilian clothes" are you talking about some other occasion?'

'Different time,' Fyodor agreed.

'Why were you talking about a different time?'

'You are asking me how he was attired; what clothes did he wear.'

The video was played again. This time Fyodor shouted his answer. 'I'm sixty-seven-years-old. There's no need to twist my brain. The same and the same thing being said. I'm some sort of man as I'm telling the truth, convinced that that is the truth. We could badger the person for years but for fifty years – '

'Stop,' David demanded loudly. He turned and leaned over the bar table to magistrate Prescott.

'Could I ask for an adjournment?'

But Fyodor hadn't stopped. He continued yelling as Reid led him through the gallery, and his untranslated shouts could be heard as they walked out the door into the street. Fyodor was explaining to Reid that, back in Ukraine, they would have shot Polyukhovich by now.

When the court resumed ten minutes later Prescott took over the cross-examination. Slowly, carefully, the magistrate told Fyodor that the video would be played, and that he'd then be asked to repeat word-for-word what he'd said on the television.

The video was played more than twenty times, rewound and played again, in smaller and smaller portions, until they contained grabs of only two or three words. At one point Reid left the court. The reporters wondered if he had an errand to run or just needed a smoke.

They were still going after four, trying to work out whether Fyodor had seen the column through a window of his house or a crack in his barn wall. Prescott asked if the witness was getting tired.

'Naturally . . . I don't know how many times the same thing is being said and said.' Fyodor sounded exhausted.

'Just calm down for a moment. Now, would you like to have a rest?' Prescott asked.

'Let us continue and finish with me because I'm also human. There is no need to hold me here for months.'

———

'It's just ridiculous,' Big Ivan announced to the rest of the group sitting in the coffee shop. 'I don't mind if someone asks me a question once, even twice, and if he's really stupid maybe three times. But when he asks the same question twenty times, it's ridiculous.'

The other Ukrainians sitting with Big Ivan and investigator Reid nodded in agreement. Reid, as always, had a translator with him.

'It's like this,' Big Ivan said, directing everyone's attention to a circular plate that moments before had held his sandwich. He began rotating the plate in his large hands. 'It's the same, all the time, isn't it?'

Reid couldn't help but think that Big Ivan had made a point. No matter how many times the plate was turned it was still a round plate.

———

The Ukrainians didn't ever remain upset for long. Even Fyodor seemed to have forgotten his outbursts within a day a two. Perhaps they had a very short attention span; perhaps, after fifty years of punishment, they had learned to take each day at a time. Reid was pleased that they had all so far kept their promise not to shout any abuse at Polyukhovich in court. He thought they'd all behaved themselves remarkably well.

None of them really understood the Australian court process or why the federal government hadn't sent Polyukhovich back to Ukraine for trial. Certainly none of them could fathom why Polyukhovich was on bail, allowed to go home each night to what they perceived as luxury. This would have been unheard of under a Soviet regime. They were struck by how fortunate Polyukhovich was to have spent the past forty years in Australia.

Apart from trying to fathom the curiosities of the Australian legal system, several of the witnesses were also concerned about the weather back in Ukraine. They should be home sowing their crops.

———

By the time the proceedings reached count ten, the defence and prosecution had become efficient at homing in on the important issues. The progress had actually been quite swift for a case involving so many witnesses and so many allegations. The whole of the committal transcript would end up being a little over 1600 pages. Only the need to take a rest day once a week to allow Polyukhovich to recuperate, and the need for every word to be translated, were stretching the proceedings.

When prosecutor James had given his opening six months earlier, he'd promised that five witnesses would testify about the events of count ten – the tragic meeting of the Delidon and Turuk families in the forest during 1943 during which six people had been killed. Three of the witnesses would say that Ivanechko was responsible for opening fire on the families. One of these witnesses, however, Vladimir Delidon, had failed to make it to Adelaide. When the second crucial witness, Elena Sologuk, gave her evidence, she admitted that she'd not seen any policemen on the day of the shooting. Her mother had told her that policemen were responsible. Elena also testified that one of the victims named in the charge, Nadia Turuk, hadn't died on that day. She'd died later.

This left just one witness, Ivan Turuk, to say who was responsible for the killings. Turuk told the court that his village, Brodnitsa, not far from

Serniki, had been burned to the ground in 1943. His and several other families had set up camps in the nearby swamp not far from the forest. He remembered that, early on the Sunday morning after Easter 1943, his mother had just lit a fire to cook breakfast when they had heard yelling. His father had kicked the fire out. Ivan said that he and his family had run from the camp-site and collided with another group, comprising of Kondrat Delidon, who was a neighbour from Brodnitsa, and his two sons Alexei and Vladimir. They were being escorted by two armed men.

'Had you seen either of these two armed leaders before?' James asked.

'We did not see. If we did see we would have run away.'

Magistrate Prescott interrupted. 'There is a matter I want to raise with counsel. Would the witness stand down please.'

Prescott waited for Turuk to leave. 'I'm not quite sure where we are going,' he said.

During his opening James had said that Turuk had known Ivanechko and could describe him as a policeman, of medium height, thin, with dark hair, stationed in Serniki. If Ivanechko was the person named in the charge, why was it that Turuk now said he'd never seen him before that day? The witness was called back in and James's last question was repeated. The answer was the same.

'I only saw them once,' Turuk said. One of the armed men had a rifle; the other had a sub-machine gun. Turuk said that after the two groups had collided, the man with the machine gun had demanded to know why his father had not appeared in Serniki. Turuk said that his father had answered, 'There was no order for us,' and the man with the machine gun had opened fire. Alexei Delidon had risen up wounded and shouted, 'Kill me, finish killing me.' The two armed men had talked and the one with the machine gun had taken the other's rifle and shot Alexei dead. Turuk and Vladimir Delidon had escaped from the scene and Turuk had seen his sister Nadia running off. That night the bodies of those killed had been recovered. Turuk said that his father had suffered seventeen bullet wounds. His mother had also been shot.

When James asked whether Turuk recognised anyone in court, David gave his usual objection. This time Prescott said he would hear submissions before allowing any identification to take place. Turuk was again asked to leave.

Prescott wanted to know what he should make of Turuk's earlier answer that he'd never seen the person who'd carried out the shooting before the shooting took place. David said that the situation was absurd but James again requested permission to ask Turuk if he recognised anyone in court. The magistrate eventually agreed.

'As I entered the room I saw at once Ivan Timofeyevich Polyukhovich,' Turuk told the court.

'Can you see him now?' James asked.

'Over there in the middle, up front.'

'Did anyone tell you that that was him?'

'No one told me.'

After lunch Turuk said that Ivan Timofeyevich Polyukhovich had been the man with the machine gun, but he also admitted having seen an article in a Ukrainian newspaper in late 1986 or early 1987 that had carried Polyukhovich's photograph. Turuk also recalled seeing another photograph, but couldn't remember whether or not the journalist Aarons had shown this to him. After James had taken Turuk through the Special Investigations Unit photo-board shown to him in 1989, David stood up and said that his usual objection applied more than ever with this witness because the probative value of Turuk's evidence had become so slight. Turuk himself had established that he'd only seen the defendant once, and he'd also been 'contaminated' by a newspaper article and Aarons's photo.

James continued, however, to show Turuk photos and portions of the 1989 interview on the video.

Then Michael David stood up to begin his cross-examination.

'The person you say had a sub-machine gun you've said is in court. That's right isn't it?' David said, waving at his client. The queen's counsel was giving the impression that the proceedings had turned into high farce.

'He is in court,' the witness replied.

David took Turuk back over the newspaper article and Aarons's photographs. 'Before Mr Aarons spoke to you in 1987, had you ever seen a photo of that man before?'

'It is similar sort of, but the years are young,' Turuk said.

'But had you ever seen a photo of that man before?'

'No.'

Turuk said that he'd read the newspaper article about Ivanechko that was circulated throughout his district. Magistrate Prescott asked the last question. 'Did you believe what you read in the newspaper?'

'Yes, the whole district, not only I.'

———

Ivan Andreyevich Polyukhovich recognised his sister, although he hadn't seen her for nearly fifty years. His sister Maria, he said, was sitting opposite him next to a man he recognised as Ivanechko.

Ivan Andreyevich was sixty-eight. He said that he'd grown up in Alexandrovo, but remembered that Maria had lived with her first husband's family after she'd married. In about March 1943 the Germans had burned Alexandrovo, and his family had lived in a hut in the forest. He knew that Maria and her two daughters had also spent some time living in the forest. Ivan Andreyevich's father had moved into a house in Serniki after about a month, and some time later Maria and the girls had moved in. Ivan Andreyevich said he knew Ivanechko and it seemed to him that Ivanechko was always either happy or angry. His father had once scolded Maria and told her she wasn't allowed to meet Ivanechko, who had then entered the house armed with a machine gun. Ivanechko had laughed and held the gun as if he'd intended to shoot. Ivan Andreyevich said, however, that he'd never seen Ivanechko hurt anyone.

Ivan Andreyevich said that the last time he'd seen his sister he'd been standing in a boat in the River Stubla. The family had been about to leave Serniki, and a local man, Stefan Kolb, had driven up in a cart carrying Maria, the two girls and their luggage. Ivanechko had appeared and stopped her from leaving.

There wasn't much the defence could do with this witness. His credentials were good in the identification area and he didn't purport to have seen the defendant commit a crime.

Outside of court Ivan Andreyevich asked the investigators whether they could arrange for him to meet his sister. He'd thought that after fifty years he would simply come to Australia, tell Maria what he knew and then she'd leave Polyukhovich and return to Ukraine. Maria refused to meet him. He died less than three months later.

———

It had been said Fillip Ivanovich Polyukhovich knew every horse in the Serniki area at a glance. During the next five hours he would be called on to draw upon his memories of horses linked to the deaths of his father and a man called Pyotr Stepanovich Krupko soon after Easter in 1943.

Fillip, seventy-one, was one of the older witnesses. He had lived in a small hamlet not far from Alexandrovo and had no difficulty in identifying the accused as Ivan Timofeyevich Polyukhovich and his wife as Maria Andreyevna. Fillip told the court that Ivan Timofeyevich had also been known by the street name Ivanechko or Timoshko. Fillip also remembered some of the local Ukrainian police who'd worked in the Serniki region, such as Polivnyk, Martochyn and Yulov.

The witness told the court that a month or so before Easter 1943, Alexandrovo had been burned to the ground and he, his father and other members of his family had left to live in the forest. He recalled how he'd been standing near the edge of the forest on a day after Easter, when he'd heard a machine gun firing. He'd then seen Ivanechko carrying a machine gun and riding a red horse. Fillip said that from a distance of about three hundred metres he'd seen Ivanechko approach a shed and set it on fire.

A couple of hours later and about one and a half kilometres from this scene, Fillip had come across the body of Pyotr Krupko. Krupko had been shot in the forehead, the brow and cheek. Not far from Krupko's body were a dead horse, eight dead cows and a lame horse grazing. This was the horse that he'd earlier seen Ivanechko riding.

The witness said that he'd spent the next nine days searching for his father, and had eventually found him about three hundred metres from the shed torched by Ivanechko. There had been eighteen bullet wounds in his father's body. The next day his father had been buried in Serniki but that night, as Fillip looked through the window of the priest's home, he'd seen Ivanechko ride past. Ivanechko had been riding a red horse and still carried a sub-machine gun.

This was all dramatic evidence, but it was in no way proof of who had been responsible for the killing of Fillip's father or Krupko or the animals. Prosecutor James had said in his opening that Krupko's grandson Vasily would be able to give evidence that he'd seen the defendant on horse-back shoot Pyotr Krupko and then get off his horse and shoot Krupko's cattle and another horse. James had also said then that a seventy-seven-year-old woman named Tatyana Ulitko would say that she'd seen the Krupkos tending their cattle, and later seen Pyotr Krupko's corpse. James had warned that both Vasily and Tatyana were ill, however, and that it was possible they would not be able to come to Australia to give evidence.

Neither of them ever did make it to the committal and the allegations surrounding the death of Pyotr Krupko would never be heard at the Supreme Court trial.

The prosecution team didn't know that their star witness had lain on the floor of his house in Serniki for three days in a coma. Dmitry Kostyukho-vich's wife had called a doctor, who'd told her nothing could be done. If Kostyukhovich woke up, she should get him to a hospital. If he didn't . . .

Kostyukhovich was in hospital by the time investigator Reid found out what had happened. The Australian doctor sent to Ukraine to accompany the witnesses to Adelaide visited Kostyukhovich and had discussions with the local doctors. They all agreed that Kostyukhovich could die at any time. He needed a course of drugs. There was no reason why he couldn't make the journey to Adelaide, however, provided he was careful. In some ways he'd be better off in an Australian hospital.

Reid rang Kostyukhovich in the village and told him through an interpreter that the decision was his. Reid regarded Kostyukhovich as a friend, and believed that he shouldn't put his life at risk for a court case. He could, however, guarantee Kostyukhovich proper care in Adelaide. Kostyukhovich feared Australia would be like Ukraine. There would be no drugs, little food, and he'd be forced to live in a shabby hotel.

The investigator had braced himself for the possibility that Kostyukhovich's evidence might never be given. When Kostyukhovich did arrive in Adelaide on Easter Monday 20 April 1992, Reid thanked him warmly.

'I have a mission and I have to come,' the old soldier announced.

That night Reid stayed with Kostyukhovich in his room. The Ukrainian doctor slept in the big bed, Kostyukhovich in the single one, and Reid on the floor.

———

On Wednesday 22 April sickness took its toll on the accused as well as the accuser. Michael David told magistrate Kelvyn Prescott that his client had a viral infection and wouldn't be well enough to attend court until Monday.

Having at last got Dmitry Kostyukhovich to Adelaide, prosecutor Greg James didn't want anything to stop him from giving evidence. He declared that whatever ailed Polyukhovich could not be as serious as the condition of the witness. There should be a bedside sitting, said James, to preserve Kostyukhovich's evidence.

'What is to be thought of us if this witness were to die in Australia?' James asked magistrate Prescott. 'Days may well make a fatal difference.'

The next day, despite opposition from the defence, Prescott agreed to hear Kostyukhovich's testimony in the absence of the accused. Because Polyukhovich had to be present during the committal, Kostyukhovich's words would be taken down as a deposition or statement made under oath. The admissibility or otherwise of what was said could be argued later. Both the prosecution and the defence agreed that what Kostyukhovich said could not be classified as evidence until it was formally tendered. The court would have to be closed to the public.

A handful of reporters spent the rest of the sunny afternoon waiting on the steps outside the court. Perhaps an ambulance would be called.

———

Both the witness and the defendant survived the weekend and appeared at the committal hearing on Monday 27 April. Kostyukhovich was required to repeat his evidence in open court in the presence of the accused. The witness took a few careful steps into the court, removed his hat, and took his seat. From there he stared intently across at Polyukhovich seated opposite.

Kostyukhovich told James that he'd joined the partisans after the war broke out, then served nine years in the Red Army, before working as the manager of a collective farm for thirty years. He'd received the Order of Glory and the Order of the Great Patriotic War; they were among the medals pinned proudly on the jacket of his grey three-piece suit. Apart from his military service, Kostyukhovich had spent his life in Serniki. He'd gone to school with Ivan Andreyevich. Kostyukhovich said that he'd lived near Ivanechko's sister and had seen the forester visit her. He knew that Ivanechko's full name was Ivan Timofeyevich Polyukhovich.

Kostyukhovich had been seventeen when the war with Germany had reached Ukraine. He'd been working at an airfield near Brodnitsa. On being sent home, he and several other local lads had gone to the school-yard in Serniki to see the German soldiers. He'd there seen about 120 young Jewish men. The Germans were forcing them to dance.

A day or two later he'd heard shooting. Although Kostyukhovich hadn't seen the shooting, he'd known the men were being killed.

He'd joined the partisans a couple of months later and, in the autumn of 1942, he and another young man had been sent back to Serniki. Kostyukhovich said their commander had received information that the Jews were about to be killed, and that they were to observe whatever happened.

Sitting opposite this veteran, with his medals pinned to his coat, the reporters found it was easy to believe that Kostyukhovich regarded the proceedings as merely an extension of his original orders. He was still reporting his observations fifty years later.

Kostyukhovich said that he and his partner had hidden in a shed built on land owned by a Jew named Khokhum. The land had been near the wooden bridge which crossed the River Stubla. Early the next morning they'd watched through a hole in the shed wall as armed men forced Jewish men, women and children from their homes on the other side of the river.

'Who was it that you saw take the Jews out of the houses?' James asked.

'Doroctuiks, that Martochyn, Ivanechko,' Kostyukhovich answered.

He said that these men hadn't been in uniform, but had carried rifles.

'What did you see Ivanechko do?'

'Two young lads ran out. Now, whether they were afraid to run or they wanted to hide, that I do not know. They began to run towards the side of the river ... Then as soon as Ivanechko heard this he turned around, shot one and then he shot the other.'

The reporters, who had been told that this man could die at any time, were surprised by Kostyukhovich's vigour. He spoke in a forceful voice and waved his arms each time he described how one of the lads had been shot. He said that Ivanechko had followed the column as it moved off, poking the Jews to encourage them along. The shooting had started about two hours later. Two or three days later, he and a group of six or seven men had come across a large piece of freshly turned blood-stained ground in the forest.

Asked if he recognised anyone in court from 1942, Kostyukhovich gestured at the defendant. 'Over there. Who should I remember? I remember him.'

'Who is "him"?' James asked.

'Polyukhovich, Ivan Timofeyevich.'

A short time later Prescott asked how Kostyukhovich's health was standing up, and the lawyers agreed to take the lunch break early.

James played a video when they resumed. It showed the area from where Kostyukhovich said he'd witnessed the murder of the two boys. The televisions showed Kostyukhovich and SIU investigator Reid walking near the Stubla river and the street opposite the Jew Khokhum's shed. Kostyukhovich said that this street eventually turned left towards Serniki's market place. He recalled the place where Moyshe Kriniuk had his house and shop. Kostyukhovich interrupted the video after a while and said, 'That is the house of my aunt and here stood the shed where we were.'

The video showed telegraph poles in the foreground and a structure that James referred to as a transformer. The video continued, showing a tree that grew at the intersection of two wooden fences. Kostyukhovich and Reid were standing next to it. The 'in-court' Kostyukhovich said that the shed, from which he'd seen the two boys killed, had been built around about that spot.

Michael David began his cross-examination for the defence by asking whether or not the witness was sure that he'd seen the Jews dance after he'd returned to Serniki in 1941. Kostyukhovich said that he was sure. Why then had Kostyukhovich told Reid in 1990 that, when he'd returned to Serniki after working at the airfield, the Jews had already been killed? To make his point David played the video of the 1990 interview.

'Maybe I made a mistake,' said Kostyukhovich. 'But we did see as they were dancing.'

David pushed the issue. Kostyukhovich said that he couldn't have said the Jewish men were already dead. He'd seen them. The video was played two more times; Kostyukhovich became angry and started shouting. 'I did not say such, I could not have said that . . . I'm telling you now. Were I drunk or stupid or said something foolish like that? But I never said anything like that.'

Prosecutor James tried twice to object to the continued questioning, but Prescott overruled him. The defence believed that the prosecution had gone further than was necessary with Kostyukhovich. There'd been no need to ask him about the first killing of the Jewish men, since it wasn't alleged that Polyukhovich had been involved. The defence could now use this inconsistency to cast doubt over the rest of his testimony. The defence lawyers felt vindicated in their decision to question each of the witnesses in a very tight fashion. The prosecution had asked too much.

David switched to the topic of the clothes worn by Ivanechko and the others on the day the Jews had been rounded up. Kostyukhovich said curtly that they might have been wearing dark or blue clothes but not uniforms. David asked whether Ivanechko had been too far away to see what he was wearing.

'Well I'm telling you it's about sixty or fifty metres beyond the river.'

'Was he too far away to see what he was wearing properly?'

'I've just told you, for God's sake.'

It was time for a break. A nurse took Kostyukhovich's blood pressure. A nurse had also attended Polyukhovich during the afternoon. When the court resumed ten minutes later, James said that he'd been told it would be unwise for the witness to continue. Apparently it was the same for the defendant.

———

Kostyukhovich became angry again next morning. David put to him that in 1990 he'd told Reid that Ivanechko had been wearing a policeman's uniform at the time the boys were shot. Then he showed Kostyukhovich a map of Serniki. Kostyukhovich cried out that he was being tortured. He'd answered their questions a hundred times. But was it possible, asked David, that the shed had been on his aunt's land and not Khokhum's?

No, said Kostyukhovich. He'd been in Khokhum's shed and Khokhum's property was between his aunt's and Moyshe Kriniuk's. David read from the 1990 statement where Kostyukhovich was recorded as saying that he'd watched from his aunt's place. Kostyukhovich said that this could not have happened. The video was played several times, but it made no difference.

'I am not agreeing,' he said. 'Even if you cut my head off. It's no difference to me whether I observed from Khokhum's shed or from aunt's place but the truth is that we observed out of Khokhum's shed. He himself, Ivanechko, he knows where Khokhum's shed is.'

Prosecutor James asked a few questions for the prosecution after David had finished but Kostyukhovich was plainly sick of all the lawyers. James soon said that he'd finished.

'Completely?' Kostyukhovich asked. 'Thank you very much. You are at last letting me go. I could not endure. If I knew it would be so difficult I would not have arrived with my illness. You all see and judge for yourselves . . . But I came.'

Someone thanked Kostyukhovich. His loud voice filled the room again. 'You're very welcome. Thank you to all present.'

———

Bob Reid was sitting with Stefan Kolb, Ivan Andreyevich, Fillip Ivanovich and their interpreter outside a café opposite the court building. Reid, wanting to make conversation, asked them what life had been like under Gorbachev. The men seemed uncomfortable and looked around to see if anyone was watching them.

'It's all right,' Reid assured them. 'There's nobody here to listen.'

One of the men paused and then answered through the translator that back home no one listened to their conversations any more either, but that was the way they'd been brought up. The men told Reid that the nice thing about his country was he'd never had to look over his shoulder.

Reid remembered that these people had survived the German occupation, only to be punished under another totalitarian regime for the next half a century.

———

Stefan Romanovich Kolb was the last Ukrainian witness in Adelaide. Kolb's credentials in the identification area were sound. He was the nephew of Polyukhovich's wife, Maria Andreyevna, and his mother had received letters from Maria since her arrival in Australia. Photographs of Maria, his cousins, Luba and Anna, and the defendant had accompanied the letters. Kolb said that Ivan Timofeyevich had also been known by the street name Ivanechko and that before the war Ivanechko had visited his father regularly. Ivanechko had been a forest ranger who carried a gun. Asked if he recognised anyone in court from those days Kolb said that it had been a long time but: 'Approximately, approximately, Maria and Ivan Timofeyevich.'

Kolb said that his family had lived in the forest after Alexandrovo had been burnt down. Maria Andreyevna and her daughters had camped nearby. The Nazis had later issued an order to shoot anyone found living in the forest, so Kolb's family and Maria and her father had moved to Serniki. The witness confirmed that Maria's first husband was, by this time, a German prisoner-of-war. Kolb said that he remembered seeing Ivanechko in 1943 wearing a policeman's uniform and carrying a machine gun. On that occasion Ivanechko had been with Maria and her father. He couldn't remember whether they'd been arguing. Kolb remembered that later that year, as the Germans evacuated the area, the family had been preparing to leave Serniki on a boat on the Stubla. He'd been driving a cart carrying Maria and the two girls towards the river, when Ivanechko had appeared wearing a uniform and still carrying the machine gun. Ivanechko had ordered Maria and the children off the cart and threatened the thirteen-year-old Kolb. 'He says I ought to be shot up,' said Kolb.

'And what did he do?' James asked.

'He wanted to shoot, but Maria would not let him. She lifted her arm.'

'Did Maria lift the machine gun up?'

'Up. There was a round of firing, but beyond that I do not know any more. The horse by itself reached the river.'

While this dovetailed neatly with Ivan Andreyevich's recollections of the same event, Kolb's most important evidence, the prosecution believed, was that he had seen Ivanechko kill someone, a woman.

Kolb said that in late 1942 near Serniki, he and several other men had seen Ivanechko and another armed man.

'Did you see Jews shot?' prosecutor James asked.

'Yes.'

'Was Ivanechko there when the Jews were shot?'

'Two, there were two.'

'But was Ivanechko there?'

'Yes.'

'There were two what?' James queried.

'Well, he was then a militia man, a policeman,' Kolb replied.

'Was there one policeman there or more than one?'

'Two.'

'How many Jews were shot?'

'Two.'

'Who shot them?'

'Polyukhovich, Ivan Timofeyevich.'

Kolb said that Ivanechko had been wearing a black uniform with an armband bearing the German swastika. The other man had been wearing a similar outfit and had also been carrying a machine gun. Kolb said that he saw the women killed from a distance of about 250 or 300 metres. He'd been told later by the man who buried the corpses that the victims were Tsalykha and her daughter.

Magistrate Prescott interrupted. 'What was this woman's name?' he asked.

'Tsalykha, I understand,' Kolb answered.

'Did you know Tsalykha yourself?' prosecutor James asked.

'I knew.'

'Did you look at the women after they were shot to see if it was Tsalykha?'

'I did not look.'

'When they were shot, did you recognise the woman yourself, with your own eyes, as being Tsalykha?'

'No.'

This evidence was riddled with problems. In his statement to the SIU in 1989, Kolb had said he'd seen Ivanechko leading one woman, not two. He'd not seen her shot; rather he'd heard a shot fired about fifteen minutes after seeing her. Later, he'd inspected a woman's body. He'd said that these events had occurred in 1943; not 1942.

Prescott referred James to his opening, where this first version had been set out quite clearly. James replied that he'd seek to amend the charge so it read that two had been murdered not one, but there would be no attempt to attribute a name to the victims. The defence and prosecution would be meeting during the next few days and would discuss how the charges should be placed in a proper form.

The cross-examination of Stefan Kolb followed a predictable path. David put each one of the obvious inconsistencies to the witness.

The next day prosecutor James spoke to Kolb. 'Mr Kolb, the evidence you have given on oath, sworn on the Bible, is what you have given in evidence here on oath the truth to the best of your memory and belief?'

'That which I saw and knew I said, all truthfully,' Kolb told the court.

———

The committal entered its final stage after eight weeks of evidence from overseas witnesses. In light of the evidence produced, it was clear that the prosecution would have to drop several charges and amend others. Ze'ev Erdman remained in Israel, too ill to make the trip and give his evidence regarding count six – the killing of a woman, two girls and the one-year-old boy allegedly thrown in the river. The charge involving the death of Pyotr Krupko could not be sustained. The Delidon charge would at least have to be altered, since evidence had been given that one of the persons named in that count, Nadia Turuk, had not died at that time. The final form of the charges upon which magistrate Prescott would be asked to decide would be worked out during the next few days.

While this was being done, a procession of archivists from Germany, Russia, Byelorussia, Czechoslovakia and Ukraine made their way through courtroom eleven. They were there to produce dozens of documents proving that the Nazis had a policy of exterminating Jews and dissidents. The archivists also produced glazed eyes on the faces of nearly everyone in court.

The most eminent of the archivists was Dr Josef Henke, the senior officer at Germany's main archive of ss documents. He had played a role in exposing the fake Hitler diaries. He produced a report to the Adelaide court which had been given to Adolf Hitler by his second-in-command, Heinrich Himmler. James had quoted from this document in his opening. It recorded the fact that 363,211 Jewish people had been executed in the eastern territories during a four month period. Henke said that the report had been specially prepared for Hitler in larger-than-normal type because of the Führer's bad eyesight. A separate document tendered to the court had been stamped 'secret'. It recommended that local forest wardens be enlisted by the Reich as scouts and guides. A third document concerned the establishment of ghettos which, 'if the establishment is necessary or at least useful' were to be 'in places with a larger percentage of Jewish inhabitants, especially in towns'.

The following day, Tuesday 5 May 1992, Special Investigations Unit historian Professor Konrad Kwiet stood in the witness box – he preferred standing – and explained the policies and practices of Nazi Germany following the invasion of Ukraine. Kwiet had worked as a consultant with the siu since 1987, and was now based at Macquarie University in New South Wales. Nazi Germany, he said, welcomed the involvement of local people when carrying out its policy of exterminating the Jewish race. Indeed, at least in the early period, even members of the SS preferred to leave the killing of women and children to local police. Kwiet said that the unauthorised killing of Jews, however, had been punished and the issuing of firearms strictly controlled. Kwiet said that he knew of one case in which a Ukrainian policeman had been shot on the spot by the Germans after it had been discovered he'd hidden a machine pistol. The professor believed that, if it were realised that a substantial number of people had escaped a ghetto massacre, there had been 'a kind of un-spoken law to liquidate Jews on the spot'.

'A sort of process of clearing up,' prosecutor Niemann suggested.

'Yes.'

Kwiet said that despite strenuous research, there was no known documentation for the pit killing near Serniki.

————

After the archivists were finished, SIU investigator Bob Reid was recalled by the defence. He had begun his evidence the previous November, but the defence lawyers still had a few crucial questions to ask him. They'd decided that Lindy Powell would examine Reid. He might be more on his guard with Michael David. The queen's counsel might bring out the 'cop' in him.

Powell took Reid methodically through the video which showed him, investigator Dowd, an interpreter and Dmitry Kostyukhovich walking near the River Stubla. At one point it showed the place at the water's edge near the old bridge where Kostyukhovich said the two boys had been shot. Later it showed Gregarin Street, which runs down to the old bridge. The video played on and then Powell stopped it again. 'What's depicted there is the position that Mr Kostyukhovich told you he saw Ivanechko in?' she asked Reid.

They were looking at a portion of Gregarin Street near a building which appeared to be a shadehouse.

'Approximately, yes,' Reid agreed.

The video played on. It showed the group on the other side of the Stubla, then the telegraph line supports and the tree where the two fences joined forming a corner. Kostyukhovich had said in his evidence that the shed had stood on this spot. Reid agreed that this position was ten or fourteen metres to the right of the spot which Kostyukhovich had shown him in 1990.

'And can you say at all what view one would have had of Gregarin Street, or indeed across to the old bridge from that point?' Powell asked, referring to the place where the tree was situated.

'From that area there, from memory you would not have been able to see. Gregarin Street would have been closed off to you,' Reid conceded.

'Now I take it that you never stood in that position?'

'No.'

'That position was never pointed out to you?'

'That's correct.'

'You have no information as to the state of trees at the point of the old bridge at the relevant time?'

'Only from the witness.'

'From what he says he could see?'

'He informed me there was a clear view, and with every witness that I interviewed I went into that aspect – what they could see, what impeded their view. And from what he told me, there was nothing that could impede his view.'

Sometimes the destruction of a prosecution occurs without drama. None of the reporters seemed to take much notice of this discrepancy.

———

The committal had one last surprise: a surprise witness. It had always perplexed Reid that the Special Investigations Unit had found people who claimed they'd seen the round-up, the murders and the pit being filled in, but had never discovered any of the locals who'd dug the massive grave. Reid's colleague Blewitt wasn't convinced that the Soviets had done everything possible in this regard. The procurator Melnishan, who'd been present during most of the SIU interviews in Ukraine, had travelled to Adelaide for the committal. So Reid had raised the matter of the diggers with him.

'Oh, we think the diggers came from the village of Solomir,' Melnishan had said.

'Why didn't you tell me this earlier?' Reid demanded.

'Well, I didn't think it was important.'

Reid had told the procurator that when he got back to Rovno, he was to go straight to Solomir and try to locate more witnesses. Blewitt also hoped that more people would be prepared to come forward with information after seeing the witnesses return home safely. He decided that two of his officers, Anne Moore and Keith Conwell, would accompany one group of witnesses back to Ukraine and then stay on to make further enquiries while the committal continued in Adelaide.

Melnishan collected a few people during their first day in Serniki, 1 May 1992. One of them suggested that the Australians should speak with Sergei Potapovich Polyukhovich, a quiet, sixty-six-year-old deacon in the Orthodox Church, who lived in Zarechnye, not far from Serniki.

Moore and Conwell were spending the night at the Zarechnye 'Hilton'. Sergei was brought there late in the afternoon. He was not one of the diggers, but it became clear that he was a relevant witness. He said that he'd seen Ivan Timofeyevich at the pit when the Jews were being killed.

The two officers were curious why this man had suddenly appeared after the investigations had been going on for so long. They were aware the defence might try to capitalise on the late timing of Sergei's appearance. Sergei told them that he'd simply not wanted to be involved.

The next day, the investigators took a formal statement from Sergei. Moore and Conwell also had to get signatures from several witnesses who'd refused to come to Australia: people such as Olga Polyukhovich, the defendant's sister, and Maria Stepanovna, his first wife. Then they went back to Rovno and contacted their boss Blewitt, who told them to get Sergei on a plane. Sergei, who had managed to avoid any connection with the case for more than three years, now seemed resigned to being sent to the other side of the world.

The arrangements had been so hurried that Sergei was stopped by an airport official as he was going through the barrier at Kiev. The Moscow liaison officer and translator had to promise that he'd be personally responsible for Sergei's return.

Moore was sitting behind Sergei on the Lufthansa flight from Kiev to Frankfurt. As the airline meal was placed in front of Sergei, he said that it looked like a wedding feast. The interpreter deemed this worthy of translation to Moore.

Reid never heard whether or not Melnishan found any diggers in Solomir.

———

On Tuesday 19 May 1992 Sergei told the Adelaide Magistrates Court that he remembered a man named Ivan Timofeyevich Polyukhovich, whose street name was Yanechko. He also remembered Polyukhovich's first wife, Maria Stepanovna, and he remembered a large rectangular pit dug not far from his home outside Serniki.

Sergei said that he and Maria Stepanovna's brother, Ivan Stepanovich, had been employed looking after the Germans' horses in Serniki. He and Ivan Stepanovich had been on their way to work one morning when they'd seen Jewish people approaching. Ivan Timofeyevich had walked up to them from another direction, and Ivan Stepanovich had asked his brother-in-law if they could stay. Ivan Timofeyevich had answered, 'If you are interested in this matter then stay.'

The witness said that they had stood about 150 metres from the pit. They had watched as Jewish men, women and children were herded past and told to sit a few metres away from the grave. A man, perhaps a rabbi, had taken a book. He had spoken to them in Hebrew and then said in

Russian, 'This is God's punishment, and for that we are going into this pit.'

The Jews had undressed. The shooting lasted maybe two hours. Ivan Timofeyevich had told Ivan Stepanovich to fetch some buckets of water, towels and two cups or mugs. The two youths had gone to Ivan Stepanovich's home nearby, where he'd seen Ivan's sister Maria. They'd collected the items and, on returning to the grave, had put them where Ivan Timofeyevich told them. Sergei noticed that the Germans used the utensils they'd brought to wash their hands. He said that the Germans told him he could look into the grave.

'What did you see?' prosecutor James asked.

'When I had a look I saw that they lay in there in the row, one next to each other, and there was a lot of blood poured there along this corridor.'

Sergei said that he saw the terrible sight of the bodies still moving.

'What did you do when you saw that?'

'I could not look any longer. I could have stayed there longer, but it appeared to me very frightening and I could not stay.'

Sergei said that when he'd arrived home his father had said nothing but 'took me by the ear'. He said that during these incidents he had not seen Ivan Timofeyevich shoot, beat or hurt anyone and he had not seen him with a gun.

During Michael David's cross-examination, Sergei agreed that the local policemen he'd seen at the pit on the day of the massacre had been carrying guns and wearing 'uniforms of a kind'. He said that he thought the ghetto had been liquidated in 1943, but 'maybe I made a mistake'. Significantly, Sergei identified the man Ivan Timofeyevich Polyukhovich as having had a job supplying feed for the Germans' horses.

Sergei, then, had delivered a two-edged sword. In the dying moments of the committal, he had placed a man who appeared to match the defendant in several important ways at the pit on the day of the massacre, but had said he'd not seen this man hurt or shoot anyone. Sergei also had said he had not been confident enough to identify anyone when shown an SIU photo-board in Ukraine.

——

The next day James formally closed the case for the prosecution. He also formally announced that the prosecution was no longer pursuing count six (Ze'ev Erdman's charge), count nine (Stefan Kolb's charge), count eleven (the murder of Pyotr Krupko), and was deleting the name of Nadia Turuk from count ten.

Polyukhovich remained charged with having committed seventeen individual murders and with being involved in the pit killing.

——

A week later, defence lawyer Michael David told magistrate Prescott that the case against his client was so inadequate he should never have to face a jury. David said the evidence produced during the committal had been 'incredible', 'manifestly self-contradictory' and 'totally unsatisfactory'. Generally there was only one eyewitness to each of the offences allegedly committed fifty years ago. 'Evidence of that type, as the basis for committing a defendant for trial on a serious charge is totally unsatisfactory,' he argued.

The vital charges were counts one, two and three, David said. These dealt with the round-up of the Jewish people, their deaths at the pit and the murder of the woman and the two children at the pit later the same day. But the evidence supporting these allegations rested 'entirely on the internally and externally inconsistent eyewitness accounts'. The charge involving the Delidons and Turuks relied upon the evidence of just one man, who'd told the court he'd not seen Polyukhovich before or since the event.

Regarding the law, David argued that the prosecution had to show that Polyukhovich was aware he'd been following the German policy of racial or political persecution. 'There is no evidence from which it can be inferred that the accused knew that the killings were committed in the course of political, racial or religious persecution of the Jewish people of

Europe,' David argued. Nor was there any evidence Polyukhovich had ever received any instructions regarding the Serniki extermination.

Greg James, for the prosecution, argued that the so-called 'spectacular inconsistencies' in the evidence had almost always involved peripheral issues or were not in fact inconsistencies at all. He argued that there was more than enough evidence to place Polyukhovich on trial. He said that the magistrate had to be careful he did not attempt to take on the role of a judge and jury. Prescott's function was simply to decide whether the inferences which could be drawn from the prosecution's evidence – taken at its highest – warranted consideration by a judge and jury.

'It is for a jury to decide whether a prior statement is inconsistent,' James argued. Prescott should not try to second guess what the jury might think. For instance, even if the jury found a prior statement made by a witness was inconsistent that jury might still choose to say, So what, it's been fifty years, or a jury could choose to accept one part of what a witness said while rejecting another. It was also sufficient for the prosecution to prove that Polyukhovich had been acting in pursuance of a general policy. The War Crimes Act did not require proof that the accused was a 'paid-up member of the party'. James argued that witness after witness had identified the accused in court, proving it was possible to give evidence regarding something from a long time ago. If the defence were accusing the witnesses of having lied, this was a question for a jury.

It was very wet. Reporters made their way through the rain only to find the doors to the courtroom locked. They'd come early because this was the most important day so far.

David had told Powell the day before that he didn't want to turn up for the decision. Neither did she, but she'd insisted that if she had to go, so did he. Prosecutor James had pitched the burden of proof so low that, if magistrate Prescott accepted his arguments, committing Polyukhovich to the Supreme Court was inevitable and the committal had been simply a matter of going through the motions. They would, of course, apply to the Supreme Court for a permanent stay of proceedings, but what if they failed? The defence believed sincerely that a jury should never be allowed to convict a man on the evidence presented against Polyukhovich. But what if the case did get to a jury? The defence lawyers' greatest fear was that, once the emotive testimony of survivors was heard, convictions would flow out of the jury box without proper regard for the flaws in the evidence.

Prosecutor James had provided Prescott with an easy way out. Clearly there was evidence. The magistrate could commit the case to the South Australian Supreme Court, sending it and all its problems upstairs with a clear conscience, understanding that any difficulties were matters for a judge and jury. James knew that the prosecution could always ignore an unfavourable decision and re-lay any dismissed charges directly in the Supreme Court. But it wouldn't look good. It might appear as though the prosecution was stubbornly pursuing an unwinnable case and would have a terrible effect on the prosecution's morale.

So much was riding on this day's decision.

While the defence and prosecution sincerely held opposite views about what to do with the case, they were agreed that the charges had the same basic strengths and weaknesses. The difference between the charges was only a matter of degree. Both sides expected that all of them would be committed for trial or all dismissed.

The doors still hadn't opened when James arrived, shaking the rain off his coat. The reporters, their cameramen and photographers smiled as he too was forced to wait on the small, cold porch under the majestic columns that flanked courtroom eleven. When the doors finally opened, the court filled quickly, mostly with reporters, and became noisy as they, the lawyers, the court staff, and curious and committed members of the public speculated on the decision.

The dividing lines were clearly drawn, just as they had been for weeks.

The front left row was taken by the defence; the front right row by the prosecution.

Investigator Reid turned around, tension showing, and joked with reporters. 'We've got a new last-minute witness,' he said. 'Goebbels, we found him.'

Polyukhovich and Maria, accompanied by defence lawyer Stokes, made their way to the jury box just before ten. The minutes passed and it seemed that magistrate Prescott would be uncharacteristically late. Then the translator rushed in and took his seat next to Polyukhovich. A moment later, in walked Prescott.

Everyone rose. Most probably didn't notice that Prescott was carrying a pad in his hands. Defence lawyer Lindy Powell *did* notice and for a moment wondered if the decision might go their way, at least in part. Why would the magistrate need a pad with writing on it if his decision was 'committed on all counts'?

There was silence and then Prescott spoke. 'With respect to the arraigned information containing eight counts:

'Count one, I find there is no case to answer.

'Count two, I find there is no case to answer.

'Count three, I find there is a case to answer.

'Count four, I find that there is no case to answer.

'Count five, I find that there is a case to answer.

'Count six, I find that there is no case to answer.

'Count eight, I find that there is no case to answer.

'With respect to count seven, I make no order.

'I accordingly direct that counts one, two, four six and eight be dismissed.

'Mr Polyukhovich, if you would please stand. Now that the evidence for the prosecution has been taken, do you wish to be sworn and give evidence on your own behalf or do you desire to say nothing in answer to the charges? You are not obliged to be sworn – '

The magistrate continued setting out Polyukhovich's rights but these were probably heard and absorbed by nobody. He had spoken so quickly that everyone seemed to be struggling to understand what had happened.

' – but whatever you now say may be given in evidence upon your trial.'

Prescott had finished the statutory warning. David had the presence of mind to stand up and say, 'He wishes to reserve his defence.'

'You will be committed to stand trial in the Supreme Court. You will appear on Monday the sixth of July at ten in the morning. Bail to continue in the same terms.' Prescott rose. Everyone stood as he left the room.

It was over. At first, the courtroom was silent. The prosecution and defence teams each huddled together. Polyukhovich began to cry as someone tried to explain to him what had happened. The silence gave way very slowly to the increasing noise of reporters asking each other what it all meant.

———

Investigator Bob Reid stood still, ashen-faced, his mouth a little open, his mind grasping that the magistrate had dealt the prosecution a mortal blow. A prosecution which had begun with nearly nine hundred murders was reduced to just six deaths. Only Fyodor's account of the killing of the miller's daughter and the two children, and Big Ivan's account of the shooting near the river would go to the Supreme Court. The heart of the prosecution – the pit killing – was gone. Reid had worked for three years, travelled thousands of kilometres, and studied Serniki's holocaust until it felt like he knew the victims personally. He'd conducted countless interviews with the survivors until they'd become his friends. After all his effort the case had been decimated. What was he going to tell the witnesses?

Even when the court was nearly empty Reid remained standing near the bar table, next to two or three of the prosecution solicitors. He was approached by the reporter whom he'd cursed weeks earlier over the article in the News that claimed witnesses had been mistreated. She asked him something about the cost of the committal. From a distance Reid looked as if he was still so dazed that all he could manage was a smile. In fact, he was thinking about hitting her, but one of the prosecution lawyers intervened and said some diplomatic words.

Polyukhovich walked out of the court to face a crowd of reporters staring up at him through the drizzle, cameras and microphones pointing at him. He made his way slowly down the steps. A reporter managed a question; it wasn't answered. A few people belonging to a small group from the League of Rights and National Action clapped in support. 'We're with you all the way,' one of them yelled. 'Good onya Polly,' shouted another.

If these supporters expected to be interviewed, they were disappointed. The media parted, then flowed around and crowded in on Polyukhovich as he continued slowly to a waiting car driven up by David Stokes. A camera recorded forever Polyukhovich's annoyance as Maria's open umbrella, which had given him no protection from the rain now pouring down, hit him in the head. He got in the car and it drove away.

The media people lingered, reluctant to leave in case something happened, but not knowing what possibly could. Slowly they dispersed.

Reid walked out. One of Polyukhovich's supporters thrust a placard in his face and said, 'You ought to be ashamed of yourself Mr Reid'. Forcing his anger and disappointment down inside, the investigator walked on.

———

Each of the prosecutors and investigators spent the rest of the day either bitterly disappointed or bewildered. Magistrate Prescott hadn't given any reasons for his decision: the prosecution had nothing it could analyse, understand, explain away, or attack.

Two hours after he'd given his decision, lawyers James, Niemann, David and Powell were all in Prescott's chambers. James was asking the magistrate to give reasons. Prescott was unimpressed and immediately refused. During the committal, James had asked Prescott not to give any reasons if he did in fact send Polyukhovich for trial. The prosecutor feared that, if published, the reasons might prejudice a jury. It turned out Prescott had given a mixed decision and he now made it clear that he wasn't about to sit down and write out his reasoning at this late stage.

By the middle of the afternoon the prosecution team decided to ignore Prescott by re-laying the pit killing and Kostyukhovich's allegations directly in the Supreme Court.

When it had all started, the prosecution case had looked so strong. The Special Investigations Unit had been told by its counterparts overseas that this was perhaps the strongest war crimes prosecution produced anywhere in the world for at least a decade. But in court so many of the witnesses had dropped some part of their allegations, often without any prompting. Fyodor Grigoryevich Polyukhovich, for instance, had failed to repeat his earlier claim that he'd seen Polyukhovich take part in escorting the column of Jews out of the ghetto. Others, such as Stefan Kolb, had given contradictory accounts and been exposed as unreliable. While some cracks were great holes through which allegations had fallen never to be seen again, others were hair-line fractures exposed under the strict rules of evidence. Despite these problems, the prosecution still believed that its central case was intact and that the bulk of inconsistencies were peripheral. They believed that the faults were not so much with the memories of the witnesses, as with the failure of the court system to understand them.

During the course of the committal the difficulties experienced by the Ukrainians had often seemed strangely familiar to prosecutor Grant Niemann, but the reason had only occurred to him late in the proceedings. Niemann had spent the early 1980s working with tribal Aborigines in the Northern Territory. He'd been in charge of a team of lawyers in the Northern Land Council that argued claims on behalf of Aboriginal communities. The work required great patience. Niemann had found that at first he'd often been misled because he hadn't understood the culture.

Ask the wrong person if a particular spot was a sacred site and that person would deny it, not because the site wasn't sacred, but because that person had no authority to tell its significance. The Aboriginal concepts and the language were alien to Niemann and the white legal system. If evidence for claims was to be gathered, Niemann had to know his clients intimately. He could not afford the detached lawyer–client relationship lawyers traditionally insisted on. The courts, too, had to make allowances for the cultural differences. They needed to bend and adjust. For instance, five or six individuals sometimes would give their evidence together as a group rather than separately. Niemann realised that, like the Australian Aborigines, the Ukrainian witnesses belonged to an entirely different, essentially oral society. Such people produced versions of events in which central issues were consistent but peripheral issues often were not.

Looking back on how the evidence had emerged during the committal, the prosecution believed that the Ukrainian witnesses had been disadvantaged by the Australian criminal justice system. It was a very unforgiving system. It creaked and groaned along always having difficulty dealing with anyone outside the mainstream whether they be ethnic minorities, children or rape victims. The prosecution believed that the task of drawing evidence out of these sorts of groups couldn't be approached in the same way as getting evidence from a sophisticated white, middle-class man from North Adelaide whose first language was English. While the defence believed the Ukrainians simply could not be trusted to give evidence in a criminal court, the prosecution appealed for more tolerance.

The Ukrainians would present the court with a dilemma for as long as the prosecution pursued its case against Polyukhovich. If the court was too tolerant and sympathetic towards the witnesses, there was the terrible possibility it would accept evidence from sincere but mistaken witnesses. After all, it was the prosecution that was required to prove its case beyond reasonable doubt. This wasn't a civil dispute about land claims that could be decided on the balance of probabilities. The accused, Polyukhovich, had been charged with the most serious criminal offences. It was he who enjoyed the benefits of any doubts in the case, not the prosecution witnesses.

———

Having decided the witnesses had been disadvantaged, the prosecution needed to have the committal evidence appraised by someone who could do more than give a new word-for-word translation. It needed someone who could 'interpret' the Ukrainian people to the court. The DPP found that person in Ludmilla Stern.

Stern was the head of Russian Studies at the University of New South Wales. She was born in Moscow in 1958 and had emigrated to Australia in 1979. She had worked part-time for the SIU since November 1989 as an interpreter.

Stern studied the committal transcript for three months, with a view to identifying the limits of accurate translation. In the statement she eventually produced, Stern began by saying that there was 'a natural tension' between smooth court proceedings and accurate translation. There was also a general misconception that good translating must be literal or verbatim. Because every language worked in a different way, a mechanical translation which stuck to the word-order used by a witness would result in nonsense. Ukrainian and Russian grammar allowed the most flexible word order, but it seldom coincided with English. This meant translation was, to an extent, subjective.

Stern also pointed out that there were many words which existed only in one language and were specific to one culture. The Russian and Ukrainian languages did not differentiate between 'hand' and 'arm', or 'foot' and 'leg'. English had the general term 'to go' but in Russian and Ukrainian different words were used depending on whether a person was 'going' by foot, horse or cart. Unless an interpreter was given more detailed information, the question, 'Did you go to your village?' would pose big problems. The word 'nu', used by some of the witnesses, and often translated in the transcript as 'so?' meant more precisely 'yes with some reservation'.

All Ukrainian and Russian nouns had a gender, sometimes without any obvious logic. For instance the Ukrainian word for 'child' was masculine gender and so might be translated 'he' regardless of the actual child's sex. This might be particularly relevant in Fyodor's evidence, which had referred to two *male* children being escorted into the pit with the miller's daughter. The three bodies discovered near the ramp during the exhumation had belonged to a woman and two *female* children.

Even a literal translation of the words 'yes' or 'no' was likely to cause confusion, according to Stern. In English, a question such as, 'You didn't see him, did you?' would be answered 'no' if the person interviewed agreed with the statement. But in Russian/Ukrainian a person would confirm the question by answering 'yes'.

There was also potential for problems between the Russian and Ukrainian languages. Russian was the official language of Ukraine at the time of the investigations, but the witnesses first language was Ukrainian. Although the two languages were similar, there were potentially confusing differences. For instance, the Russian word for 'week' meant 'Sunday' in Ukrainian.

Stern said it was also necessary to understand that, under the Soviet legal system, there would have been no challenge to the prosecution witnesses' credibility. The witnesses wouldn't have expected cross-examination of such persistence and intricacy as David's. In Slavic cultures, Stern said, spontaneity was valued much more highly as a sign of 'genuineness' than precision of detail. 'One is expected to demonstrate his or her emotions when discussing a moving or disturbing subject,' she said. 'A Slavic observer is likely to view a dispassionate account as a callous one, especially during the giving of evidence on emotionally-charged subjects.'

Stern said that concepts of colour and time were also different in the communities the witnesses came from. The differentiation of colours was much more elaborate when people referred to domestic animals than to clothing. Clothing tended to be divided into 'black' and 'white' which often meant 'dark' or 'light-coloured'. The term 'early morning', meaning the hours which follow midnight, could not be directly translated because in Russian/Ukrainian the concept of 'morning' implied daylight. 'It would be uncharacteristic for a peasant in war-time Ukraine to be able to be specific about the hours of the day,' Stern's statement read.

The Ukrainian concept of 'knowing' someone was also different. It could vary from 'knowing' of a person's existence to 'knowing' that person very closely. In pre-war Ukraine the social hierarchy that separated children from adults added yet another dimension to the concept of 'knowing'. Most of the witnesses had been children or adolescents during the war.

Stern wrote that long, badly worded questions usually compounded these sorts of problems, but that breaking up questions into small segments often only destroyed the logical links between sections. The practice of breaking up questions had been used repeatedly throughout the committal. Stern pointed out that the witnesses' earlier statements given to the SIU in Ukraine, which had often appeared so inconsistent with the in-court evidence, had themselves been translated. By the time these statements had been read in English by a lawyer standing in court and then translated again through the court interpreter, they might have only remotely resembled their original words. No wonder the witnesses had been confused. Stern concluded that the witnesses had been disadvantaged.

A lay person might think that such basic problems with translation meant the bulk of the committal had been a waste of time.

The prosecution team knew that it did not have public support. The meagre demonstrations held outside the court didn't get them down so much as the widespread indifference they encountered, and the media's constant emphasis on the cost of proceedings. The prosecution lawyers and investigators had hoped that public opinion would turn as the evidence emerged from the courtroom. It hadn't. Even members of their own families sometimes challenged them, and they tended to avoid telling people what they did for a living. They weren't ashamed. They still believed the prosecution of suspected war criminals was morally right, an exercise in meeting Australia's international obligations, no different from sending a warship to Somalia. But they were tired of answering the same question over and over again: Why are you wasting all our taxpayers' money?

It had become increasingly obvious that the federal government wouldn't consider extending the SIU's investigative life. The government had always said that the unit would have a limited life, and any hope of an extension had disappeared with Bob Hawke's leadership and Lionel Bowen's departure as Attorney General. Both of these politicians had personally supported the unit's work, but a new regime was in power in Canberra. Heinrich Wagner and Mikolay Berezowsky, the two other South Australian war crimes suspects, had been charged but the government refused to allow a fourth investigation, which had been under way for months, to proceed to court. This investigation had centred on a seventy-nine-year-old man who lived in Melbourne. An independent queen's counsel had reviewed the case, a search warrant had been executed on his home, and the SIU had been optimistic that charges would be laid. Some members of the unit had believed that there was even scope for the SIU to be given a new mandate to investigate other theatres of war. They had argued that it would be a logical progression. They could investigate allegations, for instance, that Australian citizens were taking part in war crimes committed during the conflict tearing apart former Yugoslavia.

When the SIU was established, its members had felt some pride. They had believed they were working for a government that had shown the international community it wasn't prepared to tolerate war criminals, but was equally dedicated to the Australian justice system. Now, judging from the community's attitude, perhaps war crimes prosecutions were becoming an embarrassment for the government. It was very different from those early, enthusiastic days. Different from when the SIU had made that first trip into the Soviet Union believing they were demonstrating Australia's commitment to justice to the world.

———

During July the Office of the Director of Public Prosecutions was humiliated as it tried to have seventy-eight-year-old Mikolay Berezowsky committed for trial on war crimes. Berezowsky's committal hearing had begun in the Adelaide Magistrates Court not long after the close of Polyukhovich's committal. It was alleged that Berezowsky had been involved in the murder of about a hundred Ukrainian Jews in 1942. On 2 July 1992 a Ukrainian witness, sixty-eight-year-old Pyotr Mel'nik, told the court a man named Berezowsky had been head of the Ukrainian police in the small village of Gnivan during 1943. Mel'nik was asked to stand up and identify Berezowsky. The witness explained he had a bad eye, put on his glasses and then glanced around the court. He'd then pointed into the public gallery and asked, 'Is that him?' Mel'nik was pointing to an American tourist, Robert Carswell, who'd come to the court that morning to observe the hearing. The next day Mr Carswell's photograph, showing the American wearing his black cowboy's hat, dominated the front page of the local newspaper the *Advertiser*. The headline read, 'Who me? Robert has his own trial.'

The story explained that not only was seventy-six-year-old Mr Carswell not Mikolay Berezowsky, he had in fact worked as an allied intelligence officer during the second world war. Mr Carswell, originally from Texas but now a resident of Virginia, was in Australia to attend an international conference on human caring.

By the end of July, David Gurry, the magistrate hearing the case against Berezowsky, found there was insufficient evidence to place him on trial and the prosecution was dismissed.

The same day Robert Carswell was identified in court, the DPP sent a facsimile message to the war crimes defence team explaining that the prosecution against Polyukhovich would continue. The fax went on to explain that the prosecution had decided to re-lay the charges which accused Polyukhovich of taking part in the massacre at the grave and of killing the two young men seen running from the ghetto round-up.

The defence were not only angry, but worried. They knew that a queen's counsel from interstate had been commissioned by the prosecution to review the evidence following the committal. It seemed he'd agreed the charges should be re-laid in the Supreme Court. What then were Powell and David overlooking? They'd hoped that, following Prescott's decision, the prosecution would give up. In a rare statement to the media, Michael David said he was 'extremely surprised and disappointed' at the 'regrettable' decision which would lead to a long and expensive trial.

———

David Stokes was reflective, perhaps even melancholy. After nearly three years as Polyukhovich's solicitor he was leaving the case.

Looking back over that time, he was struck by how much Polyukhovich had aged. His hair was whiter, his face more wrinkled, and his walk shakier. Polyukhovich had rarely shown emotion. Even during the committal hearing, when he'd been forced to sit and hear the villagers accuse him of murder, Polyukhovich had given little away. His blood pressure would soar sometimes, but Stokes had noticed that Polyukhovich did not often become angry. He just seemed to absorb all that had happened, all the allegations. Maria, on the other hand, was much more fiery. Her anger would erupt in her home, or driving away from the court, or during a break in the evidence, when she would declare the witnesses had no right to say what they were saying. Other times it seemed that Maria felt betrayed or sad.

In some ways Stokes regretted having ever taken on the case. There were many within Adelaide's small community of criminal lawyers who would have loved the chance to defend Polyukhovich. He knew they hadn't been slow to find faults in his handling of the case. Looking back, he could see that at times he'd been overwhelmed by the prosecution in those first few months. He knew that he'd been too quick to agree to the on-commission hearings. Instead of trying to shape a defence and then bringing in a queen's counsel to argue the case in court, he should have hired a QC within a week of Polyukhovich being charged. He'd do things differently if given a second chance. But he could reassure himself with the thoughts that no one in Australia had ever before faced the task he'd taken on and Polyukhovich's defence was now doing well.

Since David and Powell had taken over the defence, Stokes had been relegated to the role of an instructing solicitor. He'd found it frustrating. In court he'd been like an understudy, waiting for either of them to take sick. Unfortunately for him, they'd remained healthy throughout the committal. Money had finally forced Stokes out. He was finding it difficult to maintain his city practice and take part in a full-time war crimes case. The federal government wasn't prepared to compensate him beyond a legal services rate, and he believed that this just wouldn't pay for the practice. Brenton Illingworth, the former state prosecutor who'd joined Stokes in Polyukhovich's defence early in the case, had left the defence team weeks earlier.

Craig Caldicott, another well-known Adelaide criminal lawyer, was ready to step into Stokes's shoes as instructing solicitor. He'd been associated with Polyukhovich's defence from the very early days during the arguments over the on-commission hearings, but had not quite been able to find a permanent position on the team. Caldicott would now stay with the defence until the very end.

———

The defence lawyers made a flying visit to Ukraine during October 1992. Michael David hated it. The hotels stank. The food was foul. He nibbled on chocolate and peanuts and slept in his clothes for the two days of the trip.

Walking through Serniki, however, he found fascinating. It was strange to visit a place for the first time and yet find it so familiar, like going home to memories of things he'd never experienced but had studied until they'd become his own.

They had to go to Serniki to view the river and Gregarin Street from the positions described by Dmitry Kostyukhovich. It was from Khokhum's shed that Kostyukhovich had claimed he'd seen Polyukhovich shoot two boys during the ghetto round-up. Given Reid's evidence regarding Khokhum's shed at the end of the committal, they were amazed the prosecution weren't there as well.

There was no need for David or Powell to linger. They arrived in Serniki from Rovno in the morning. After spending the day looking over the village and visiting Alexandrovo, they were driven straight to Pinsk. It was very late when they got to their hotel, but David wouldn't spend another night in a Ukrainian hotel and asked the drivers if they were prepared to keep going on to Kiev. The drivers agreed, but decided that they shouldn't turn on their vehicle's heating because the cold would help keep them awake. The Australians sat together exhausted as the little Lada van sped through the freezing night.

———

On Monday 30 November 1992 the defence began to tell Justice Brian Cox why it was wrong to continue the prosecution of Ivan Polyukhovich. Cox was one of the more senior judges in South Australia's Supreme Court. If the defence application failed, he would oversee Polyukhovich's trial before a jury.

Over the next few days the defence continued to whittle away at the prosecution case, while the prosecution fought all over again to justify its charges. This time it did so without the witnesses. The court worked from the transcript of the committal which, in the opinion of the prosecution, concealed as much as it revealed. Prosecutor James tendered Ludmilla Stern's affidavit. Cox didn't take long to make his own criticism of the translation. He said that he marvelled how so much had been spent in preparing and presenting the case and yet, at the practical stage of taking evidence, the interpreting was obviously deficient. James quickly pointed out that the interpreters had been supplied by the South Australian Courts Department, not the federal Director of Public Prosecutions.

The main theme of the defence application was that the passage of time between events in occupied Ukraine and Polyukhovich's pending trial made it impossible for the Adelaide pensioner to get a fair trial. Later, David focused on each of the charges individually, starting with Dmitry Kostyukhovich's allegations regarding the ghetto round-up and the killing of the two boys. Prosecutor James saw some strength in the fact that Kostyukhovich had been sent to the village on the morning of the liquidation with the specific task of observing events. But David argued that the court had been placed in the awful position of not being able to make an objective assessment of what Kostyukhovich had seen.

'He might be honest, but wrong,' David told Cox. 'He might just be wrong when he says "It is him." '

The defence argued that it was difficult to test Kostyukhovich's story. Firstly, there was confusion over where exactly he'd been standing on the day of the round-up. Secondly, the landscape had changed since the war.

'We are talking of an untestable piece of evidence that is vital to the case,' David said.

The QC argued likewise with Fyodor's allegations regarding the miller's daughter. The mass grave had been filled in, making it impossible to test what Fyodor could have witnessed. Moreover, the court had to rely solely on Fyodor for an account of this killing.

Cox said that this submission often arose in sexual cases where only one person had witnessed a crime and a conviction relied on that person's credibility. The judge reminded David that rape cases weren't stopped from going ahead just because they rested on a single victim's testimony.

James went further, saying that Fyodor's evidence had been supported by the exhumation. The pit had been uncovered in the exact location Fyodor had said they would find it, and the clothed bodies of the woman and two children found near the ramp had corresponded neatly with Fyodor's allegations regarding the miller's daughter having been escorted down into the grave and shot.

David attacked the evidence supporting the pit killing charge, just as he had in final submissions to magistrate Prescott. He said it relied on witnesses who individually could not be trusted and who, when taken together, conflicted with one another. One witness had Polyukhovich with a gun; another had him without a gun. A third witness who saw the massacre did not see Polyukhovich there at all.

Prosecutor James said that the evidence suggested Polyukhovich had in fact participated in the massacre from the very beginning and then throughout the day. The fact that Fyodor had not been prepared to put the accused with the round-up was a credit to him. It showed that the prosecution had found a man who was not prepared to accuse Ivanechko on a wholesale basis.

Regarding Big Ivan's allegations, David conceded the prosecution were in a stronger position in terms of recognition. Big Ivan had claimed that he'd seen Polyukhovich emerge from a forest, try to kill three people with a single bullet and then club the third victim with his rifle butt. There was evidence that Ivan had known Polyukhovich much better than the other witnesses. Even so, the court was again faced with just one witness viewing events from a distance of, at best, about a hundred metres. If the court tried to test Big Ivan's evidence by returning to the scene, it would find the river was gone, replaced by a canal. And there were no bodies; there was nothing to examine forensically.

'What we have, in this case, is just the bold assertion that it happened, and really nothing else,' David argued. To warn a jury that, after fifty years, the witnesses might have made a mistake, would be 'with the greatest respect, meaningless'. A modern jury couldn't comprehend what it was like to remember something over fifty years.

Prosecutor James said that it was plainly open to the defence to remind the jury they were only hearing the evidence which had survived the ravages of time. But James turned this to his advantage. He said that it was equally open to the prosecution to point out that it defied coincidence that the only surviving evidence either incriminated Polyukhovich or supported the case against him in some way. Murder, James pointed out, had never required more than one witness. Anyway, he said, each of the charges, with the exception of Big Ivan's, had some corroboration. James was telling the judge that there was nothing in the prosecution case that couldn't be scrutinised by a properly instructed jury.

———

Justice Cox published his thoughts on 22 December 1992.

It would be a rare case, he wrote, which was stopped from going ahead simply because there had been a delay between events alleged and a trial. Cox said the delay in this case had not been caused by any tardiness on the part of the prosecution. The legislation allowing the case had come into force only a year before the charges had been laid. Even a very long delay, said the judge, was not by itself fatal. He cited a case where a woman had accused her step-father of indecently assaulting her more than twenty-five years before speaking to police.

'Of course, the delay of fifty years in this case is enormously long – of unprecedented length, so far as I am aware – but I do not think it can be said that a fair trial must be impossible, after such an interval, no matter what the circumstances.'

The circumstances surrounding Dmitry Kostyukhovich's evidence, however, were inadequate. Cox found that the old veteran hadn't had sufficient time to look at the man responsible for shooting the boys to identify him reliably. And this was from a shed the position of which was not certain, and that had overlooked a topography which had changed. 'In my opinion, this is one of the very rare cases in which one may say, on the totality of the material, that there is nothing the court can do to ensure that the accused will get a fair trial,' said Cox. Kostyukhovich's allegations would not proceed to a jury.

Cox said that Fyodor's evidence had similar problems. There was corroboration, however, that the sort of killing he'd described – the shooting of a woman and children at the pit – had occurred, and that Polyukhovich had been at the pit during the afternoon helping the Germans. Fyodor also claimed he'd seen the accused at close quarters and knew him before the murder of the miller's daughter and the children. Fyodor's allegations would go to a jury.

Cox ruled that Kostyukhovich's evidence could not be used to incriminate Polyukhovich in the pit killing but, based on Sergei's and Fyodor's evidence, he would also allow the pit killing charge to proceed to a trial.

Lastly there was Big Ivan's allegation regarding the murder of the three people in the field. Justice Cox said that this situation was similar to Kostyukhovich's, but that Big Ivan's evidence had some advantages. He'd known Polyukhovich well, had more time to witness the killings, and had been more consistent when speaking with the authorities. Big Ivan seemed honest and intelligent and hardly likely to make a mistake about witnessing a triple murder. Cox was prepared to let a jury decide Big Ivan's credibility.

But, and it was a big 'but', Justice Cox would not let one jury hear everything. The miller's daughter and the pit killing were alleged to have occurred in the same place and on the same day. Big Ivan, however, had witnessed the three killings outside Alexandrovo perhaps several weeks later. His allegations were quite separate. There would be a real risk of prejudice if one jury heard both this and the other allegations. A jury could too easily slip into the notion that Big Ivan's allegations supported the others or *vice versa*, and this would be unfair. A caution to the jury would not be enough to guarantee against this. If the prosecution insisted on pursuing all the remaining charges there would have to be two trials.

The prosecution had known all along that a judge might sever the charges. It also knew that it wouldn't be possible to bring the witnesses out two more times, one for each trial. Big Ivan's allegations would be discarded for good.

The prosecution felt that it was as if South Australia's courts were minded to slowly torture them. Prescott and Cox had each left some hope alive, enough for the prosecutors to rise up once more. But each time a magistrate or a judge looked at their case, a vital piece was removed.

———

Justice Cox's decision to stop only Kostyukhovich's charge, involving the two boys allegedly shot during the round-up, had taken the prosecution by surprise. To them that count seemed no more 'contaminated' than any of the other charges. They'd believed that the position of the disputed shed could easily be sorted out when the Jewish witnesses were brought back for the trial. It had simply been unfortunate that all of them had left by the time Kostyukhovich had given his evidence at the committal. Reid had contacted them since, however, and several were confident they knew its position.

Prosecutor James wasn't willing to let the matter rest. He suggested that they now take one of the Jewish witnesses back to Serniki to locate Khokhum's shed once and for all. If that could be done, he might be able to convince the judge to lift the permanent stay now in place. Without Kostyukhovich, they'd go to trial relying on Sergei's allegation that Polyukhovich had ordered him to get towels and water for the Germans working at the pit.

Bob Reid had left the Special Investigations Unit six months before, but the unit now brought him back to make another journey to Serniki. This time he'd take Milton Turk from Toronto, who had grown up in Serniki, and together they would try to find Khokhum's shed. Jack Kriniuk had wanted to return to the village with Reid and his old friend Turk, but Kriniuk was seriously ill. He'd injured his legs during the war and his circulation was becoming worse. Flying was out of the question.

Turk, however, was well qualified to do the job on his own. He was a builder, able to give expert evidence about the use of technical measuring equipment. Turk would be able to locate the various spots in question down by the river and then draw precise maps.

———

Grant Niemann's head suddenly appeared from out of the dark train doorway. 'Oh, you're here,' he said with obvious relief.

It was four in the morning and the train he was standing in had just pulled into the freezing Kiev railway station. Reid and Blewitt laughed as they saw the worry disappear from the prosecutor's face. Niemann had travelled from Moscow alone, and by some miracle had made the rendezvous as planned. Standing with them on the platform was Milton Turk. Next to him was his son-in-law, Victor. Turk's family had insisted Victor accompany him for support.

Reid had been trying to reassure Turk ever since Frankfurt that he didn't have long to wait. Now they set out on the journey to Rovno. When they arrived on 18 January 1993, they were met by their old friend, procurator Melnishan, who insisted they couldn't go up to the village without first having some lunch. After lunch he explained that it was too wet to travel and they would make the trip the next day. The last twenty kilometres to Serniki were nerve-racking for both Reid and Turk. Melnishan had wanted to stop for a meal on the way, but Reid had insisted they continue, and the procurator had known better than to argue. Word had got out that Reid was coming back to the village, and quite a few locals were there to greet them.

Turk knew that he'd been recruited to help locate Khokhum's shed, although Reid hadn't told him its significance. Now the sixty-five-year-old man began walking the streets of the village he'd grown up in half a century earlier.

'I'm not going to tell you anything,' Reid said. 'No hints.'

Turk gazed from side to side as they walked along the main street.

They were actually walking through a village built on the ruins of the Serniki that the Germans had burned to the ground not long after the destruction of the ghetto. When they came to the old market, however, the memories fell into place. Turk knew where he was. He began pointing to houses, explaining that they'd been built on the sites of Jewish homes. This was where Zaltzman had lived; the synagogue had stood there. Then they made their way into Gregarin Street, where dozens of frozen puddles had begun to thaw.

'Nothing's changed,' Turk said. 'It was exactly like this in 1942. This is my village.'

As they approached the bend in the road which led towards the river, Turk told Reid he knew what was beyond. 'You look straight down and the old bridge is there,' he said.

'I'm not going to give you any hints,' the policeman repeated with a grin.

The old bridge had gone, but as they reached the pylons which had survived, sticking out of the muddy banks, Turk pointed across the water and said Khokhum's shed had stood over there. Jack Kriniuk's place had been next to it. Zamal Kaz had lived over there. Turk pointed along the boundary of the old ghetto naming every house. They crossed the river and Turk showed Reid where he believed the shed had stood. The rest of the afternoon he made Reid work like a navvy as he set about measuring lines of sight, recording distances and angles.

The next morning Turk insisted that they all go to the grave: Turk, Victor, Reid, Blewitt and Niemann.

'Do you want me to come with you?' Reid asked Turk when they reached the site.

'Yes, please,' Turk answered.

Turk stood over the grave, took out his prayer book and placed his *kippah* on his head. Reid realised he didn't have his hat, and the Ukrainian driver fetched it from the car. Then Turk began to pray in Yiddish. Reid understood German, but was having trouble following the words. Turk began reciting the names of people lost to the pit. He cried, but kept reciting the names. He gasped for breath, but still kept reading. The other men stood by silently, as the tragedy of the pit they were standing on was recounted in this poor man's prayer. It was a mixture of tears, words and agony. Reid looked around for Victor but he was somewhere taking photographs. Turk couldn't breathe properly, but somehow managed to finish.

'Come on, we'll sit in the car,' said Reid, putting his arm around Turk.

'No, not yet.'

They walked to the other end of the clearing, where a large stone had been placed after the exhumation nearly three years earlier. Victor took some photographs of his father-in-law standing next to the memorial and then Turk turned to Reid. 'Get me out of here,' he said.

———

Turk worked for the rest of the afternoon taking measurements all over the village. Reid didn't realise at first just how much the grave had upset Turk, who refused to stop for lunch until Reid explained that the village's mayor was hosting a meal for them. It would be rude to refuse. Turk agreed he couldn't insult these people who'd welcomed him back so enthusiastically.

The next morning Turk said that he wanted to go to the Jewish cemetery.

'Look, you don't want to go there, Milton,' Reid warned him. 'It's awful.'

'Well, I've got to see that it's awful,' Turk said. 'And I don't want you to come. I'll just go with Victor.'

The Jewish cemetery had been left in ruins since the war. The fence marking its perimeter on a barren hill was falling down. Headstones lay broken and smashed, overgrown with weeds. A portion of sunken ground showed where the Germans had buried the hundred men killed during the first sweep through the village in 1941. Turk's father had been among them. Turk returned about an hour later, clearly distraught.

'That's why I didn't want you to go,' Reid explained to his friend.

'I know, and that's why I didn't want you to go,' Turk answered. 'Because you'd have got upset taking me somewhere like that.'

———

The pre-trial argument began on 1 March 1993. For the prosecution, James started by tendering a copy of the plan drawn by Turk. He argued that, together with Reid's statement regarding the trip, the videos made around the Stubla, and the evidence given at the committal, there was sufficient evidence to justify reinstating Kostyukhovich's allegations. The prosecution, James said, could prove that on the morning of the liquidation there was nothing impeding Kostyukhovich's view from any of the suggested positions. The reason for staying the charge – concern that the witness's account couldn't be tested – had been refuted.

The defence responded with two arguments. Firstly, Justice Cox's order simply couldn't be changed. It was a permanent stay. Cox did not have any power to re-open it, review it or to make an order inconsistent with it. Secondly, and here the defence were much more confident, it would still be unfair to put Polyukhovich on trial over Kostyukhovich's allegations, despite Turk's evidence.

Cox heard the lawyers argue these points for two and a half days. On 4 March he gave his decision. His order could be recalled. The judge said that it was always possible circumstances could change dramatically, and it might turn out that an accused could have a fair trial on charges earlier thought unsafe. 'As Mr James put it, a permanent stay may be forever but not forever no matter what,' the judge said. But whether or not the order should be put aside in this particular case, he continued, was a different matter. Back in December, he'd made his decision based on the totality of the circumstances, of which the extraordinary delay was by far the most important. He dismissed Turk's plan and Reid's statement, saying that their effect was minor and would not have altered his decision. The judge still wouldn't allow a jury to hear Kostyukhovich's allegations.

'Finally,' said Cox, 'the crown asked me to have a view of the village of Serniki before reaching my decision on this application. The request is not supported by the defence. It seemed to me that there was very little, if anything to be gained by having a view of the scene and it would obviously have caused considerable trouble and expense as well as delaying the trial. I therefore decline the crown's request.'

The court was adjourned at 9.45 AM.

The prosecution had started the week optimistically. It had been a new beginning with fresh evidence. Turk's plan had been confirmed by sketches drawn by other survivors, and they were confident that there was plenty of material the defence could use to test Kostyukhovich's story in front of a jury. Before long, however, they'd had that familiar sinking feeling. James had won a major legal victory in getting the judge to say that he could recall the stayed charge, but now their key witness again had been put beyond their reach.

An hour later they were all back in court. 'Where do we go now?' Cox asked.

James said that he wanted to know exactly how much of Kostyukhovich's evidence they couldn't use. The judge asked whether the prosecution was suggesting that Kostyukhovich should be allowed to give evidence he'd seen Polyukhovich take part in the round-up, even though his evidence regarding the shooting of the two boys had been stayed.

'That's the submission,' James said.

The judge must have marvelled at James's resilience. 'You have a job in front of you,' he warned him.

The prosecutor spent most of the next two hours trying to convince Cox to let Kostyukhovich say something incriminating, but the task was hopeless.

Investigator Blewitt sat in court devastated by what he was hearing. After so many adverse decisions, he'd become cynical about the South Australian judiciary. He knew that he'd probably become too close to the case, but why didn't the judge just kill off the prosecution cleanly? Why did the courts remove one vital organ at a time, but still leave the patient on life support? He picked up a folder containing Sergei's evidence and read it from beginning to end. When he finished, he believed that there was nothing in it that could substantially link Polyukhovich with the events at the pit. They'd needed Kostyukhovich. With his evidence, Polyukhovich had been seen at the beginning of the liquidation process, with a gun, killing two boys who'd been running from the ghetto as the Jews were chased from their homes. Then Sergei had seen him at the pit ordering two young men to get towels and drinks for the Germans. Finally, Fyodor had seen him near the end of the day escorting the miller's daughter and the children into the grave. Pull Kostyukhovich from the case and it began to crumble. Fyodor would still be able to stand, but he alone couldn't support the allegation that Polyukhovich had been involved in the wider massacre, and Sergei's story was simply circumstantial. Blewitt could see the defence explaining away Sergei's account by saying Polyukhovich had been forced to obtain the towels and water.

Towels and water. Was this all they were left with after so much work?

Blewitt passed Reid a note and then moved next to him. James and David were still giving submissions but Blewitt whispered to Reid that it was time to pull out. They could not go on any longer. 'I'm going to recommend to Greg that we drop the charges,' he said.

'Oh, right, okay,' was all Reid said.

Just before the court adjourned for lunch, two lawyers from the media turned up to argue about suppression orders. Prosecutor James, aware the case was hanging in the balance, said cryptically that it might be best if they waited until after lunch. As soon as Cox left the bench, Blewitt asked James if they could appeal to the High Court against Cox's rulings, but James said there was no point. The High Court wouldn't intervene. Someone suggested that they should ring Grant Niemann, who was in Brisbane for a meeting of commonwealth deputy directors. Blewitt used a public phone on the first floor of the Samuel Way building to tell Niemann about Cox's rulings and that he thought it was time to quit.

Reid was becoming angry. As they walked out of the building, Blewitt tried to make him understand that continuing was pointless. There simply wasn't enough evidence to continue with the mass murder count that had always been the heart of the prosecution. Blewitt believed that, if the trial went ahead, the judge would simply intervene at the end of the prosecution case and tell the jury they had no alternative but to acquit Polyukhovich. Blewitt had witnesses all around the world waiting for his office to tell them whether or not to make the journey to Adelaide. If they were ever going to stop the prosecution, now was the time to do it.

The prosecution team stood in the street outside the court building and took a straw poll. Blewitt repeated that it was time to stop and Bob Green, the deputy director of the war crimes unit, agreed. Prosecution solicitors Nick Goodenough and Rocky Perrotta sided with Reid, who flatly refused. 'You can't do this,' Reid said angrily. 'We've done all this work.' James could sense a fight brewing, and stepped in to calm the situation.

Reid stormed off towards Grote Street. The group followed him to a small café, where the debate continued. Reid and Blewitt, two friends who'd travelled the world piecing the case together and then spent nearly four years maintaining it, understood each other, but now it was time to sort out their roles. Were they lawyers or investigators? Reid insisted that the case was out of their hands. It was in the court's hands. They'd done their job to the best of their ability and then handed it to the court. And they had been justified. There had been a case to answer. Magistrate Prescott had allowed something through and Justice Cox was prepared to allow two charges to go before a jury. James was senior counsel, and he had not yet recommended they pull out. Reid was prepared to accept that Cox might throw the case out, but he wasn't going to do it for him. This wasn't the Soviet Union. Everyone had a separate role, the investigators, the prosecutors, the defence lawyers, the magistrate and the judge. Each was accountable for their own decisions. Besides, in a strange way, Polyukhovich had a right to a trial. To pull out now, at the last moment, leaving the charges unresolved, would be unfair. Let Polyukhovich be convicted or acquitted. One or the other.

Blewitt left the others and walked back to the court by himself. Perhaps he'd been too hasty. He rang Niemann and said that he'd had a change of heart. Niemann told him that the deputy directors had spent the last hour discussing the matter, and they too had all agreed the case should proceed. Blewitt rang his office in Sydney and told them to give the witnesses the green light.

The court had reconvened while Blewitt was making his calls but, within a few minutes, the judge had adjourned again. Cox wanted to inspect a machine the prosecution intended using during the trial. It took an image of a document or photograph and displayed it on several television screens simultaneously. At 2.43 Cox had resumed his seat. By this time it was obvious to everyone that the prosecution had been holding intense discussions.

'Mr James, I presume we just proceed?' asked the judge, showing a respectable amount of curiosity.

'Yes we do, your honour,' James answered. 'I have literally just now received instructions as your honour was walking back into court and we do proceed.'

The rest of the afternoon was taken up discussing how much of the interview conducted on the day of the arrest should be allowed to go to the jury. James threw himself into the fray with as much enthusiasm as he'd displayed at the start of the committal.

Justice Cox interrupted him toward the end of the day. 'You made an enigmatic remark before lunch which I suppose puzzled more people than just me,' the judge said. 'Can I take it to be fairly enigmatic in the way I deal with it too? That we are going on?'

'We are going on,' James answered again. 'Your Honour described me as responsible senior counsel earlier. I will let the court know.'

'I'm assuming we are going on and we will be engaged in the exercise for the next few weeks,' Cox said.

'We are going on and we are engaged in a very real exercise.'
James said.

They were still arguing about the admissibility of evidence eleven days
later. On 15 March Justice Cox delivered another blow to the prosecution. From the start of the committal, the defence had said they would
challenge the photo-board evidence. Cox had concluded that the photo-
boards did contain a real potential for unfairness. The judge said that the
trouble with the boards was that they each contained only one photograph of a person from Serniki – the accused Ivan Polyukhovich. All the
other photographs were of people of a similar age, but they would not
have been known to any of the witnesses. The witnesses, presented with
only one familiar face, were likely to point to the accused's photograph.
They would consciously or unconsciously pick out the photograph of
someone they'd seen before, whether or not they knew him to be the
forester. Cox said that he wasn't sure what to do with this vital identification evidence. So he had to rule in the accused's favour. The jury would
not be shown the photo-board evidence.

As for the interview conducted on the day of Polyukhovich's arrest,
Cox was satisfied that the answers had been voluntary until 4.20, when
the accused had said he'd had enough.

This last ruling was only a minor setback for the prosecution compared to the decisions about the photo-boards and Kostyukhovich. Nearly
all the vital information had been gleaned by investigators Reid and
Huggett in the first half of the interview.

During the two further days of the pre-trial argument, Cox said that
the prosecution could use the photographs seized from Polyukhovich's
home. As a measure of safety, however, only those witnesses who'd successfully picked out Polyukhovich from the flawed photo-boards would
be allowed to identify the seized photographs. This ruling affected the
key witness Sergei Potapovich, who had been unable to pick anyone with

confidence when shown a photo-board at the committal. The defence lawyers still weren't satisfied and asked that Fyodor Polyukhovich not be allowed to make any identification from the photographs. They argued that Fyodor hadn't known Polyukhovich well enough to be trusted. The judge said that he'd hear that application after Fyodor had given his evidence. The pre-trial argument finished just before four, on 17 March 1993.

James went back to the DPP office to begin fashioning an opening address in accordance with Justice Cox's latest rulings.

The jury would be selected the next day.

The trial

The trial

Polyukhovich used his walking stick to make his way slowly up the few steps which took him to the first level of the Samuel Way building. Maria was by his side. Defence solicitor Craig Caldicott was standing there. He asked how his client was feeling; Polyukhovich shrugged his shoulders and said a few quiet words.

The rain which had been falling steadily through the night and morning had cleared, leaving the city a humid place. Courtroom three was warm and, despite its size, quickly became stuffy as a large group of potential jurors was ushered in. Polyukhovich took his seat in the dock next to his interpreter. Maria found a seat in the body of the court, but was brought down to sit with the defence in the front row.

Court staff had called in about seventy people to make up the jury pool, many more than were usually deemed necessary. They filled what was normally a drab, silent public gallery with colour and a low hum of conversation. Spaces not taken up by people were filled with books and folders containing notes and transcripts, the baggage of a long court case. Most of the journalists and artists covering the case were forced to stand along one wall. The defence lawyers, sitting at the bar table, were poring over the list of names of people in the jury pool.

Justice Cox's associate read out the two charges, which had to be translated. Polyukhovich pleaded not guilty to having taken part in the pit killing and the murder of the miller's daughter and the two children.

The judge told the potential jurors that there was no need to follow the convention of reading out the list of witnesses who would give evidence. The jurors were unlikely to know any of them, since nearly all were either from interstate or overseas. If they knew any of the lawyers or the accused, however, they should disqualify themselves. He added that the trial was expected to take five or six weeks and then asked if anyone wanted to say anything.

More than half the people in the gallery rose as one to their feet. Faced with this extraordinary sight, Justice Cox said that the response wasn't what he'd hoped for, and that he would need a good reason to dismiss any of them from the jury selection. Three people said they knew either the defence lawyers or the defendant and were excused immediately. As for the rest, Cox said he would hear their reasons for not wanting to sit on the trial one at a time. Thirty people walked up to the judge during the next half hour. One woman tried twice. Only the judge's staff sitting near him and the court-appointed reporter could have heard what was said. When all the potential jurors had resumed their seats, Cox announced that the vast majority of objections were of the usual kind, business and personal reasons, which weren't satisfactory. A handful of people had told him they had family in Ukraine or Poland, and one middle-aged man claimed he'd spent his early childhood in Holland. Justice Cox said he understood their concern. He wouldn't order that they be removed from the jury pool but, if they wanted to be excused, he would allow it.

It was eleven, nearly an hour had passed, and only now was the court ready to select the jury. The judge's associate began reading out names chosen randomly from a box. Six had been called before defence lawyer David challenged the selection of a man with a Slavic sounding name. Nervous laughter was heard from the gallery and the man returned to his seat smiling. An elderly woman was called and then a woman who'd earlier told Cox she had family in Kiev. David challenged her and she returned to her seat. Two more people were challenged – one by the prosecution and one by the defence – and then three women and nine men sat in the jury box. A collective sigh of relief could be heard from those people left in the gallery. Someone even clapped. The associate read the charges again and declared that the accused was now in the hands of the jury. Those people not chosen to serve on the trial were told to return to the jury room in case they were needed for other cases.

Prosecutor James then asked for count two to be amended so that it no longer referred to the sex of the two children murdered along with the miller's daughter. Justice Cox explained what this meant to the jury.

At last all of the preliminaries were over. More than three years after Polyukhovich's first appearance in the magistrates court, the prosecution was about to put its case to a jury. Prosecutor James began. 'Ladies and gentlemen my name is James. I appear on behalf of the prosecution with my learned friend Mr Niemann – '

James spent most of the rest of the day outlining the nature of the charges, the reasons for the charges, the evidence the crown would rely on, and who would be called to give testimony. James stressed that he was simply a barrister. What was ultimately important wasn't what the lawyers said, but what the witnesses said and, regarding the law, what the judge said. Despite James's explanation that he was probably superfluous the jurors continued to look at him. Some looked tired already. It was still very warm in the court.

'You may well find that in the context of this case the crucial question is not even whether the murders alleged occurred, but whether or not the accused was party to those murders in the way alleged,' James said.

The prosecutor once interrupted his address, saying that there was something most important the jury should remember regarding the burden carried by the crown. It was the crown that had brought the charges and the crown that had to prove them beyond reasonable doubt. The jury might wonder why these matters that occurred 'over there' were being tried in Australia. The short answer, James said, was that Polyukhovich was an Australian citizen and had to be tried in Australia.

He said that the witnesses would fall into two classes: those Jewish people who had fled from Serniki, emigrating to North America and Israel, and those non-Jewish people who still lived in the Serniki area. It would be for the jury to assess the witnesses in the light of their background, literacy and intelligence. The witnesses might be elderly and frail. Some would not speak English. The Ukrainian witnesses, in particular, came from a small remote rural community. The jury would need to remember that these witnesses would be in a position to know the local population and the dramatic events alleged by the crown. But the jury would also need to keep in mind that, while Australia had changed greatly since the war, these Ukrainian witnesses were from a part of the world which had changed little. James played a video of the Serniki area and explained some of the historical background to the case.

Before Justice Cox would let the jury go to lunch, he had a warning for them. Much publicity had been given to this case, he said, but the jury's verdict had to be based solely on the evidence presented to them in court. 'Don't discuss this with anyone else. I would say keep it to yourselves even after the trial,' Cox warned. He said that he believed the integrity of the jury system was best maintained if jurors didn't later tell-all about their deliberations. The prospect of one of them later speaking out could serve only to seriously inhibit the freedom of their discussions.

The judge had made it clear it was very important for them to keep their deliberations secret forever.

———

Juries never walk into empty courtrooms. The different parties are always sitting waiting for the jury's return, just as they sit during the jury's departure. It must seem to jurors that they are the only ones who come and go during a trial. A long loud squeak was heard throughout the court as these particular jurors resumed their seats and the door through which they'd just walked closed.

James continued his address. He was speaking about the role of foresters in occupied Ukraine. In the Pinsk area, which included Serniki, a number of locals were employed by the forestry department. Among them was Ivan Timofeyevich Polyukhovich, the defendant. Since the committal, investigators had found a second world war forestry document in the former Soviet archives containing Polyukhovich's name. James promised to show this to the jury along with an identity card issued to Polyukhovich by the forestry department and seized from his home in Adelaide in 1990.

The prosecutor said that it was admitted by all that Ivan Timofeyevich Polyukhovich had been living in Alexandrovo at the time of the alleged offences and that a number of witnesses would give evidence he was known by the street name 'Ivanechko'. In 1939, he'd married a local girl, Maria Stepanovna Polyukhovich, whose father lived in a house about two hundred metres from what would become the mass grave. The defendant had left his first wife and, by the early 1940s, had developed an association with another local woman, Maria Andreyevna Polyukhovich. This second Maria was married to another man and had two daughters. Later, as the Germans had retreated from the area and the partisans had taken control, collaborators had left the country regions and concentrated themselves in the towns still controlled by the Germans. Evidence would be given that, between October and November 1943, Ivan and Maria Andreyevna Polyukhovich and her two daughters had arrived in Pinsk. Eventually Ivan had been given work in Germany. Documents would show that this was the same man who now sat opposite the jury.

———

During the next two weeks the prosecution team's confidence began to grow again. Cox's decisions had cut a swathe through their case but the rulings also had a purgative effect. They felt that everything left was virtually unchallengeable.

The court made good progress. As soon as James finished his opening, defence lawyer Powell read to the jury a list of facts conceded by the defence. Some of these were obvious. Other concessions saved the court much time. Polyukhovich agreed that Germany had established a policy of exterminating the Jews of Europe and that, in pursuance of that policy, the Germans had established a ghetto in Serniki. In September 1942 hundreds of its inhabitants had been murdered by a German execution squad and their bodies had been exhumed in June–July 1990. Polyukhovich also agreed that he had been born in Serniki, but maintained that at the time of the alleged offences, in 1942, he'd been living in Alexandrovo about six kilometres from Serniki. His father was Timofey. His mother was Eva. He had five brothers and sisters. By the time of the liquidation he'd separated from his first wife. Finally, Polyukhovich agreed that he'd emigrated to Australia in 1949 with Maria Andreyevna and her two children. He'd become an Australian citizen in 1958.

———

On the third day Michael David applied for a mistrial after Milton Turk slipped in a comment during his evidence. Turk had expressed the view that where Ivanechko was 'you didn't want to be'. Cox, however, wasn't convinced this warranted such drastic action. They continued.

Early in the trial the court was moved to complete silence as Nathan Bobrov senior described the last time he'd seen his mother. The proud, stern man had struggled to speak, pausing for a minute or more before finding the strength to move on. Each person in court had seen his pain as he recalled his mother's instructions to run to safety.

———

The prosecution had to 'cleanse' many of their witnesses before allowing them in court. The witnesses were told that, although they'd given evidence of many offences during the committal, there was a lot of evidence that the judge had decided they couldn't repeat in the trial. Nathan Bobrov junior wasn't allowed to describe Alter Botvinik's death. Dmitry Kostyukhovich had become an evidentiary eunuch, and Big Ivan was instructed not to accuse Polyukhovich of murdering the three people in the field. They were angry at being muzzled, but remained controlled and resigned in court.

'Well, I'm here now,' Big Ivan had told investigator Reid. 'Whatever you want me to do I'll do.'

Several times Reid would watch anxiously as the witnesses worked their way through their testimony. No, you're going to go too far, he'd think. You're not going to stop. And then the witness would stop exactly where he or she had been told to stop.

Reid would lecture each of them before they went into court. 'Don't look at Polyukhovich. Don't say anything to him. Just walk straight past him, go into the witness box and, when you've finished, don't look at him. Just walk straight to me and out the back door.'

For Abe Dinerman, however, the emotions were too great. Dinerman had suffered from nightmares for a year since giving evidence at the committal. He stared intently at Polyukhovich as he walked into the court. Dinerman was the last witness for the day. When he finished his evidence, he got down from the witness box, stopped in front of the accused and exploded with emotion. He demanded to know how Polyukhovich could have done these things. The jury had just left but Justice Cox was still there. Reid leapt up and quickly took Dinerman outside.

Ivan Mikhailovich took the stand two days later. He'd always been a supporting member of the cast but on 1 April 1993 he decided to elevate himself to the status of a main player. Ivan's evidence related to the ghetto round-up. He'd consistently said, since the first interviews with the Special Investigations Unit, that he had not seen Ivanechko escorting the Jews. Now he recalled seeing Ivanechko with three other policemen forcing Jewish families from their homes.

Investigator Reid and defence lawyer David were suddenly listening more intently. But prosecutor Niemann didn't pursue Ivan Mikhailovich's statement, which seemed to be referring to the morning of the massacre.

David began his cross-examination slowly and pleasantly. 'Just one thing I am a little confused about. I think you have said that Ivanechko, during the German occupation was a forest ranger, is that right?'

'Yes,' Ivan Mikhailovich answered.

'You also told the court that in 1942 you saw him acting as a policeman, in a policeman's uniform. Is that right?'

'First he was a forest guard and then he joined the police force,' Ivan said.

David took his time and then asked, 'Are you saying to the court that on the day of the liquidation, he was one of the people escorting the Jews?'

'Yes, yes, I saw it.'

Oh no, I'll kill him, Reid thought.

David hadn't finished setting the scene. A couple more questions and it would be time for the kill. 'You have told us about a time . . . in Serniki when he was with other policemen.'

'It was in the market later. It was the day where the Jews were forced out of the ghetto,' Ivan said.

'That's right, and that was the day that you watched them being taken off to be liquidated, is that right?'

'Yes.'

'And you saw Ivanechko in Serniki on that day, is that correct?'

'Yes, from the market place I could see it.'

Now it was time. 'About a year ago, on 30 March 1992, do you remember coming to Australia to give evidence in this case?' David asked.

Ivan remembered, but he couldn't remember being asked whether he'd seen Ivanechko at the round-up. He also couldn't remember saying that he had *not* seen the forester take part. 'Maybe I was wrong,' he said.

David asked him if he could remember telling Reid in March 1990 that he hadn't seen Ivanechko at the round-up.

'Maybe it was so, maybe,' said Ivan.

'But you now say he was there?' asked David.

'Yes, I say he was there.'

David suggested that perhaps Ivan had been right three years ago and was wrong now.

'Okay, let's say it was my error, maybe, maybe, yes,' Ivan said. 'Let it be the way it used to be three years ago.'

But David wasn't going to let it be. 'We don't want to let it be the way it used to be. In fairness, what do you say – having heard what I have put to you – the situation was? Was he there or was he not?'

'I must suggest he was.' But a moment later Ivan changed his mind again. 'No, he wasn't there. Let it be so.'

'What you said in court today, namely that Ivanechko was there, is not correct,' David said.

'It was my mistake, probably, maybe he wasn't there because I was far away on the other side of the river.'

Ivan Mikhailovich left the court despondently. The prosecution team knew that his performance would reflect badly on all the Ukrainian witnesses.

———

Four days later one of the women in the jury wept openly as Fyodor Polyukhovich described the murder of the miller's daughter and the two children.

Fyodor said that the men conscripted to fill in the grave told the police that they should cover these latest three bodies themselves. Then he said, 'I heard the policemen telling people, "We covered them, continue filling in the pit." So we returned back to the edge of the pit and continued shovelling in the earth . . . All of a sudden I saw the earth moving and a child's voice could be heard from underneath, something like, "Mamma," and I couldn't see anything more after that. I almost lost my consciousness and I began to cry because, well, if it were an old person and guilty of something it would be maybe different, but it was a child.'

This was the sort of emotional evidence the defence feared.

The next day James told Fyodor that he wished to show him some photographs. David objected. These were the photographs seized from Polyukhovich's home. Several of the witnesses had already identified them as being of Polyukhovich. Justice Cox had said weeks earlier that he would consider whether Fyodor should be allowed to see them after hearing his evidence. David now contended that Fyodor's credentials simply weren't good enough. While other witnesses who'd known Ivanechko well were qualified to say whether or not they recognised him from the photos, Fyodor clearly wasn't. Fyodor had admitted seeing Ivanechko once or twice from a distance of between one hundred and two hundred metres. On one other occasion Fyodor had looked through the window of a house at Ivanechko's wedding reception. There was a real risk, David warned, that Fyodor would pick out the correct person in the photographs only because he remembered viewing the photo-boards that Cox had ruled out of the trial.

Cox said it was a borderline case and consequently he had to rule in favour of the defence. James asked if Fyodor could make an in-court identification. Cox refused to allow it.

The prosecution would now have to rely on circumstantial evidence to link the accused with the person Fyodor described as Ivanechko.

It was Sunday afternoon and Reid was reading in his apartment. The phone rang. It was Mira Grinberg, one of the Special Investigations Unit translators. Dmitry Kostyukhovich had collapsed in the car park outside his motel.

When Reid got there an ambulance was parked outside. Kostyukhovich had suffered a fit and needed to be admitted to the Royal Adelaide Hospital. Reid and Stas Kostesky would go with him. Stas was the translator and guide who'd told the investigators about the radiation clock in

Rovno so long ago. He'd travelled with the Ukrainians as one of their translators.

Reid, Kostesky and Kostyukhovich were left alone for a while in the hospital's casualty area, and then another seizure gripped the old man. Reid's brother was an epileptic, so he knew what to do, but Stas had never seen anything like this before.

'Stas, hold his hand,' Reid said. 'Put his hand down on the bed. Don't grip it so tight, you'll break his arm. He's gonna be really, really strong. Just hold it so it doesn't hit the sides of the cot.'

Reid had turned to look for the nurses when he heard a thud. 'Stas are you okay? Stas?'

Stas had fainted.

The medical staff came running in. Kostyukhovich soon fell into a deep sleep, but fifteen minutes later he was convulsing again. Eventually the staff drugged him. Reid left after telling Kostesky to stay at the hospital and call him if anything went wrong.

The next day Reid took one of the Ukrainian women to see Kostyukhovich; that night he returned to the hospital, where Kostesky swapped shifts with the other Ukrainian translator, Igor Milyukov. Just after midnight Reid received a call from the hospital. He could hear Kostyukhovich screaming in the background.

He arrived to find the Ukrainian restrained by the arms and legs. Igor explained that Kostyukhovich had been running through the wards screaming that 'they' intended to kill him. Kostyukhovich didn't recognise Reid, and was convinced that Igor was an American spy who spoke very good Russian. The staff pumped him full of drugs again, telling Reid that he should be asleep in half an hour. Two hours later, Kostyukhovich was still pulling at his restraints and shouting at the top of his voice.

'That should have downed a water buffalo,' the nurse told Reid, pointing to the drugs.

'Yeah, but he's Ukrainian,' the investigator replied.

Kostyukhovich dozed off eventually, and Reid went back to his apartment to win a couple of hours sleep before another day in court. Mid-morning Reid's pager sounded. 'Please ring Royal Adelaide Hospital urgently.'

He could hear Kostyukhovich's screams over the phone again. The doctor, who thought that Kostyukhovich might calm down if he was with his own people, asked Reid to get the patient out of the hospital as quickly as possible.

Reid walked in to the hospital to find Kostyukhovich sitting in a crowded ward talking to an elderly man named Walt. Neither Walt nor Kostyukhovich seemed to have any idea what the other was talking about, but neither seemed to mind. Kostyukhovich saw Reid. 'You are here to kill me, are you?' Kostyukhovich asked.

'No, I don't want to kill you,' Reid answered. The policeman denied the allegation as though people accused him of murder every day.

'We're going home,' Reid told Kostyukhovich.

'No we're not,' he answered.

Kostyukhovich refused to enter the elevator, so Reid and Igor walked him down eight floors and dragged him towards the car.

'You've got a pistol!' Kostyukhovich exclaimed.

'I haven't got a pistol,' Reid said.

'I've seen it and you're taking me out to shoot me in the forest!' Kostyukhovich shouted. He had regressed to his partisan days.

'I'm not going to kill you. Search me!' Reid said.

Kostyukhovich searched Reid; the old soldier still remembered all the places a person could hide a gun.

Kostyukhovich seemed to calm down in the car and Reid hoped he'd be fine once he was back with the other witnesses. When they got to the motel, however, Reid realised the witnesses had all been taken on an excursion. He opened the car door and Kostyukhovich bolted. Igor, Reid and the son of the motel owner caught and subdued Kostyukhovich. Then Reid remembered that Stepan Sidorovich was on call as the next witness. Sidorovich should be around somewhere. Kostyukhovich calmed down when he saw Sidorovich, but refused to go into his room. He began to accuse Sidorovich of being a 'collaborator'. Suddenly Kostyukhovich leapt up onto some frame-work attached to the fence outside his room. On the other side a dog began barking viciously, but the old man was nearly over the top of the fence when Sidorovich, considered the slowest-moving of the witnesses, grabbed Kostyukhovich's ankle. As Sidorovich lost his grip, Reid grabbed Kostyukhovich's leg. As Kostyukhovich was dragged back down, he grabbed Reid's thumb and pulled it back. There was a cracking sound, and Reid winced. Sidorovich realised that the policeman had been hurt and decided the nonsense had to stop. He belted Kostyukhovich.

Kostyukhovich was exhausted by the time the doctor arrived. Reid was showing him the medals on his coat. When the doctor tried to take his blood pressure, Kostyukhovich told her to go ahead and kill him, if that's what she was going to do. He was too tired to fight any more. He slept the rest of the day in his room.

That night Reid went with Stas Kostesky to the old man's room to see if he was all right.

'Hello Bob. How are you?' Kostyukhovich asked. His voice was frail.

'It's time for dinner. Are you going to come up for some dinner?' Reid asked.

'Yes, I'd like some dinner. I'm a little bit hungry. Did you take me to the hospital?'

'Yeah, you were very, very sick.'

'Oh, thank you very much. What happened to your hand?' Kostyukhovich was pointing to Reid's now bandaged hand.

'I got drunk last night and fell over.'

'You shouldn't drink so much, I've told you that you shouldn't be drinking,' Kostyukhovich scolded.

Stas started to tell Kostyukhovich what had happened. Reid told him to shut up.

———

A few days later Bob Reid was standing with the Ukrainians at the air-port. They'd given what evidence they could and would be leaving in a few moments. Kostyukhovich was crying.

'That's enough of that,' Reid told him.

The old soldier composed himself.

Reid had tried hard not to think about this moment. Whenever it had occurred to him that he'd probably never see them again after they left, he'd pushed the thought to the back of his mind. Several of them had said, 'You must come and visit,' and of course Reid had agreed. Now Big Ivan stood in front of him. He was a very practical man who didn't suffer from any false hopes. He was upset.

'Well,' said Big Ivan, 'this is the last time I'll ever see you.'

'No, no, don't be silly. I'll come over and see you,' Reid said, refusing to be morbid.

'Why?' asked Big Ivan.

'Well, I'd like to come back,' Reid explained.

Ivan looked at him and said, 'There's far better places to go than Serniki.'

———

On 14 April Michael David told Justice Cox that the defence had found another reason to stop the case from proceeding. Junior defence lawyer Craig Caldicott had just returned from Ukraine, where he'd visited and interviewed Polyukhovich's first wife, Maria Stepanovna. A few days ago she'd signed a statement that showed she could provide evidence vital to the defence. David said that her account contradicted important parts of the testimony given by the two key witnesses, Fyodor Polyukhovich and Sergei Potapovich. Unfortunately she was confined to her room in Serniki. It would be unfair, said David, to try his client without the jury hearing the evidence of the first wife. The trial should stop. Greg James said that the prosecution didn't accept Maria Stepanovna as a truthful witness but that the offer to take evidence in Ukraine remained. Her evidence could be taken on video and played back to the jury.

The next day the judge said that he couldn't stop the case from proceeding while the possibility of taking the evidence in Ukraine existed, no matter how much the defence disliked this type of hearing. David then asked Cox to authorise an on-commission hearing and the judge agreed. Cox would go to Serniki, along with Powell, Caldicott, James and Reid. David was happy to stay in Adelaide.

Before the trip could happen, however, it would have to be organised, and then it would probably take a week to get there, get the evidence and return. The defence still planned to ask Cox to find that there was no case to answer when the prosecution had finished its evidence. If that was accepted, there'd be no need for this special hearing to take place. Meanwhile the jury wouldn't be told what had been discussed.

———

Historian Konrad Kwiet was half a day into his evidence for the prosecution when the jury were told to leave the courtroom. They'd spend nearly all of the next two days cooling their heels in the jury room while the lawyers sorted out how much the professor would be allowed to say regarding the involvement of foresters in the execution of 'the final solution'.

Five months after the end of the committal hearing, Anna Terebun, the director of the Brest archive in Eastern Europe, had contacted the Special Investigations Unit with news of the discovery of previously unexamined documents. They related to the control of forests in German-occupied Ukraine. Kwiet had spent four days in late December examining the documents. He'd incorporated his findings in a statement where he outlined his conviction that foresters had played an 'integral part' in the war-time German administration. Kwiet wrote that the German army had used local foresters as scouts in the early battles with partisans and that they'd become indispensable auxiliaries to the local police, the ss and the army. The German foresters simply hadn't had the numbers to do their job without help, and relied heavily on their Ukrainian, Russian and Polish staff. Like the local police officer, the local forester had been given an armband which showed he was working for the Germans. A special uniform had also been issued to foresters. Forest wardens and guards, however, had belonged to the lowest-ranking group of workers.

Kwiet wrote that there could be no doubt that the forestry administration's role had been to pacify and exploit the occupied territory. It had been there, he said, 'to represent the interest of the Reich'. The forester's job had been to administer timber, a very important raw material, but he'd also carried out a police function and this had been closely related to the repressive German policy towards the region. 'In forest areas, foresters, forest wardens and gamekeepers often appeared as the sole protectors of the German kind of law and order,' Kwiet's statement read.

Foresters had been linked with the persecution of Jewish people in at least two ways. They'd supervised Jews conscripted to work at sawmills and they'd possessed an intimate knowledge of the woods which hid escaped Jews. Jews found in the aftermath of a ghetto-liquidation were killed, Kwiet wrote. 'These killings did not appear to be subject to the usual restrictions on the use of weapons.'

Kwiet claimed that foresters had taken part in the mopping up operations carried out by police in forest regions after ghetto liquidations. While this hadn't been outside their general role as pacifiers, special arrangements had needed to be put in place before foresters could take part in the rounding up, guarding and killing of Jews from ghettos.

Kwiet said that the name 'Ivan Polyukhovich' had appeared in a list of 330 workers in the Stolin Forestry Inspectorate – a part of German-occupied Ukraine – in January 1942. In March 1943 the name 'Johann Poluchowitsch', also written as 'Johans Poluchowitsch', 'Hans Polucho-witsch' and 'Johann Poluchowich', had appeared on application forms for ration cards. This person had been described as a member of the Forestry

Protection Commando. These forms had been found in the Brest archive.

As the Germans had been forced to abandon vast areas, the centres that they still controlled filled with refugees. Kwiet said that among those who came to Pinsk were Ivan and Mariya Polyukhovich. As the German fortunes had waned, the civil authorities had sent local employees, including foresters, to Germany. These people had been given papers stressing their wholehearted commitment to the German war effort. In March 1944 'Johann Polichowicz' came to Stade in Germany and was issued with a workbook.

It was up to Justice Cox to decide how much of this material would be admissible in the criminal court. An historian assesses evidence in a different way from a judge. The historian deals in generalities, but the judge must always keep in mind that a single individual will end up carrying the weight of any allegations. Cox had to make sure general statements were not unfairly placed around Polyukhovich's neck like some academic hangman's noose. David worked hard to limit the professor as much as possible and finally a formula was worked out. Cox warned Kwiet not to stray outside the guidelines he eventually imposed.

'I was already warned about this approach,' Kwiet answered the judge. The professor was clearly unimpressed that he was being placed in an intellectual strait-jacket.

'That's right,' Cox told him. 'The battle is over now and it is most important Professor Kwiet, I want to emphasise this, that in your answers you keep within the limits of that formula. Did you hear? You heard the formula? I will repeat it because it could be very serious if you strayed outside it.'

Kwiet could tell the jury only that the historical documents tendered in court showed that the Germans had sometimes been helped by local people, and not just the police, when they carried out their policy of exterminating the Jews. There were recorded instances of local forest wardens or guards helping in this way, but no record of any local forest warden or guard taking part in a pit killing.

'I want to say something more to Professor Kwiet,' the judge said. 'That formula is the result of a lot of debate you have heard . . . It is my responsibility to say what may or may not be said in evidence and there are limits according the rules which bind me, bind the parties and bind the witnesses, and it is very important in front of the jury that these guidelines be obeyed by counsel and by the witness. So do you understand you can't go outside that?'

'This is the strict limits in which I have to answer?' asked Kwiet, not hiding his distaste.

'Yes,' said Cox.

'Even if I disagree?'

'Yes you probably do disagree. You probably think the evidence shows more than that.'

'That's correct,' Kwiet said.

Cox said that he didn't think there was enough evidence to allow a jury to hear all of Kwiet's views and that that was the end of the matter. Kwiet asked whether, rather than saying there was no record of a forester taking part in a pit killing, he could say 'no record had been found'. But Cox thought that would carry a sinister overtone.

———

Investigator Bob Reid was the last witness in the prosecution case. His evidence was dominated by the recordings made on the day of Polyukhovich's arrest. The jury listened to the audio tape made at the house and then watched the video of the interview at the Australian Federal Police headquarters. The latter showed Reid sitting at a long pine-coloured table. Behind him, partially concealed, was investigator Bruce Huggett. Opposite them was Polyukhovich. Next to him was the translator. In the background a clock hung on the wall next to a map of Australia. The jury watched this scene for the rest of the afternoon.

David's cross-examination the next day was very brief. Reid conceded that the first time he'd heard Fyodor talk of hearing the sound 'Mamma' coming from beneath the ground was at the trial. The prosecution closed and the judge sent the jury home with the instruction to watch the newspaper to find out when they'd be needed next. The jury wasn't told the reason for this, but the defence had told the judge that it was again going to ask him to stop the case from proceeding.

Before Justice Cox began hearing submissions he raised the issue of the on-commission hearing in Ukraine. He understood that the accused didn't want to go to Serniki. 'Am I right about that?' Cox asked.

'Yes,' David answered.

'I don't want to go,' a voice said.

It was Polyukhovich. Apart from the words 'not guilty', this was the only time he spoke during the whole of the trial.

———

David told the judge that it was time for him to direct the jury to hand down verdicts of not guilty. If he wasn't prepared to do that, he should at least let the jurors know that they could, if they wanted, acquit Polyukhovich before hearing any evidence from the defence. The queen's counsel said that the allegation Polyukhovich had aided the massacre at the pit by ordering towels and water to be brought to the scene was clearly inadequate. A lot of preparation had been put into the ghastly massacre. To talk about a single person who was there encouraging it was absurd. It was also apparent that the prosecution could now offer no direct identification of the defendant regarding the pit killing. Sergei Potapovich hadn't identified him from any photos; nor had there been any in-court identification from this key witness. As for Fyodor's testimony, David said that witness's recognition wasn't sufficient. With the photo-board gone and an in-court identification ruled out, it was based only on Fyodor claiming that the person he'd seen at the pit was the man he'd seen at the defendant's wedding reception. That had been fifty years ago and through a window. Fyodor claimed also to have had two other 'glimpses' of the defendant.

The legal argument continued until late on Friday afternoon.

The following Tuesday, 23 April 1993, Cox found that there was still a case to answer on each of the charges. He refused to tell the jury that they could deliver not guilty verdicts without hearing any more evidence. Then the court adjourned again for another twenty-four hours. After a week's absence, the jury would be brought back, only to be told they wouldn't be needed for at least another week.

'Good morning ladies and gentlemen,' the judge told the long-suffering jury.

They seemed to have spent as much time out of court as they had hearing evidence. Polyukhovich's poor health had caused some of the delay, but legal argument had been mostly to blame. The jurors had hardly started the trial with a spring in their step. Six weeks later they looked fed up. And then the judge told them the trial would be interrupted again.

'I have been asked to suspend the trial while further investigations are made in the Ukraine,' he said. 'Obviously that's an unusual thing to do but this is an unusual trial. It's very unusual.'

Justice Cox said that the trial wouldn't proceed for the rest of the week. In fact the earliest it was likely to resume was Monday week, 10 May 1993. Until then they were free to go about their normal duties.

The jury foreman, a portly man with a beard, stood up. 'Does Mr David have an estimation of the length of his case?' he asked. 'Our employers would be interested.'

David got up quickly and said he couldn't say, because the matters were beyond his control. The defence, however, wouldn't take as long as the prosecution.

The foreman didn't look impressed.

Cox raised another matter. He said that the charges had to be amended in a technical fashion but the jurors were not to worry. 'I will be astonished if anything turns on the difference,' Cox told them.

The jury didn't look at all astonished.

David had second thoughts about guessing the length of his case. Better not to get an obviously annoyed jury offside by giving the impression that he couldn't say or didn't care. He told them that he'd need no more than four days.

————

Michael David walked out of the court building onto the footpath.

'Where's Craig?' he demanded impatiently.

His partner Lindy Powell shrugged her shoulders and tapped the ash off her cigarette. Investigator Bob Reid took a puff of his cigarette and looked down the street. Each of them had returned from Ukraine within the last three days. They looked desperately tired. Reid had come back a day early with the video of Maria Stepanovna's evidence and spent the weekend working on the transcript with Ann Sutherland, one of the defence staff. The video had been given to defence solicitor Craig Caldicott and prosecution solicitor Rocky Perrotta, who were to edit it.

The jury had been kept waiting all morning; finally they were told that the video wouldn't be ready for some time and they should come back at 2.15. It was now nearly three and there was no sign of the video.

David walked back inside. He wanted to give the impression that the defence team were clean, concise and, above all, swift. This jury had been messed about too much by delays and now the defence were keeping them waiting.

Moments later, Caldicott and Perrotta walked around the corner and were ushered into the court. But there was a problem. In their haste they'd chopped out a portion of the evidence that should have been kept in. It would just have to be read to the jury. The solution was messy, but it would have to do. The jury could not be kept waiting any longer.

David apologised to the jurors for the delay and explained the significance of what they were about to view. He told the jury that, although it was now some time since they'd heard the evidence, they would remember that the only witness to count one – the pit killing – was Sergei Potapovich. That witness alleged that he'd seen the accused help the Germans by arranging for a bucket of water, towels and chairs to be brought to the mass grave. Sergei claimed that, at the time, he'd been with Maria Stepanovna's brother. When they'd gone to Maria's home to get the items requested by Ivanechko they'd seen Maria and her mother.

'Ladies and gentlemen, the evidence you will hear from Maria Stepanovna is that no such thing happened,' David said confidently. 'It is just untrue.'

He said that Maria also had important evidence to give regarding Fyodor Polyukhovich. Fyodor claimed that he'd seen Ivanechko wearing a suit on the night Ivanechko married Maria. This was important because it established Fyodor's credentials to recognise the accused later at the pit. But the woman herself was adamant that her husband had never worn a jacket on the day of their wedding. So the jury had to be suspicious about exactly who Fyodor had seen at the wedding and, by inference, who he'd seen at the execution of the miller's daughter in the pit.

Polyukhovich poured himself a glass of water. He was about to see his first wife for the first time in half a century.

A loud hum poured out of the television speakers and then a tiny woman appeared on each of the sets spread around the court. She sat on the edge of her bed. She was the size of a small child, but looked terribly old, with a bright red shawl draped over her head like an ancient Red Riding Hood. White daylight shone through a window behind her, forcing the video camera to adjust and make the room appear even darker than it had at the time.

Powell winced as she heard her own voice, horribly distorted, ask the first question. It seemed a pity that after spending so much money gathering this last piece of evidence, the lawyers hadn't thought to hire a professional camera-and-sound person. The old woman shouted her answers; her right hand shook uncontrollably until she stuck it under her left armpit.

The Powell in the video asked the name of the man the witness had married.

Maria Stepanovna's voice became high-pitched. 'Ivan – Timofey,' she managed slowly.

'Surname?' Powell asked.

Maria's right hand was shaking again. 'Polyukhovich,' she said. The witness explained that she had met Ivanechko only shortly before they were married. She'd been seventeen. 'I was engaged, poor me,' she said. 'When I saw him my thought was he is not handsome; I wouldn't like to marry him.'

Powell wanted to know about the wedding and Polyukhovich's wedding clothes.

'No, there was no jacket, only shirt,' Maria said. 'I asked him why don't you have a jacket and he said "It's not looking very nice, it's rather old." '

Maria remembered that it had rained at dusk on the day of their wedding and that the wreath and dress she wore were wet as they walked from the church to her father's house just outside Serniki. She insisted Polyukhovich hadn't worn a jacket. He'd worn a beautiful shirt but not his old jacket.

Regarding the morning of the liquidation, Maria said her brother Ivan – Sergei's alleged companion on the day of the massacre – hadn't slept at home for about two weeks before the massacre and hadn't been there during that day. She insisted that she and the rest of her family had spent the day hiding in a ditch face down after being warned that the Jews were all about to be killed.

'At any time during the course of that day, did anyone come and ask your mother for water or towels or chairs?' Powell asked.

'No, no, no, it didn't happen, because I was with my mother all the time. It didn't happen.'

Powell asked if Sergei came into her yard that day.

'He never, never came to our yard. He didn't used to come to our place that Sergei.'

Now prosecutor James's voice was heard asking Maria if she remembered any other foresters, but she said no to each of the names he suggested until he mentioned Stroinyak, Grytsevich.

'I don't know where he is, that Grytsevich,' Maria answered.

The SIU had actually traced this man Stroinyak to Adelaide. He had lived in the same suburb as Polyukhovich but had died some time ago.

James showed Maria several photographs and asked if she recognised her husband.

'I don't know him, I don't want to know about him, I throw him out of my mind because he's got involved with another woman. He's not in my head anymore. I forget his face.'

'Did you know a man named Polivnyk?' James asked her.

'I don't know him, I don't know anybody. You should ask some smarter people. I'm a silly old woman.'

'Should we ask your brother Vasil?' asked James. Vasil was in the house.

'Why should you ask?' Maria demanded. 'Why should you involve him?'

A moment later, James asked, 'You have been very concerned, haven't you, to keep your family separate and away from Ivanechko?'

'Well, when we separated, did I think about him? Could I think about him? I didn't need him any more after that.'

A few moments later this woman, who seemed to have led such a miserable life, finished her evidence with better memories – spoken, it seemed, more for herself than for the lawyers. 'Ivanechko used to take money to the forest and he paid people and people, of course, were eager and were happy to earn something. And they respected him very much and he respected people. They loved him because he provided them with a job. I remember that event, even because people were singing when they were coming back from the forest in the evening. All the workers were so happy, they were singing songs . . . Under Soviet rule, people were paid a lot.'

And then the screens were blank and the loud hum was silenced.

It was nearly finished. All that remained was for the lawyers to give their final addresses and for Cox to sum up the trial to the jury. Then there'd be a verdict.

Greg James took more than a day to sum up the prosecution case and argue its merits. He began on 12 May 1993. The decades which separated the trial from war-time Serniki made it difficult to mount a case; the adjournments which had dragged the trial out made it difficult to maintain any momentum. James was conscious that so many of the crucial witnesses who'd given evidence weeks before must now be just dim memories to the jurors. He faced the task of recounting the evidence without boring and alienating the already weary jury.

James told the jury time had been a handicap for the prosecution, which had to prove its case beyond reasonable doubt, but not for the defence, which had to prove nothing. He reminded them that Polyukhovich had been identified in court and from photographs by eight witnesses, some of them Jewish, others Ukrainians. 'An enormous procession of witnesses' – including Polyukhovich's first wife – had given evidence that his name was Ivanechko and that no-one else in the area had used that name. As well, there was evidence from witnesses and from documents that proved he'd been a forester.

'There is simply nothing left, no challenge, no dispute, no suggestion of any dispute, that this accused was Ivanechko,' said James. 'That leaves little room in this case for any real issue to be drawn except whether Sergei Potapovich and Fyodor Grigoryevich on that dreadful day in Serniki got it right when they say he was present ... when they say that the person they saw do these things was Ivanechko.'

Much of James's address focused on the statements Polyukhovich had made during the interview with SIU investigators Reid and Huggett on the day of his arrest. James said that Polyukhovich had portrayed himself as merely a 'humble forester' who'd had nothing to do with the police or the Germans and had been either in Germany, Pinsk or the nearby town of Alexandrovo at the time of the offences. But there was a wealth of evidence to show that Polyukhovich had gone to Serniki during the occupation. The official documents retrieved from the former Soviet archives placed Polyukhovich in the nearby town of Alexandrovo at least between January 1942 and March 1943. One document showed a list of people who'd arrived in Pinsk from 20 October to 15 November 1943 – after the time of the alleged offences. It contained the names Ivan and Maria Polyukhovich. Next to their names had been the years 1916 and 1918, the years of Ivanechko's and Maria Andreyevna's births. It was obvious Polyukhovich had been in the area at the time of the offences, contrary to what he'd suggested to the Special Investigations Unit.

Polyukhovich had told the SIU that he'd gone to the forest twice a week to look around, but hadn't liked to report people for offences because there were heavy fines. 'If that's his duties, what's he doing with a gun?' James demanded to know. 'What's he doing in those circumstances in Serniki with a gun?'

The prosecutor said Polyukhovich had claimed that the allegations were propaganda, but this was nonsense. The prosecution witnesses had come from all over the world. James said that Polyukhovich had made this accusation at a time when he'd also declined to recognise his own photograph, his own signature and his own processing documents. He'd claimed that he'd only been married once – to Maria Andreyevna, his present wife. Polyukhovich had told a 'pack of lies'. He'd lied during the interview when he'd stated that he hadn't known about the ghetto. He'd lied when he'd said that the allegations against him were made up by people he'd caught stealing wood. There was no suggestion that the two chief witnesses, Sergei or Fyodor, had ever been caught stealing wood.

After waiting so long to hear Maria Stepanovna's evidence, James said that the jury might have felt a little disappointed. She had recalled that Ivanechko sometimes had grown feed on his land to supplement his income. This tended to support Sergei's assertion that Ivanechko had supplied feed for the German horses. But, James suggested, this first wife couldn't be trusted entirely. She'd consistently shown she wasn't prepared to remember anything about Ivanechko from the moment he'd left her. She'd also detached herself and her family from the events at the pit. Maria Stepanovna was adamant that she wasn't in her house when the Jews were being killed. There was a problem, however, with this. If she had spent the day hiding, how could she be so sure that Sergei and her brother had not gone to her house to get the water? Maria Stepanovna couldn't have it both ways. Besides, she hadn't challenged Sergei's central allegation that it had been Ivanechko who ordered him, on the day of the massacre, to get the towels and water.

James argued that Polyukhovich had shown some authority when he'd allowed Sergei and Ivan Stepanovna to stay at the pit. 'If the accused was simply the forester in Alexandrovo, then what was he doing at the pit?' asked James. 'What was he doing allowing the boys to stand by?'

Both Sergei and Fyodor had refuted Polyukhovich's claim that he'd not been in Serniki at the time of the liquidation. They'd recognised him at a time when Polish conscriptions had cut the number of eligible males living in the already small community. Their testimony had been supported by the forensic evidence and other descriptions of the ghetto round-up.

Aware the defence would try to exploit the fact that Sergei had not seen the killing of the miller's daughter and the two children as described by Fyodor, James tried to paint a picture of what it must have been like at the pit. There would have been one hundred, maybe two hundred conscripted men working among the piles of sand heaped next to the grave. Consequently these men would only have been aware of what was happening close by. They would have done their work as quickly as possible while under the watchful eye of German officers. It wasn't surprising that Sergei hadn't seen the incident described by Fyodor. It seemed that they were at different ends of the pit. But, in that situation of heightened perception, wasn't it likely that if they had seen the face of the man they'd known as Ivanechko it would be imprinted on their minds forever? There was no reason to doubt that Fyodor had seen the incident or to think he was wrong when he said Ivanechko was at the pit with the miller's daughter. On this last allegation Fyodor had been rock-solid. Apart from the issue of whether or not Polyukhovich had worn a jacket, Fyodor's description of the wedding reception also fitted nicely with Maria Stepanovna's own recollections. Indeed, James argued, the defence questions had tended to concentrate on guns, hats, uniforms, noises and glances, rather than the identifiability of Ivanechko's face.

'What are the essential matters?' James asked. 'They are very simple, very simple indeed. Ivanechko did those acts and this accused is Ivanechko.'

———

Michael David began his final address for the defence by saying that he'd be as brief as possible. He told the jury how difficult their task was – enquiring about events of fifty years ago through interpreters, events which had occurred in a foreign country during the second world war. For those over fifty, to remember back fifty years would seem impossible. 'For those of us who are fifty or under it's something that is out of our experience.'

David said that juries were selected because they possess the 'collective experiences of the community'. 'They come together with their accumulated knowledge of the society they live in and give a decision on facts that deal with our society. Well, we haven't got that benefit here because, of course, we are talking about a society that took place and existed fifty years ago and, indeed, in a sense, doesn't exist any more because it existed during a time of war.'

The jury had the problem of judging people's behaviour during a time of war from a position of peace and stability. 'I don't hide behind any of that, but they are factors that we must realise and bear in mind when we are making decisions about this case, decisions about the accuracy of witnesses, and decisions about where the truth lies.'

David had skilfully raised the philosophical arguments that challenged whether an Australian European war crimes trial could ever be fair. Having planted that seed, he'd told the jury that was not Polyukhovich's defence. It was simply a fact of life.

The prosecution had argued that the long delay was only a handicap to them and not the defence. That wasn't true. If the defendant had been accused of a crime committed a year ago, he'd be able to think of people he'd been with and provide accurate answers to the authorities. Polyukhovich had simply said, 'I didn't do it'.

'What else is he going to say?' David asked the jury. 'How on earth could he go into any more detail than that? You see, the prosecutor has said, "No problems for the defence. Everything's all right," and, in the next breath and for the greater part of his address, he has pilloried the accused for the inaccuracies he has made during that record of interview. Give him credit. He said, "No, I wasn't there," straight away.'

David said that it was much more difficult for a man nearly eighty to defend himself than for someone younger. 'There's matters of intellect, memory, health, nerves, strain, the fog of time.'

With great courtesy David reminded the jury that they mustn't dwell on things they shouldn't consider. 'This is not a trial about whether the Holocaust took place. We are not debating history . . . This case is about two specific charges . . . It is a very simple case with a lot of extraneous padding. But it's pretty simple: he was there at the pit, or he wasn't. We are not concerned so much about documents of the International Refugee Organisation and how he came to Australia.'

David said that it might be tempting for the jury to think this case was a 'pretty big deal'. Would all of this effort, all of this money, be spent, if they didn't have the right bloke? But to think like that would be danger-ous and unfair. 'Because we don't know what reasons the government might have for passing this legislation, for someone being charged . . .

There may be many agendas of an international nature that might have caused the government to pass its legislation.'

The lawyer said that actual evidence of who'd been seen at the grave was pitiful. Neither of the two key witnesses had said that the person whom they saw at the grave was the accused. While some witnesses had pointed to Polyukhovich in court, others had identified him from photographs. Sergei and Fyodor, however, didn't fall into these categories.

'Let's say there's no doubt about the accused being Ivanechko,' said David. 'Let's say there is no doubt that there is only one Ivanechko in the area . . . That's fine ladies and gentlemen. That doesn't mean that if any other witness in the case just mentions or bandies the name "Ivanechko" fifty years later and says, "That's Ivanechko, can't describe him, can't tell you any details of him but it was Ivanechko," therefore it is necessarily him. It is absurd. That is all they have done – bandied the name "Ivanechko" around and said, "The person we saw had that name." '

David said that Sergei appeared simply to be talking about another man. Sergei had said that the 'Ivanechko' he'd seen at the pit had worked for several months supplying feed for the German horses. There wasn't one line of evidence from any other witness to suggest that the accused had such a job. Every other witness had said there was no permanent German garrison in the ghetto. Professor Kwiet had said that there was no permanent presence in Serniki until after March 1943. The defence questioned whether Sergei had even been at the pit. His description of the rabbi, viewed from two hundred metres away, a distance longer than an Australian Rules football oval, smacked of unreality. Sergei had initially said that only one person had performed the shooting at the pit. This was plainly nonsense. David said that it was tempting for the defence to dismiss Sergei's allegation by simply asking how a direction to get towels and water could amount to a war crime. But the defence was not arguing that. The defence simply asked, Who had really given that order?

With Fyodor, David said, again all the jury had was the bandying about of the name 'Ivanechko'. 'There will always be a crown case while that name is hanging around the place,' he said. Fyodor had never spoken to the accused. He hadn't even been a guest at the wedding reception used by the prosecution as a previous sighting. The jury might think that Fyodor was also guilty of 'gilding the lily' a bit when he said that he'd heard a voice cry 'Mamma' from beneath the ground. This evidence had emerged for the first time at the trial.

David asked the jury to think about the witness Stepan Sidorovich. He'd given evidence of filling in the grave and knew Ivanechko well enough to identify him from the photographs. Even so, he hadn't seen the forester at the pit. That hole was sixty metres long. The killing of the miller's daughter and the two children was alleged to have occurred near the ramp in the centre. This meant that Stepan Sidorovich could have been no more than thirty metres from the scene described by Fyodor.

What of the gun? David said that there was no doubt Polyukhovich had been a forester and had carried a gun during part of the German occupation. But this was meaningless. The accused had also carried a gun during the Polish and Soviet regimes.

David said that he frankly admitted his client had told one lie. He had been married before his relationship with his present wife. But it was nonsense to say that because Polyukhovich had lied about his marriage, he'd also lied about committing a war crime. The jury might think that for older people, particularly someone from another culture, having had two wives was a very sensitive matter. 'For the crown to almost greedily grab hold of every little detail that an illiterate old man has given during a record of interview of this nature, where he himself has got no assistance, is really the bottom of the pile.'

David said that Polyukhovich had never tried to hide his identity. There had even been correspondence over the years with the people back in the village. As for his job, under the Germans the documents showed that in 1942 Polyukhovich had held the lowest ranking possible for a forester. By March 1943 his ration document showed that he'd been promoted to the next rung.

Finally there was the evidence of Maria Stepanovna. Her evidence did conflict with Sergei's and had to be considered in relation to the 'very strange' identification process involving Fyodor and the wedding reception. Why would she try to help the accused when she obviously wanted nothing to do with him?

'It is my earnest submission to you that a verdict of guilty on any of these counts would be a very savage miscarriage of justice,' David concluded.

———

David had started his final defence address at about midday on Thursday 13 May 1993 but had spilled over to the next day. Justice Cox was very conscious of the time left to him and that Monday was a public holiday. He knew that he wouldn't be very long summing up the trial, but wondered whether he should send the jury out on the Friday. Once out, they couldn't go home and he was reluctant to keep them cooped in over a long weekend. He decided to start his summing up and, towards the end, ask the jury for their preference.

'Some might take the view that it is better to put these things behind us after such a long lapse of time and not pursue people, anyway, for crimes committed, it is said, in another country,' the judge told the jury. 'The other view is that no lapse of time can be too great for bringing to justice anyone who has committed what was really a crime against humanity.'

Cox said that he mentioned this only to say that those issues were matters for parliament, not the court. The jury, the lawyers and he were there only to bring the trial to a conclusion consistent with the evidence and the laws that bound everyone. The jury must put aside the emotions they must have all felt while listening to the evidence and any sympathy they might feel for the accused, who was an old man. Cox reminded them that Polyukhovich had entered the court with the presumption of innocence. The burden of proof – beyond reasonable doubt – lay solely with the prosecution.

Cox said the case against Polyukhovich rested in a large part upon circumstantial evidence. This simply meant that the prosecution was asking the jury to draw inferences or conclusions from proved facts or circumstances rather than base their decisions solely on direct eyewitness accounts. Like eyewitness evidence, circumstantial evidence could be strong or weak or indifferent. But, the judge told the jury, wherever the prosecution tried to use circumstantial evidence it also had to prove that there was no reasonable, innocent explanation to that evidence. If a reasonable, innocent explanation could be produced to explain the circumstantial evidence the jury had to accept the offence had not been proved by the prosecution beyond reasonable doubt.

The judge moved on to the actual evidence given in relation to the two charges against Polyukhovich. He said that he expected the jury would find the prosecution had proved that a large number of people had been killed by, or on the instructions of, the Germans at the pit outside Serniki in about September 1942 and that most, if not all, of them were Jews from the Serniki ghetto. He said that as far as he was aware this was not disputed by the defence.

The judge summed up the crown case. 'As you know, the crown's case on the first count is that the accused, by telling a couple of the villagers to bring water, towels and chairs to the pit, was helping the Germans to carry out their plan of executing the Jews of Serniki.

'As to the second count, the crown says that the accused and two other Ukrainians marched a Jewish woman and two young children into the pit and killed them.'

Cox explained that it wasn't necessary for the prosecution to prove that Polyukhovich had actually fired the shots that killed the miller's daughter and the two children. It would be sufficient for the crown to show that Polyukhovich had actively helped the other two armed men escort the three victims into the pit knowing they would be killed. He also reminded them that while some of the evidence could be used to support both of the charges a conviction on one count would not automatically mean a conviction on the other.

Cox warned the jury to be careful when considering evidence regarding events other than on the day of the pit killing. He used the example of Nathan Bobrov junior, who had described seeing the accused armed with a rifle. On one view of this evidence, Polyukhovich had appeared to be escorting a group of people at gunpoint. Cox said it was important that the jury realise what they could *not* make of this evidence. They could not say that it showed that the accused was the sort of person who might have committed one of the crimes charged against him on the day of the pit killing.

'The most that you could draw from any evidence like that, if you accept it, is that at least at the time deposed to, the accused was armed in a way that might be thought to be inconsistent with the duties of a forester.'

Cox pointed out that simply because a witness might have given different versions on an issue such as the clothing worn by someone at a particular time didn't mean that all of that witness's evidence was worthless.

'In many cases, particularly after this long lapse of time, I would think that you would regard the assessment of many of the witnesses as a matter of degree, that you would make allowances for the lapse of time.'

Cox said experience in the courts had shown juries had to be very careful where a witness claimed to identify someone whom he did not know previously or did not know very well. 'The fact is that mistakes of visual identification have been known to happen, however honest or careful the witness might be,' he said.

'That does not mean that you must automatically disregard the evidence of Fyodor Grigoryevich, for instance, when he says that the man who told him and his companion to fetch the water and towels and chairs was the man he had seen once or twice on a farm at Alexandrovo, whose name he believed was Ivan Timofeyevich Polyukhovich, with the street name Ivanechko – '

Confused looks appeared on some of the jurors' faces and the lawyers moved uncomfortably in their seats. Cox had obviously made a mistake.

He'd mixed up Fyodor's and Sergei's evidence. Sergei was the witness who had claimed that Ivanechko had told him to help fetch the water, towels and chairs. Fyodor had given evidence regarding the miller's daughter and the two children. Cox stopped himself.

'Did I say that was Fyodor?' the judge asked. 'It should be Sergei. You will understand it should have been a reference to Sergei Potapovich. I suppose it was too much to expect that I would get through this trial without confusing those two yet again. All right, you understand the man I am referring to.'

Cox pressed on. His point, he said, was that the jury must consider how well any witness knew the accused, if indeed the witness knew the accused at all. So far as Sergei was concerned the jury would have to consider carefully the opportunity he had to consider the man he said spoke to him at the pit. The jury had to keep in mind the frightening circumstances of the occasion. 'And having in mind also the circumstances of his claimed identification of the same person as the groom through the window – whether he got a good enough look at him, for instance, and whether the man he was looking at was, in fact, the bridegroom, and not simply one of the guests.'

The jurors looked confused again. Cox was again mixing up Sergei and Fyodor. The media reporters stopped taking notes. Some of the journalists had completely lost track of what Cox was saying, and others thought he had made a mistake but were slow to judge him. The judge stopped himself a second time.

'That is confusion again, is it?' the judge said, realising that he had made a mistake. 'Yes, I'm sorry, that was Fyodor. Sergei was the one who says he knew him not at Alexandrovo, but simply as supervisor of the Germans' stable. Anyway, the details are unimportant; the issue is, obviously, that the extraordinarily long lapse of time will be an important consideration in all these identifications – '

Cox told the jury that they would have to consider the circumstances under which the witnesses claimed they'd seen the defendant. How close had they been? Did the witness get a good view of the person's face? Were there any distinguishing features about the person's appearance? The jury would have to consider the intelligence and perception of the witness and perhaps the character of the witness. 'Is he the sort of person who is likely to have jumped to a conclusion hastily?' Cox asked. 'May he have been influenced in his judgment about the person's identity by what other people might have said to him, either at the time or later . . . Remember, this is not just a matter of a witness's honesty. As I said to you, disastrous identification mistakes have been made in the witness box by witnesses who are honest, but wrong.'

Cox returned to Sergei's evidence regarding the man who had ordered him and Ivan Stepanovich to get the towels, water and chairs. Sergei had claimed this was the man who supervised the feeding of the German horses. The jury would have to decide whether or not it had been proven this man was the accused. But, Cox reminded the jury, there had been no photographic identification by Sergei. To prove the link the prosecution relied on circumstantial evidence.

'There is also the circumstance, if you accept the witness, that he had seen the same person a couple of times, maybe, in 1940 in the yard of Maria Stepanovna's house.'

Michael David stood up. Cox had made another error and the defence were not prepared to let it pass. David explained that there was no evidence Sergei had seen the same person he'd seen at the pit on two other occasions. 'That was the basis of my address,' David said.

'I'm sorry, you're right,' Cox conceded. 'I shouldn't have said the same person. It would be accurate to say, would it not, the crown asserts the person that he has seen a couple of times maybe in 1940 in the yard of Maria Stepanovna's house was the accused.'

David said that he didn't know what the crown was asserting.

Greg James got to his feet. 'I concede the crown does not assert there is any direct evidence,' the prosecutor said. 'There is some circumstantial evidence. I think that's what my learned friend said in his address to the jury.'

Cox accepted the guidance being offered from the bar table. 'So, ladies and gentlemen, even with that last correction, there is certainly circumstantial evidence linking the person who allegedly spoke to Sergei Potapovich and Ivan Stepanovich at the scene with a man called Ivan Timofeyevich Polyukhovich, known as Ivanechko, and evidence identifying that man with the accused himself. That's a question of your assessment of that evidence, taken as a whole.'

Cox said that it was a 'little difficult' to reconcile the evidence given by Sergei and Fyodor. Sergei had seen the accused in a uniform but said that he was not carrying a rifle. Fyodor had said that the accused was not in uniform but was carrying a rifle. While anyone could obviously pick up and put down a rifle during the course of a day, the jury might find it more difficult to reconcile the different clothing. Cox also pointed out that the witness Stepan Sidorovich had been at the pit and had not seen the accused there.

Regarding Fyodor's identification of the man who'd taken part in the murder of the miller's daughter and the two children, Cox reminded the jury that this was the same witness who said that he'd seen the accused on a previous occasion at the wedding. But the wedding had occurred some three years earlier.

Referring to the lies Polyukhovich was alleged to have told the Special Investigations Unit on the day of his arrest, Cox said innocent people sometimes tell lies. 'You could only take these lies – if that is what you think they were – into account against the accused if you have excluded all reasonable possible grounds for telling lies that are consistent with his innocence. I suggest to you that the nature of the accused's false answers, if that is what they were, doesn't, in the circumstances, enable you to draw the conclusion that he told lies to the police because he knew that he was guilty.'

The judge turned his attention to the defence case. The only witness called by the defence was Polyukhovich's first wife Maria Stepanovna. She had insisted that on the day she married the accused he had worn a shirt but not a jacket as claimed by Fyodor. This discrepancy supported the theory that Fyodor had not in fact looked at the accused on the night of Polyukhovich's wedding and so cast doubt on Fyodor's ability to recognise the accused at the pit some three years later. Maria Stepanovna had also denied that anyone had come to her mother on the day of the liquidation and asked for water, towels or chairs.

Then Cox said that he wanted to talk about the person who had *not* given evidence – the accused, Ivan Polyukhovich. Polyukhovich had the option of giving evidence but had chosen to remain silent. Had he given evidence he would have done so from the witness box, under oath, like any other witness. Cox said it would be wrong for the jury to conclude from the fact that Polyukhovich had not given evidence that he must be guilty. Polyukhovich was entitled to rely upon what the defence would call the inadequacies of the crown case to ensure his acquittal. But, if the jury was satisfied that there was reliable evidence implicating the accused in either of the charges, they were entitled to take into account the fact that the evidence had not been contradicted by the accused.

Cox summed up the final prosecution and defence addresses and then said, 'Let me finish with a few words of my own. They are offered for your assistance, but, as they amount to comments on the facts of the case, you are entirely free to accept or reject them as you please.'

Cox said that the delay between the alleged crimes and the trial had been extraordinarily long and its effects could not be ignored. He also disagreed with James that only the prosecution had been disadvantaged by the years. 'Witnesses who may have given evidence for the crown or the defence – who can tell which? – are no longer available, and the difficulty for those who did give evidence was plain for all of us to see.'

If Polyukhovich was innocent and the trial had occurred closer to the alleged offences, he would have been able to explore the evidence more thoroughly and find support for his defence among those now dead or disappeared.

'Of course, it may be that he is *not* innocent. But you would have to be very sure of that, don't you think, before you could ignore the possibility, in a case such as this, that the accused might have been placed at a marked disadvantage by the sheer lapse of time?'

Cox said that the evidence did make out a case for the accused to answer. The accused had also chosen not to go into the witness box. The defence had offered to explain why Polyukhovich had chosen not to give evidence by pointing out the infirmities of age and memory. But, the judge said, the jury might think those explanations would have been more persuasive if they had seen the accused give evidence. Cox said that he could see no reason why the jury would not have made allowances for any memory difficulties Polyukhovich might have suffered.

Then Cox returned one last time to the issue of the identification evidence. 'It could hardly be regarded, with respect to either count, as outstandingly strong,' he said. 'There are difficulties, as it seems to me, about the crown's evidence on both counts, particularly on the vital issue of identification, but perhaps also, so far as the first count is concerned, on the question of whether the acts or words alleged against this man at the pit site really did happen. Proof beyond reasonable doubt is a pretty high standard, and it does not become any easier to achieve when the crown has only one eyewitness for each count and he is talking about events that are said to have happened such a long time ago.'

Cox said that neither Sergei or Fyodor could be said to have known the accused well.

'It may be, ladies and gentlemen, you found the prosecution evidence more impressive than I have implied in what I have just said and that, in the end, will be for you to judge, not for me. But these considerations are matters which I am sure you will weigh very carefully.'

Cox paused, then said that he'd nearly finished but, once he was done, the jury would have to begin its deliberations. Having begun, they'd not be allowed to separate until they reached a verdict. Monday was a public holiday and it was very important that they not feel under any pressure to reach a verdict until they were ready to do so. Perhaps they would like to stop there and resume on Tuesday.

The jury went out and came back two minutes later. Now it was their turn to cause an adjournment. They'd hear the rest of Cox's summing up next week.

When the jurors had finally left the room, Cox asked the lawyers whether he'd made any mistakes that hadn't been corrected immediately. There was considerable anger among the prosecution ranks over what Cox had said during the last hour and a half. He'd made several confusing mistakes and they felt his comments on the prosecution case amounted to the kiss of death. Cox's cautions to the jury sounded like a repeat of the arguments used by the defence months earlier during the pre-trial legal argument. Why hadn't he stopped the whole thing then? At the time, of course, the prosecution had poured all their efforts into convincing Cox not to stop the case.

Prosecutor James asked for the lunch break to think about the summing up. An hour later he said the prosecution had nothing to say.

The prosecution had come to the conclusion that it would have been pointless to ask Cox to redirect the jury on any of the evidence. They believed that the only solution would be for the judge to start all over again. That was out of the question.

Some of the prosecution members took comfort from the fact that the jury had asked for the case to be adjourned until Tuesday. The jurors were clearly tired, surely eager to finish, yet they believed they'd need more than an afternoon to reach a verdict.

———

When defence lawyers David and Powell returned to the court on Tuesday morning, it was as if the jury had already been out for three days. The pair had suffered an awful weekend. David had slept very little. They lived near each other and on Sunday morning had met accidentally in the local delicatessen. Powell had never seen David look so dark.

The jury's request to adjourn until after the long weekend terrified them. Surely the issues were straightforward, the doubts obvious and a verdict easy to reach? The defence submissions had been so fundamental that, if they'd been embraced, a verdict should have been reached swiftly. Perhaps Cox's summing up had been so much in favour of the defence that the jury were defying him. That was a dangerous thought. The prospect of a hung jury loomed as a dreadful prospect. Whatever the reason for the jury's request, long deliberations could only mean that the prosecution had gained a foothold.

Investigator Reid had tried without any success to forget about the case for three days. The policeman didn't allow himself any false hopes. David's final address had been brilliant, and Cox's summing up fatal. The best Reid could do was to try to keep his mind on other things.

Prosecutor James had taken some encouragement from the jury's request for an adjournment, but even the irrepressible Sydney queen's counsel believed that rational hope for a conviction had been dashed the moment that Cox had said, 'I'd like to add a few words of my own.' But he knew that juries are curious and unpredictable, and he arrived at the court expecting a long day.

———

The judge and jury were running late. Most people sitting in the court seemed to be occupying their time talking about the state of origin rugby match played the night before.

A bell sounded from somewhere out the back. It was the judge's lift. Cox entered and the jury was ushered in. It was 10.06 on 18 May 1993.

The judge began, 'Members of the jury there's not much more I want to say to you, but I did want to refer to one thing I said on Friday towards the end of my summing up. What I want to say is really by way of a correction to the direction I gave you on the subject of delay . . . On reflection it's not really correct to say that the factor of delay is just an option that you may consider or not. I should have put it more strongly than that. You are bound to have regard to the possibility that, had the accused been charged with such offences as these much closer to the time when the offences are said to have taken place, he would have been able to explore the circumstances when they were still fresh, as it were, and perhaps chase up witnesses who could have thrown doubt on the crown evidence. Witnesses who, perhaps, for one reason or another, are not now available. Given that possibility it would be dangerous for you to convict the accused on the evidence that has been brought against him unless, having scrutinised the prosecution evidence with great care and paid heed to this warning, you are satisfied of the truth and accuracy of that evidence. In making that evaluation of the prosecution evidence you are entitled to take into account the fact that it remains uncontradicted by the accused, who, you might think, should have been able to contradict it if it's not true.'

Cox finished by reminding the jury that the exhibits would be sent out with them and that any verdict they reached had to be unanimous.

The tipstaff said loudly, 'Would the sheriff's officer please take charge of the jury.'

The jurors retired to consider their verdict at 10.11. Cox left the bench. Prosecutor James went over to the judge's associate, and asked how late juries in South Australia were kept out at night considering verdicts and for the name of a nearby hotel where he could spend the night, if necessary, without the embarrassing prospect of bumping into jurors. Then James and Niemann left to find a cup of coffee.

The defence remained sitting at the bar table. Reid walked over to David after a few minutes and joked, 'You must be worried. It's been fifteen minutes and they're still out. Something must be up.'

'Don't joke about it,' David replied. The look on his face showed that he wasn't amused.

Just after ten thirty the sheriff's officer was told that the jury had their first question. Neither side could take any comfort from this development. Reading a jury is like trying to understand the cultural gestures of a tribes person never encountered before. The two prosecutors and Justice Cox were brought back into the court.

Cox read out the message. ' "We would like to review the evidence of Sergei Potapovich Polyukhovich or an identification of photographs," ' read Cox in a puzzled voice. 'The message goes on, "Can a transcript be made available to the jury or a reading?" '

The message was confusing for two reasons. While it began to list the requests with numbers, the jury hadn't got past the number one. More puzzling still, however, was the fact that Sergei Potapovich hadn't identified any photographs. He hadn't been shown any photographs during the trial. The defence and prosecution confirmed this.

At 10.46 the jury was brought back in. Cox told the jurors that he wasn't entirely sure what their question meant. He explained that there was no evidence of Sergei Potapovich identifying photographs or dealing with the question of identifying photographs. Cox also said that he could not let them have a printed copy of the transcript of the evidence but they could have it read to them.

Normally any communication between the jury and the court is done through the jury foreman but, after so many weeks, the court had lost any power to intimidate. A juror in the back row spoke up. It was the middle-aged man whom some of the lawyers had come to refer to as 'the bus driver'.

'Well was he given the opportunity to ID?' he asked.

Cox replied that the issue simply had not been raised. Sergei had not been asked, as some other witnesses had, to look at photographs or to look around the courtroom to identify the accused. Several of the jurors turned and looked at the bus-driver, who raised his eyebrow and managed to combine a nod with a shrug.

'I think it illustrates the passage of time, your honour,' the foreman said knowingly. The jury retired again.

Defence lawyer Powell had a terrible thought. Could the jury possibly think that the lawyers had simply forgotten to show some witnesses photographs? It worried her that the bus driver had used the word 'opportunity'. Perhaps the jury would conjecture that Sergei might have been able to identify the photographs if he'd only been given the opportunity. That possibility would never have occurred to any of the lawyers. Lawyers are aware of each stage of the trial process, why some evidence is excluded and why some witnesses are asked to do some things while others are not. This jury, however, had spent days outside of the court unaware of what had been argued and how the case came to be presented.

All but one of about a dozen media people left the court. After this false start, they expected the jury to settle down to consider its verdict. They could afford to congregate in the nearest coffee shop.

Prosecutor James, however, had watched the jurors while Cox answered their first question, and had guessed that there wouldn't be any more. He knew now, beyond reasonable doubt, what the verdict would be and that it would be returned soon.

Just after eleven there was a knock on the door through which the jury had disappeared. Ann Sutherland, the law student who'd worked for the defence during the committal and trial, called out to the orderly, who fetched the lawyers. None had strayed far this time. Polyukhovich had gone down into the public gallery to sit next to Maria, but now she helped him make his way past investigator Blewitt to his seat in the dock.

The lawyers resumed their positions. From the public gallery the orderly could be seen talking into a telephone at the front of the court. From the public gallery the word 'verdict' could just be heard. At 11.09 Justice Cox entered and the jury filed in.

'I don't want to know for the moment what the jury's verdicts might be,' Cox told the foreman. 'I just want to be quite sure, first, that you have reached a verdict on each count.'

'We have,' the foreman answered.

'And the verdict is unanimous on each count?'

'It is.'

Cox asked the associate to read out the charges.

'On the first count, of being knowingly involved in the murder of 850 people, how do you find the defendant, guilty or not guilty?'

'Not guilty.'

Someone in the gallery loudly breathed the word 'yes'.

'On the second count, of having murdered a woman and two children, how do you find the defendant, guilty or not guilty?'

'Not guilty.'

Gabby Brown, the lawyer who'd been part of the defence team since the High Court's ruling, reached behind her and held Maria's old hand while a broad grin appeared on Lindy Powell's face.

Justice Cox began thanking the jury for their service. Ivan Polyukhovich's face became red. The old man lifted himself up so that he could reach deep into his trouser pocket, from which he took out a crumpled white handkerchief. He used it to wipe away tears and then drank from the glass of water next to him.

At 11.13 the court was adjourned. A Salvation Army officer leapt from his seat to meet Polyukhovich and shake his hand as he walked out of the dock. A crowd gathered quickly around the old man, but Powell had reached him and was shaking his hand vigorously.

The court emptied quickly. For a moment only James and Niemann were left standing there together while they took off their wigs and slowly unbuttoned their black vests. As Niemann was about to leave, SIU officer Anne Moore walked back into the room. 'Could I leave this here?' Niemann asked her, gesturing with his empty bag at rows of folders which suddenly seemed unkempt, the rubble of a prosecution.

Niemann stopped, took more notice of Moore and forgot about the folders. Although everyone within the prosecution team had expected the verdict, no one was up to sorting out or transporting documents. 'Never mind,' Niemann said softly and walked out.

Five minutes after the court adjourned, the discharged jury were walking out the front doors of the Samuel Way building. At the same time a pack of journalists rushed in from the opposite direction. The news of the verdict had finally reached them in the coffee shop. A reporter tripped in the panic and slid along the foyer. In one motion he picked up himself, his pen and pad and continued on. But it didn't matter how fast any of them ran. After three and a half years of waiting, they'd missed the verdict by ten minutes. Polyukhovich's lawyer Craig Caldicott was forced hastily into an impromptu media conference outside the door of court-room three.

———

Polyukhovich and Maria walked slowly out into the brilliant sunshine with their arms around each other. Caldicott followed behind them. Polyukhovich ignored the microphones and the questions and let Caldicott speak.

'Mr Polyukhovich is reasonably upset and relieved that after such a lengthy period of time he's finally had it all over,' Caldicott said. The words were jumbled but the meaning was clear. 'He's been going now, he's been under investigation, for three to four years.'

Asked how his client had reacted, Caldicott said that he'd cried. 'He was very, very emotionally upset. He has been through the entire trial process but it all became too much for him. He's been waiting for this moment for three years and he's an old man, we must remember, he's seventy-seven years of age. A very old man.'

———

Bob Reid and some of the other members of the prosecution team were still standing inside the building, just outside the courtroom, at a loss as to what they should do. 'I'm going to go for a walk,' Reid told Anne Moore. Then he turned towards the doors of the Samuel Way building. Seeing the wall of television cameras, photographers and reporters, he hesitated.

———

'Nine's got nothin', Nine's got nothin'.'

One of the commercial television reporters was gloating to his camera-man that a rival hadn't been there to video the lawyers' departure. Reid took a deep breath, tightened his stomach and moved towards the doors. He'd taken half a dozen steps outside when the gloating television reporter spotted him and yelled out, 'Bob, Bob.'

Reid kept walking quickly; he stayed close to the building. The camera crews chased after him.

'How do you react to the verdict?'

'I've got no comment to make.'

'It must be a severe disappointment for the prosecution?'

Reid's cheeks filled. He blew air through his lips as he sighed, but he didn't slow his pace. Another reporter caught up.

'I've got nothing to say,' Reid told the reporters.

'Where do you go now, professionally, where do you go now?' the television reporter asked.

Reid's red face and tired eyes looked down and then forward. He took a deep breath, as if he was going to answer the question, but then walked on silently.

'Is it a worry, that the jury took such a short time?'

Reid looked up and saw the jury foreman standing close by on the footpath, waiting for something or someone. Reid said nothing.

They'd passed the Hilton hotel and a third camera crew had caught up. 'Can you stop and give us a few words?'

Reid walked on.

———

Michael David was trapped. He'd managed to leave the building imme-diately after the verdict, but had been forced to return on discovering that he'd lost his glasses. Although nearly an hour had passed since the verdict was announced, the media people were still lingering outside the court, waiting for anyone connected with the case. They'd pounced as soon as David tried to make his second exit. Surrounded by cameras, the queen's counsel explained that he couldn't comment. The reporters ignored this, and enquired about the welfare of his client.

'He's a very old man and he's very upset. I assume he's all right now.'

Epilogue

War crimes prosecutions continued to feature in the Australian media after Polyukhovich's acquittal. The most famous of the American prosecutions, the case of Ivan Demjanjuk, re-emerged with the news that the Israeli Supreme Court had overturned the conviction that alleged he was 'Ivan the Terrible', a notorious Treblinka camp guard. Allegations continued that Demjanjuk had been a guard at camp Sobibor and had worked at the Flossenburg and Regensburg camps, but the Israeli court found those accusations had not been in the original indictment and could not be tried. Demjanjuk was returned to his home in Cleveland, Ohio, after seven years in Israeli custody.

In Adelaide, the case against Mikolay Berezowsky had been dismissed by a magistrate months before Polyukhovich's trial, but the crown continued its case against the last Australian charged with European war crimes, Heinrich Wagner. Greg James, who had shown so much enthusiasm for war crimes prosecutions, was enlisted as the DPP's senior counsel in the Wagner case. On 10 December 1993, however, the Director of Public Prosecutions, Michael Rozenes QC, chose to stop the case on the basis that Wagner was too ill to continue. Wagner had suffered a heart attack and evidence had been given that a trial would put his life at risk. Graham Blewitt and Grant Niemann were in Germany collecting evidence against Wagner when they learnt of the decision. Blewitt later said that he was bitter Rozenes had not consulted him before making the decision. He said he was sure that critics of the war crimes prosecutions would 'love this result' but said that didn't worry him.

Members of the federal Liberal opposition soon declared that Australia's war crimes prosecutions had been an extraordinary waste of taxpayers' money. South Australian senator, Nick Minchin, said the exercise had done little more than line the pockets of a bevy of lawyers. The federal government confirmed that just under twenty-five million dollars had been spent on war crimes investigations and prosecutions. The final figure on the current year, however, wasn't yet available.

Michael David, who had defended Wagner as well as Polyukhovich and Berezowsky, said the three cases had ended with just results. 'There's a lot of differing opinions in the community about whether they should have gone on and on or whether the money could have been spent better elsewhere,' David said. 'All I can say is they were three very hard fought, difficult cases. They weren't very easy from a legal point of view and they were very difficult to defend, as well as prosecute, I should imagine. As far as whether the money could have been better spent elsewhere, that's a very personal opinion and many members of the community have got very different ideas. I'm not sure myself. All I can say is . . . I'm sure on the evidence that was presented in these three cases that those three results were just results.'

The federal government defended the prosecutions. Attorney General Michael Lavarch pointed out to reporters that the cases were, after all, about the most serious allegations and not speeding tickets.

Increasingly, however, media reports about war crimes did not refer to events of half a century ago. Instead they spoke of atrocities some-times committed only hours earlier in former Yugoslavia. In November 1993, the first international war crimes tribunal since Nuremberg was inaugurated at The Hague. The United Nations had voted to set up the tribunal to try people accused of murder, rape and other serious offences committed in the republics of former Yugoslavia. During February 1994 the Australian federal government introduced an international war crimes bill designed to meet its obligations to the United Nations. The bill allowed Australia to hand over accused people for trial by the tribunal and to cooperate with investigations and prosecutions of alleged offenders. It also allowed the tribunal to sit in Australia.

That same month Graham Blewitt was appointed an interim chief prosecutor with the United Nations war crimes tribunal. Before leaving, Blewitt said that he was concerned his final report on the work of the SIU and the War Crimes Prosecutions Support Unit had not been made public. Blewitt conceded that his report contained a fair amount of criticism of the courts that had dealt with Australia's three European war crimes defendants.

The other investigators and lawyers went back to doing what they had done before taking on war crimes prosecutions. Ivan Polyukhovich returned, much older and weaker, to suburban obscurity.

Then, as if the shadow of the second world war was stubbornly refusing to fade away, one more case unexpectedly appeared to annoy the Australian government. In March 1994 eighty-year-old Konrads Kalejs lost a battle in the United States Supreme Court that had stretched over about a decade. Kalejs had been accused of having served as a company commander in the Latvian auxiliary police during the Nazi occupation. It was alleged that he was responsible for acts of persecution against Jews, gypsies and other civilians and that he'd misrepresented his wartime activities on entering the United States in the late 1950s. The court found Kalejs should be deported. Throughout his case Kalejs had said Australia was the place he would nominate if deported. It was reported that Kalejs had lived in Australia immediately after the war and had become an Australian citizen in 1957.

Early on Sunday 10 April 1994 Kalejs arrived in Sydney. Immigration officials were satisfied he was an Australian citizen and he was formally allowed to enter the country. The Executive Council of Australian Jewry said the Australian government had a moral obligation to investigate claims against Kalejs and should put him on trial if the evidence existed.

Although the war crimes legislation still stood the SIU had long since been disbanded. Federal Attorney General Michael Lavarch said the Australian Federal Police now had reponsibility to investigate such cases and the AFP would have to decide if there was any basis to the allegations. At the time of publishing it is unclear whether the authorities will embrace another legal and moral crisis.

Index

Wakefield
Press

SENTENCE: SIBERIA
A STORY OF SURVIVAL
Ann Lehtmets and Douglas Hoile

Ann Lehtmets is one of few people alive in the western world to have
lived through Stalin's holocaust. This is her tale of survival in a world
where existence was difficult for all and deadly for most.

ISBN 1 86254 313 5   RRP $18.95

—

IN HER OWN NAME
A HISTORY OF WOMEN IN
SOUTH AUSTRALIA FROM 1836
Helen Jones

This book tells the history of changes, from 1836 to the present,
that have helped women in South Australia move from
subordination towards equality. It includes much new
material on the leaders of the suffrage movement.

ISBN 1 86254 321 6   RRP $16.95

—

Wakefield
Press

BEAUTIFUL LIES
AUSTRALIA FROM KOKODA TO KEATING
Tony Griffiths

Beautiful Lies is an original account of the people, events and trends
that have shaped Australia since Menzies declared war on Germany
in 1939. It is racy, maverick and impartial – a *tour de force*.

ISBN 1 86254 284 8   RRP $14.95

—

SCANDINAVIA
A MODERN HISTORY
Tony Griffiths

Tony Griffiths tells the story of two centuries of change in the Nordic
nations, focusing on the exchanges between Scandinavian artists and
their politicians that have produced many of the western world's
archetypal cultural and political motifs.

ISBN 1 86254 263 5   RRP $19.95

—

Wakefield
Press

WAKEFIELD CRIME CLASSICS

This series revives forgotten or neglected gems of crime and mystery
fiction by Australian authors. Most of the writers, published between
the 1920s and 1970s, became international stars, while remaining
little known in Australia. Several of the novels are being published
in Australia for the first time.

———

PATRICIA CARLON
THE SOUVENIR: A guessproof whodunnit
THE WHISPERING WALL: Lethal house, silent witness, talking wall

———

S.H. COURTIER
DEATH IN DREAMTIME: A mystery of masks and ciphers
LIGNY'S LAKE: The race to solve the riddles of a vanishing man

———

PAT FLOWER
VANISHING POINT: Where intimacy turns to violence

———

ARTHUR GASK
THE SECRET OF THE GARDEN: Criminal? Surgeon? Jockey? Friend?

———

CHARLOTTE JAY
ARMS FOR ADONIS: Blood and love in Lebanon
BEAT NOT THE BONES: A tale of terror in the tropics
A HANK OF HAIR: An exquisite danse macabre

———

A.E. MARTIN
COMMON PEOPLE: Murder in sideshow alley
THE MISPLACED CORPSE: Introducing Rosie Bosanky, alarming, disarming
and altogether charming
SINNERS NEVER DIE: A savage small-town saga

———

Wakefield
Press

Wakefield Press has been publishing good Australian books for
over fifty years. For a catalogue of current and forthcoming titles, or
to add your name to our mailing list, send your name and address to
Wakefield Press, Box 2266, Kent Town, South Australia 5071.

TELEPHONE (08) 362 8800   FAX (08) 362 7592

———